Arizona
Day Hikes

A Guide to the Best Hiking Trails

from Tucson to the Grand Canyon

Dave Ganci

Illustrations by Jana Lunt and
Kathy Humphrey

Sierra Club Books
San Francisco

The Sierra Club, founded in 1892 by John Muir, has devoted itself to the study and protection of the earth's scenic and ecological resources—mountains, wetlands, woodlands, wild shores and rivers, deserts and plains. The publishing program of the Sierra Club offers books to the public as a nonprofit educational service in the hope that they may enlarge the public's understanding of the Club's basic concerns. The point of view expressed in each book, however, does not necessarily represent that of the Club. The Sierra Club has some sixty chapters coast to coast, in Canada, Hawaii, and Alaska. For information about how you may participate in its programs to preserve wilderness and the quality of life, please address inquiries to Sierra Club, 730 Polk Street, San Francisco, CA 94109.

Library of Congress Cataloging-in-Publication Data
Ganci, Dave.
    Arizona day hikes / Dave Ganci.
      p. cm.
    Includes bibliographical references and index.
    ISBN 0-87156-597-8
    1. Hiking—Arizona—Guidebooks. 2. Arizona—Guidebooks. I. Sierra Club.
  II. Title.
GV199.42.A7G26 1995
796.5'1'09791—dc20   94-32235
                                                          CIP

Production by Janet Vail
Cover and book design by Mark Ong
Illustrations by Jana Lunt and Kathy Humphrey
Composition by Wilsted & Taylor

Printed in the United States of America on acid-free paper containing a minimum of 50% recovered waste paper, of which at least 10% of the fiber content is post-consumer waste

10 9 8 7 6 5 4 3 2 1

Cover printed on recycled paper containing 50% recovered waste, of which at least 10% is post-consumer.

◆

Dedicated to the hardworking personnel of the
National Forest Service,
Bureau of Land Management, and
National Park Service
who assisted me in the research for this book.

◆

With special thanks to Deanna Ashcraft,
Alice Long,
and Merrill Glustrom of Yavapai College.

Contents

Part Two   **CENTRAL MOUNTAINS
PROVINCE   143**

Preface

Why Day Hike in Arizona?

Arizona offers the greatest variety of outdoor landscapes of any area of similar size in North or South America, which makes it great day hiking territory. Its kaleidoscope of biotic life zones starts at the driest and hottest sea-level deserts along the Colorado River and climbs up to the 12,633-foot subalpine volcanic summit of Humphrey Peak northwest of Flagstaff. Hikers, campers, photographers, and naturalists come from all over the world to sample Arizona's palette of geology, plants, animals, colors, shapes, and shadows.

Geologists love this state's topographic diversity, with its great exposures of ancient rock formations. They can explore the jagged fault-block mountains and silt-filled valleys of the southern deserts, then examine the bedrock granite and ancient uplifts of the central mountains, and study the lava-covered limestones and sandstones of the northern plateau.

Botanists love Arizona for the fact that over 3,700 plant species inhabit the state. Their variety extends from the southern desert cacti and creosote bushes, up through the central mountain pinyon, juniper, and oak, and up to the northern plateau sagebrush, yucca, ponderosa pine, and Douglas fir. The range of Arizona's plant communities spans that found from Canada to Mexico.

Zoologists love Arizona for the mammal, reptile, rodent, and insect varieties that live within the state's diversity of geologic, plant, and weather patterns. From kangaroo rat and fringe-toed lizard, to pronghorn antelope and javelina, to the Wyoming elk and black bear, this state is a wildlife biologist's heaven—containing 138 native mammal species and 32 native fishes.

Ornithologists love Arizona because of the many overlapping biotic communities that support 258 bird species—from southern desert cactus wrens and buzzards to the central mountain hawks and falcons to the northern plateau ravens and eagles.

This book helps readers become naturalists in that it describes the natural history of the state in Part One and continues such descriptions throughout the day hikes in Part Two. If day hikers follow the landscape narrative as they trek along, they will gain a basic understanding of why this state is world famous for its great diversity of outdoor scenery. The kicker is that this day hiking scenery is accessible within a short driving distance of the major freeway system, which runs north-south across the state.

In addition to helping you become an amateur naturalist, day hiking in Arizona provides you with the physical benefits of cardiovascular fitness, the mental and emotional benefits of reconnecting to the outdoor environment, the purse-strings benefits of inexpensive recreation, and, finally, the educational benefits of learning to appreciate the natural environment for its own sake—and why some of it should be preserved for future generations.

Perhaps you picked up this book to satisfy your curiosity about what Arizona's landscape is all about. Perhaps it's your desire to get out on the land with the carefree day hiker's stride, taking in all the sights, sounds, smells, touches, and tastes of this great state. Perhaps by taking this book out on the trail and following the natural history descriptions, you will fall in love with this state, and walk in joy across its landscape. Maybe you are like that person described by John T. Nichols, author of *The Milagro Beanfield War*: "A naturalist is a person who tries to delight in everything, is in love with the whole of life, and hopes to walk in harmony across the earth."

To help you approach your day hiking with increased awareness of the outdoors, here are a few observational techniques:

1. Stop and look around: We humans have to turn our heads a lot to see things around us. It's one of the limits of our binocular eyesight. It's also why we should stop every so often and look around. Like the coyote, keep your head turning so you know what is going on. Look up at the sky to see what the clouds are doing. Look behind and to the side to see what you may have missed. Many times, you'll see creatures that have waited for you to pass before crossing the trail.

You might notice a water hole, bee hive, or bird nest you missed because the sun was in your eyes.

When you stop, close your eyes for a few moments and just listen. Focus your entire awareness on the sounds around you. Listen for bird sounds, ground sounds, tree sounds, air sounds, and animal sounds.

With your eyes still closed, take ten deep breaths through your nose and try to pick out scents. Breathe from your diaphragm in slow, deep breaths. What "green" smells do you notice? Pick up and smell rocks, plants, and anything else that interests you. The memories that the sense of smell produces will last a long time, because the olfactory nerves are directly linked to memory banks. Perhaps this is a holdover from earlier times when the sense of smell was more important for human survival. When you pick up objects to smell, hold them in your hands and "feel" them as well. Close your eyes and "memorize" the texture. Is it coarse, smooth, bumpy, striated, brittle, sharp, soft, hard?

By practicing such techniques and experiencing your surroundings with multiple sense organs, your overall memory capacity will increase. Memories created in this manner will often make recall easier when you again encounter "memorized" objects.

In addition, try using binoculars and a magnifying glass to increase both your far and near visions of the world.

2. Record your observations: Take some time to record your adventures as you trek. Use written notes, poetry, drawings, photographs, or a tape recorder. This way, you'll have a permanent record of the landscape—and a permanent memory of the experience.

3. Make a file for your observations: Make a special space at home for your observation records so you can refer to them later.

4. On the road, take time to notice the environment as you drive to the trailhead: What rocks does the roadcut expose? How is the plant life changing as you gain or lose elevation? What is the weather doing as you drive to the trailhead?

5. Expand your library: Collect natural history books at the many museums and gardens available in Arizona. Many of these oases of information offer classes and field trips to specific areas of interest.

Introduction

Arizona—the name is magic—ever changing, always exciting. It's a day hiker's state. Its climate, color, landforms, and scenery provide the foot-tramper with endless varieties of outdoor joys and adventures.

Hikers are adventurers, but they are also an important group of environmental protectors because they relate directly to the landscape. They get out on the ground—get their feet wet, their hands muddy—and really feel the land. They stop along the way to really see, hear, smell, taste, touch, and absorb the natural history surrounding them. This book provides descriptions of the natural history of the hiking terrain in Arizona. That helps the hiker reconnect to the land. And reconnection to the land is what's needed if future generations are to be successful stewards of this earth.

Day hiking gets us back to the country. It shows us how to become one with the coyote—adapting to the challenges and rewards of the landscape. By doing this, our cares, in the words of naturalist John Muir, "will fall off like Autumn leaves."

Day hiking has been a natural human exercise since our ancestors stood upright a couple of million years ago. Our bodies then, like now, were built for hiking. Our feet evolved to walk on uneven ground. Our upper body was built for climbing trees, boulders, and mountains. Our senses evolved to take in the clouds, hills, winds, rain, animal cries, and flower scents. This book will help you—the hiker—reawaken those senses. It will do that by taking you on 109 of the best day hikes in Arizona's three provinces. Those provinces are (1) the Southern Deserts, which includes Phoenix and Tucson; (2) the Central Mountains, including Payson, Prescott, and the Verde Valley; and (3) the Northern Plateau, including Flagstaff and the Grand Canyon.

The hikes follow showcase trails, chosen for their scenic beauty, dramatic vistas, photo opportunities, outdoor educational values, and representations of the state's many biotic life zones. These trails are a large part of Arizona's history. Indian tribes, Spanish explorers, trappers, miners, farmers, cattle ranchers, missionaries, Mormon pioneers, and California-bound gold seekers have all traversed Arizona—leaving their marks, memories, and tracks. Often they followed animal trails. Some of those trails have become train tracks, some dirt roads or highways. Some remain as hiking trails for foot-trampers like us. Follow along with this book for 109 of Arizona's best.

The I-17 freeway runs through the middle of the state, providing easy and quick access to the day-hike trailheads in this book. The exception to this is the Grand Canyon area, which is still easily accessed by State Routes 180 and 89.

Due to the ease and speed of accessing these hiking areas—and the relatively short driving distances between them—six of the seven population centers (Tucson, Phoenix, Payson, Prescott, Verde Valley, and Flagstaff) can be reached from any of the other centers in a half day's driving time. Tucson and Phoenix are two hours apart. Payson, Prescott, and the Verde Valley are two hours from Phoenix and four hours from Tucson. Flagstaff is three hours by freeway from Phoenix and five hours from Tucson.

The Grand Canyon (South Rim) is one-and-a-half hours from Flagstaff. The most isolated area is the Grand Canyon (North Rim), which is three hours from Flagstaff and five hours from Phoenix. But the drive to the North Rim is so scenic, just getting there is worth the time.

(See Figure 1.)

A beginning reference location (freeway, highway intersection, Forest Service office, or visitor center) is noted for each of the seven population centers. From such reference points, you'll be directed to each Day Hike Area Takeoff Point. From there you will be directed to Trailheads. Selected campgrounds will be noted for each hiking area, usually in nearby national forests or county parks.

Open camping is permitted on Forest Service land unless posted to the contrary. The drawbacks are lack of water supply and toilet facilities, dry conditions preventing campfires, and potentially damaging environmental impact. In choosing open camping, use the same approach as if camping in your own backyard: Dig latrines at least 200 feet from water sources. Bury human waste. Carry out all trash, toilet paper, and food scraps. Pour wash water in a hole. Avoid building camp structures—use tarps instead. Pick up all ground scraps. Burn only downed wood and bring some extra with you.

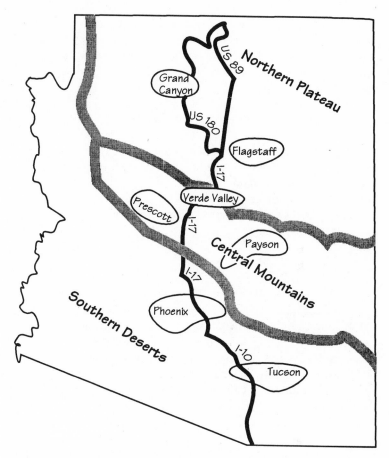

Figure 1. The three provinces of Arizona.

Cover the latrine thoroughly before leaving camp. Use existing fire circles and clean out the fire pit. Don't build fires in meadows or against large rocks. Do not camp next to water sources.

TRAIL DESCRIPTIONS

Each trail description contains information organized according to the following categories:

Time: Most times are figured at about 1 mile an hour, taking the leisurely naturalist's approach.

Distance: This will be within 100 yards or so. Some of the hikes are described as part of a longer trail and some require a car shuttle.

Elevation Gain: Described one way to within about 100 feet. When "Level" is used, it means flat, undulating, or with a few short ups and downs.

Rating: Easy, Moderate, or Challenging, based on hiking at a leisurely pace. Easy will designate a less-than-half-day trail. Moderate will be half-day hikes, and Challenging will be for trails of over half a day or those that include heavy climbing.

Trailhead: Obvious starting point of the trail, usually signed.

High Points: Outstanding features of the trail, why this trail was chosen as one of the best day hikes in Arizona.

Hiking the Trail: A narrative of the route, including discussion of the trail's natural history.

PREPLANNING

Preplanning is the single most important contribution to the enjoyment, appreciation, and benefits derived from day hiking. Preplanning includes reading this book, checking weather reports, and, perhaps, visiting one or more of the many natural history museums and gardens scattered throughout the state. These include the Desert Botanical Garden and the Phoenix Zoo; the Boyce-Thompson Southwest Arboretum; the Arizona-Sonora Desert Museum in Tucson; the Tucson Botanical Garden; the National Forest Museum in Payson; the Northern Arizona Museum; and the Flagstaff Arboretum.

These precious sources of information and education contain microcosms of the natural and cultural history of Arizona. They all have excellent book sections, and the gardens sell potted plants to visitors. If there is a local visitor center near the trail you wish to hike, make time to go there first. If you sit down and read through information before heading out on the trail, you'll get a lot more out of the experience. These gardens and museums will be discussed in more detail in later chapters.

WEATHER

This is the single most important element of preplanning. It determines everything else about your day hike, including road conditions, how long it will take to get to the trailhead, how long it will take for the hike, and what you should take on the hike. The long-term weather forecast can be accessed on the local television and radio channels, but the best thing to do is call the Forest Service office or visitor center closest to your destination.

In mild weather, day hiking can be the freest of outdoor pursuits. You can literally get out of your chair and head out the door with whatever you have on—well, almost. The point is, day hiking in mild weather requires a minimum of hassle and gear. By tanking up on water before heading out, you can probably hike for half a day with nothing but loose change in your pockets.

But then, the weather doesn't have to be perfect to enjoy the trail. In fact, the more temperature and precipitation variations you hike in, the more you will experience and learn. If you only hike in room-temperature weather, you will miss 80 percent of the fun of outdoor tramping. Don't be afraid of a little rain or snow or wind. Just be cautious of a lot of it.

In the summer, you can often hike in shorts and a T-shirt and brimmed hat. In addition to preventing sunburn, a hat will protect your face and neck from excess radiated heat gain, which occurs due to the limited expansion and contraction capabilities of the blood vessels of the neck and head. Take along a sun-blocking agent if you are sun-sensitive.

By traveling light, with minimum weight on your back, you cut down on metabolic heat gain and use less energy and less water. That makes more energy available for enjoyment and awareness. But be sure to carry enough water to stay comfortable on the hike. What's enough? That's an individual answer and will be different for each hiker. Take a quart along for short hikes and two quarts for a half day or longer. You'll get to know your water needs as you do more day hikes.

Use available stream water to cool your head, neck, and face as you go. Soak your hat and bandanna and T-shirt—they will then act like an evaporative cooler as the air evaporates the water and cools you down—or jump in and take a dip.

Put your half-full water bottle in the freezer the night before heading out. Fill it up in the morning and stuff it into the bottom of your day pack. The ice will keep the water cool for quite a while.

Plan for a slow, leisurely hike and don't build up metabolic heat gain by moving too fast. When it's hot, start just before dawn. That's the coolest it's ever going to be, and the time when most animals are up and moving around. In winter, with the right clothing, there is no reason to avoid that light rain, snow, or mist that puts everything in a different light.

OUR BODIES

The human body tries to maintain an inner temperature of about 99 degrees Fahrenheit with a skin temperature of about 80 degrees Fahrenheit. It likes a relative skin humidity of 70 to 90 percent. The body tries to keep a quarter-inch envelope of warm, moist air around it for maximum comfort against chilling. If this "second skin" is removed by wind, cold air, or water, the body tries to replace it with more heated vapor—which dissipates internal heat. This happens up to a point, then the body starts to constrict the blood vessels and outer capillaries to cut down blood supply to the hands, feet, and limbs in order to conserve the warmer blood in the vital organs. The head is the only part of the body in which the capillaries scarcely contract, because the body wants to keep the brain functioning with the most adequate blood supply.

Wind and water are the two greatest threats to body heat and can quickly wipe out the layer of moist, warm air around the body. Water has twenty times the conductivity of dry air, and wet skin can lose heat 200 times as fast as dry skin. Most cases of hypothermia (cold stress) happen in temperatures of 40 to 50 degrees Fahrenheit, when the skin has gotten wet and wind is blowing and the hiker isn't prepared with additional dry clothing. You need to preserve that quarter-inch barrier around you, and you can do this with vapor barrier clothing.

DRESSING FOR THE WEATHER: THE VAPOR BARRIER CONCEPT

The vapor barrier concept of heat retention is somewhat opposite from the breathability concept. A pioneer in this idea is Robert S. Wood, author of *Pleasure Packing* and *The 2 Oz. Backpacker*, excellent references for further detailed discussions of vapor barrier clothing.

Simply stated, vapor barrier clothing is waterproof fabric worn close to the skin to keep body moisture in. This sealed fabric protects and maintains the body's moist layer of vapor around the skin and protects the wearer's outer clothing from dampness. Sweating is minimized, but that can increase body heat—which must be reduced proportionally. The key to this concept is to maintain a moderate pace so as not to build up body heat. When it does build up, one should vent at the neck, armpits, and cuffs.

Shirts

The cheapest and lightest vapor barrier shirt is a plastic garbage bag with a couple of holes cut out for the head and arms. Wear it over underwear and tucked inside pants to form a barrier that can add up to 20 degrees of warmth with practically no additional weight. Cheap plastic rain ponchos, available at many retail outlets, are a bit better. Some have arm covers and hoods. Any waterproof shirt can act as a vapor barrier. It is a matter of weight and cost. Our goal is to keep both to a minimum.

In cold, dry weather, wear a light pile shirt or sweater over the vapor barrier. In wet weather, wear the vapor barrier on the outside as raingear. If the weather turns especially nasty, keep the lightweight vapor barrier on the inside of the shirt and wear another lightweight waterproof garment on the outside.

Outerwear

The outer protection garment can be anything from the garbage bag or cheap plastic rain poncho discussed above to a more sophisticated wind- and waterproof parka. Since a garbage bag might last for only one day hike as an outer garment, spend a few more dollars on a good abrasion-resistant garment for consistent protection from wet weather.

The best outerwear fits loosely and contains large zippered pockets—where you keep those "extras" like keys, money, binoculars, small camera, notepad, and candies, and where you can put your hands.

The total weight of the upper garments—vapor barrier, outer shirt, or sweater and outer parka—should not exceed three or four pounds.

Pants

When it's too cool for shorts or light cotton pants, a vapor barrier for the lower body can be formed from simple lightweight rain pants. If it's cold, wear a thin polypropylene layer under the rain pants. If it's still cold, put on some thicker underwear. Like the shirt, lightweight rain pants double as an outer layer in case of rain. The best vapor barrier pants for the money are made of urethane-coated nylon that can weigh as little as eight ounces. The cheapest and lightest are those from a plastic storm suit that can be bought in outdoor stores, usually for less than $10.

Again, if an outer layer of weatherproof clothing is consistently needed, get one that's abrasion resistant and has big pockets.

Socks

The lightest vapor barrier for your feet are the free plastic baggies found in the produce section of your local grocery store. Put one around your foot some freezing morning—under your socks. Leave the baggie off the other foot. Walk around in the snow. Your baggied foot will stay warmer and it won't be that damp when you take your boots off. The sock you wore over it will be clean and dry.

How about the socks themselves? Synthetics surpass cotton or wool because they dry quickly and don't shrink when washed. Orlon, stretch nylon, Lycra spandex, and polypropylene are all good synthetic fibers and last longer than natural fabrics.

For subfreezing weather, wear a thin pair of polypropylene socks under the baggies, with heavier synthetic socks on the outside.

Headwear

Headwear is extremely important for cold weather because—as mentioned—the head is most sensitive to heat loss and heat gain. The best headwarmer is either a wool or synthetic watch cap that pulls down over the ears. In cold and windy weather, wear a full-face balaclava that can be pulled down into the outer shirt for face and neck coverage. These can be found in outdoor stores and thrift shops for less than $10.

Hats protect against eyestrain, sunburn, rain, wind, and blowing dust. I've used them as water basins, cups, dog dishes, rear-end ground protectors, water-soaked head coolers, camera shades, siesta face covers, fly and mosquito swatters, even frisbees.

Handwear

A thin pair of polypropylene gloves worn underneath heavier outer gloves reduces the chances of chapped, dry hands and finger "splits." They can be bought cheaply in drugstores, supermarkets, and paint stores.

DAY PACKS AND FANNY PACKS

The ideal day pack is no day pack—just a few things thrown into large, baggy pants pockets. That's the ultimate day-hiking freedom. And for short day hikes, that may be all you need.

When you want to carry a few more items, invest in a day pack or fanny pack. Personal preference determines whether you carry your day-hiking gear on your back or on your fanny. Some folks hate shoulder straps, some hate the feel of anything bouncing on their derrieres.

There are literally hundreds of styles of both packs, and the selections would fill a catalog. Prices start in discount stores at under $10 and go up to $50 or more in specialty shops, depending on the material, number of pockets, zippers, and amount of padding. The more items you carry in a day pack, the more padding you want in the shoulder straps. A fanny pack should always have a wide belt strap.

I like backpacks because I don't like things hanging off my waist. I use one with a belly strap to keep it from swinging when I take off on my aerobic jaunts.

Start cheap and buy up. Remember, the idea is to travel as light and unencumbered as possible. If you buy a large day pack you will find a way to fill it.

FOOTWEAR

You may already have some old tennis shoes, running shoes, or work boots to hike in. They are fine and have already been determined comfortable. If you don't have these, try the new generation of light-weight fabric/leather boots that have revolutionized the footwear business. They come in all shapes, colors, fabric combinations, and price tags. Since you will be limiting your day-hiking carry-weight to the absolute minimum, start out with the lightest, cheapest shoes and buy up from there. The most important consideration is a comfortable fit. These types of shoes require a minimum of break-in time.

Keep 'em light. Every extra pound on your foot has to be lifted every time you take a step. Five hundred steps with two extra pounds requires the energy to lift 1,000 pounds in that distance. Think how much that is over a 5-mile hike. Remember, the game is to conserve energy so that you can travel farther and see more. Stay light! Stay free!

CARDIOVASCULAR CONDITIONING

A little cardiovascular conditioning will help you enjoy day hikes even more due to the increased endurance level attained through training. And how do you train? Simple! By day hiking! While on the trail, hike at a faster pace, in short spurts, for 20 minutes. This increases your oxygen intake and heart rate and can be done right in the middle of your "smell the roses" pace.

Your speed, in order to gain conditioning level, is determined by your heart rate. The following chart shows you how to compute your heart rate (pulse).

Age	Pulse/10 Seconds
10–19	25–30
20–29	24–28
30–39	22–27
40–49	21–25
50–59	20–24
60–69	19–22
70–79	18–21
80–89	16–19

Find your age group and the 10-second pulse rate you need to maintain for 20-minute intervals. Walk at a pace that maintains that rate—somewhere between the two numbers. That's it. Don't stop during the 20 minutes—keep going. Then take a break and get back into the observation and outdoor awareness mode. You can do this for as many intervals along the trail as you want, but once or twice every other day is sufficient to keep your conditioning at a good level.

Another physical benefit of day hiking over uneven terrain is the overall toning and flexing of a great many lower-body muscles. When the route gets steep and rocky, even more muscle groups are used. It's not like running or jogging, where you use the same muscles to the point of boredom.

VEHICLES

More problems, delays, cancellations, and hassles are caused by vehicle failures than by all other causes combined. Since all the trailheads in this guide are easily accessible from good roads, most backroad problems are minimized.

The most frequent vehicle problems, no matter what road you are on, involve batteries and tires, so always carry jumper cables and a couple of spare tires. Have a good bumper and axle jack. Carry extra water and oil, just in case. Keep a small shovel in the trunk, along with a tow chain or rope.

The worst situation you're likely to encounter on any of this book's access roads will be surfaces slick from heavy rainfall.

FIRST-AID KIT

A first-aid kit is probably the most unused, unopened item in the history of day hiking—that is, after the snake-bite kit. But, as Murphy would have it, if you don't carry a few things for scratches, blisters, or chapped skin, you will surely need them.

In over 30 years of hiking, backpacking, river running, mountain and rock climbing, survival courses, and long-distance desert treks—both as a soldier and as a civilian—the most used item in my first-aid kit has been the band-aid. Ninety-five percent of all injuries I've encountered in the outback—both in myself and others—have been either cuts, scratches, blisters, or skin chapping from dehydration or wind.

A comb and tweezers for removing cactus spines is on the list for desert day hiking. I can't think of much else I have ever used, except an ankle bandage. The above items weigh practically nothing and don't cost much.

"DANGEROUS" ANIMALS

Too much bad publicity has been given to poisonous creatures. Snakes, scorpions, spiders, and centipedes purportedly have laid in wait to pounce on unwary travelers. In reality, no animals out there want to eat us—or harm us—unless we threaten or harass them.

There are some 11 varieties of rattlesnake in Arizona, and the hiker will be flat-out lucky to see one on a day-hike trail. If one is encountered, note the size and color and leave it alone. If you leave it alone, it will simply slither away. Don't try to kill, capture, play with, or chase away a snake in order to make your path "safe"—that's when people get bitten.

The Arizona Game and Fish Department statistics show that 90 percent of all recorded snake bites have occurred because people were harassing the snake. It is an extremely rare instance when a person gets bitten by accident.

In the worst-case scenario, if you ever get zapped by a rattlesnake, don't try to treat your wound by cutting and sucking, with constricting bands, by freezing, electric shock, or biting the snake back. Just get to medical help as soon as possible. That's really all you can do. Try to get calm. Wash the wound and bandage it. Get to a doctor or hospital.

Scorpions are next on the list of "dangerous" critters. A scorpion bite might cause a mild numbness or the pain of a bee sting. That's all I've ever felt.

Black widows? You get closer to them around your house than in the backcountry.

Centipedes? You will be lucky to see one.

Actually, the creature most dangerous to humans is the honeybee. Why? Because there are so many and there are a certain number of folks who will react to the sting and go into anaphylactic shock.

There is one creature that does seem to go into the attack mode anytime and anyplace—the little black ant. It seems to be everywhere on earth, and its sole purpose seems to be to harass humans.

Animals demand respect for their territories and their young. Respect them and they'll respect you.

CHAPTER 2

The Arizona Landscape

An Overview

Geology

The geologic complexity of Arizona's landscape is the major reason for its great diversity of weather, plant and animal life, and scenic beauty. The three contrasting geographic provinces—Southern Deserts, Central Mountains, and Northern Plateau—are the result of geologic forces that have been acting on the earth's thin crust for a couple of billion years. That's a long, long time.

Geologists in Arizona have pieced together a good part of the earth history of that 2 billion years, thanks to the dry climate that has left rock outcroppings exposed and visible all over the state—rock strata that would ordinarily be covered with topsoil and plant life in wetter climates.

As far as we know, this one-of-a-kind, round, living ball called earth that we live on is the master artwork of the universe. In the center of this masterpiece is a red hot mass of burning material—part liquid and part solid. This hot core is surrounded by a thick mantle, thought to be semi-liquid or plastic. Floating on the outside of the mantle is a very thin crust—similar to the top layer in a cooling pan of hot pudding. This crust is attached to the upper part of the mantle and forms a layer 40 miles thick under the oceans and 60 miles thick under the continents.
(See Figure 2.)

The undersea crust layer is thinner but heavier due to its basalt consistency—rich in magnesium and iron. The continental crust layer is thicker, but made up of lighter rocks that ride up above the ocean plates, forming continents.

Earth's hot, interior core causes convection currents to travel

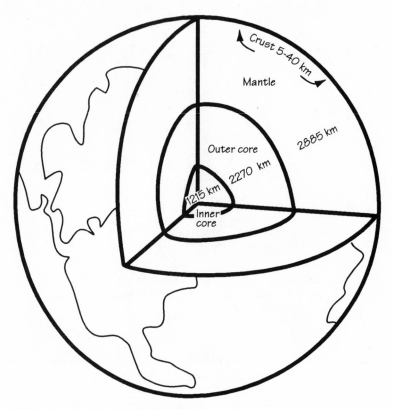

Figure 2. A view of the Earth's layered structure.

through the mantle. This creates movement and slowly tears the crust into separate plates—moving them apart and into each other—consistently reshaping the continents over millions of years. This makes the crust a living, moving layer of material—albeit an extremely slow-moving one.

The plates split along mid-ocean ridges that spread apart from the force of molten material welling up from the hot mantle. This molten material forms new crust along the edges of the splits, and in so doing slowly spreads the plates in different directions at the rate of about 1 inch per year. We call this continental drift or plate tectonics.

Other plate separations occur along the edges of the continents—where heavier undersea plates slowly slide down underneath the

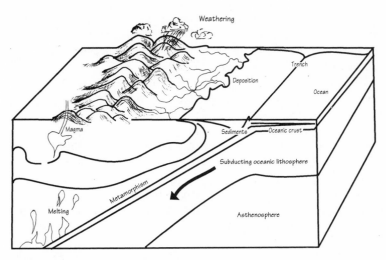

Figure 3. A plate tectonic model of Arizona's rock cycle.

lighter continental plates. We call this process subduction. As the plates slowly slide under each other, friction is formed and rocks present at such points re-melt and recycle back into molten material. The molten material rises up to the surface of the continent, causing volcanic activity and earthquakes—or it wells up at mid-ocean ridges and forms new crustal material.
(See Figure 3.)

When plates collide they create mountain ranges, more earthquakes, and all kinds of crustal deformities. These deformities are seen in the Central Mountains Province in the form of 1.5-billion-year-old mountain folds.

Plates also pull apart. This stretching action is visible in the Southern Deserts Province, where the push-pull action broke the plates up into blocks and tilted them. The tilts became sharp-edged mountain ranges that have eroded over millions of years into the present landscape of broad, alluvium-filled valleys interrupted by ghostlike ranges.

Plates get pushed up to higher elevations by collisions. This is what happened in the Northern Plateau Province with its many layers of flat sedimentary rocks that formed under ancient oceans and were subsequently pushed up above sea level.

The earth's crust is broken down into three classes of rocks:

1. **Igneous** (igniting or burning) rocks come from melted material that is either pushed up to the surface to form volcanos (called lava), or pushed up to just below the surface to be uncovered later by the actions of erosion (called magma).

The material that makes it to the surface cools quickly. It is the latest geologic event in the area before erosion, and we see it as the surface layer upon which we walk or hike.

In the past, lava eruptions occurred in many places in Arizona, most evident in the Northern Plateau Province around the San Francisco Peaks/Flagstaff area. There are over 400 identified eruption locations in this field.

Igneous evidence abounds all over Arizona—some as extinct volcanos, some as eroded remnants of old volcanos, and some as exposed lava "icing" that covers the sedimentary layercakes of the Northern Plateau Province.

The most common igneous rocks that we find in Arizona include the following:

Andesite Volcanic rock of a composition between rhyolite and basalt—with medium-size crystals.

Basalt Mostly dark and rich in magnesium and iron. Prevalent in surface lava flows and very common in Arizona. Very small crystals.

Dacite Volcanic rocks that have been welded together. Small-size crystals of varying colors.

Granite Rich in quartz and feldspars. Contains fairly large crystals. Usually light in color with dark intrusions.

Pegmatite Granitic rock containing much larger crystals than ordinary granite. Found as vertical intrusions, or dikes, in mountain areas.

Rhyolite Similar to granite but with smaller crystals. Occurs in lava flows and is scattered throughout the Central Mountains and Southern Deserts Provinces.

2. **Sedimentary** rocks consist of the eroded remains of rocks and seashells that have been broken up into fine particles to form layered sediment. Sedimentary rocks are formed both on the surface of the continents and in sea beds.

Surface sediments accumulate from wind action and water erosion that reduce rocks into grains of sand, silt, and clay. Over immense time, gravity stacks these grains into layers of sediment, fusing them with heat and pressure into solid masses. Seas advance and recede over the layers. Other layers are stacked on top. Over vast amounts of time, the layers are lifted up by continental collisions to expose them as sandstone, siltstone, mudstone, and clay.

Subsurface or ocean sedimentary layers formed when hundreds of zillions of seashell remains sank, were compressed, and eventually turned into limestone. These loose layers were fused by tremendous heat and pressure into solid layers, were later lifted by continental collisions, and are now exposed. These layers are prominently displayed in the Grand Canyon, with its layercake walls and formations.

The most common sedimentary rocks in Arizona include the following:

Breccia A jumble or conglomerate of large angular rock fragments cemented together.

Chert Associated with limestone. Usually found in small quantities or pieces that were used by early Americans for arrow points and tools. Colors are mixed and varied.

Conglomerate A jumble or conglomeration of rounded stones of all sizes, cemented together with all kinds of matrixes. Often easy to break up.

Desert Patina Dark deposits on many desert rocks, formed from iron and other dark minerals deposited on rock surfaces.

Limestone A hard rock composed mainly of calcium carbonate. Wide range of colors and textures. Often contains fossils.

Sandstone Cemented sand grains. Various colors and consistencies. Some soft and breakable.

Shale Cemented particles of clay, forming a very fine-grained rock, often soft and breakable.

3. **Metamorphic** (changed by heat and pressure) rocks are usually formed deep below the earth's surface. Over time heat and pressure have changed the original chemical composition and crystal structure to other compositions.

The most common metamorphic rocks in Arizona include the following:

Gneiss A common layered rock, originating from granites and other rocks. Appears banded and crystalline.

Marble Compressed and heated limestone. Can be almost any color, depending on trace minerals contained in the matrix.

Quartzite Sandstone that has been fused into a harder, more crystalline structure.

Schist Another common rock, sometimes greenish in color. Consists of fine, flaky particles. Different schists are named for their principal mineral—for example, mica-schist.

Arizona Over Time

Arizona is 395 miles long from north to south and 340 miles wide from east to west—almost a square. Elevations range from 137 feet above sea level near Yuma to 12,633 feet at the summit of Humphreys Peak just north of Flagstaff. This large elevation difference within a relatively short horizontal distance (275 miles to the northeast) is typical of the great variation in Arizona's topography. The elevation differences combine with the geographic positioning of the state at the center of weather-transition areas to create the kaleidoscope of overlapping plant and animal species that makes Arizona an outdoor lover's paradise.

Arizona landscapes were formed as part of the western edge of the North American continental plate. They presently contain observable rocks that date back 2 billion years. Over millions of years, these and other rock formations have been pushed, pulled, lifted up, lowered, covered by seas, eroded, covered by seas again, eroded again into flat plains, and raised again in a time-machine jigsaw puzzle that geologists are continually piecing together.

It is now known that about 200 million years ago the North American continent was part of one huge land mass that contained all the continents. As the forces of plate tectonics broke the mass apart, the North American continent broke away from Europe and headed west at a rate of about 1 inch per year.

As the continent was pushed west, it collided with other plates—mainly the huge Pacific plate. At the edge of the collision, land mass was added to the west coast, whereby California, Oregon, and Washington were born. This same collision pushed up the Rocky Mountains and the Sierra Nevada. It caused the volcanic chain of mountains along the west coast, still actively spewing lava in our lifetime. It also caused the formation of the three provinces evident in Arizona today.

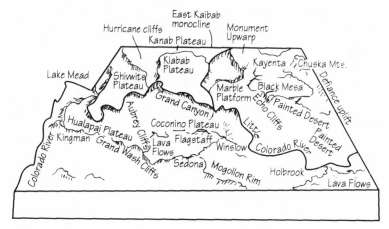

Figure 4. The plateaus and mesas of Arizona.

At first, most of the state's geographic area was covered with the layers of sedimentary rocks that presently form the Northern Plateau Province. They were raised up above the ocean surface by the plate collision. Over millions of years, parts of these layers were eroded away so that what remains to the south of them are the other two provinces—Central Mountains and Southern Deserts. This erosion line can be plainly seen as the present-day Mogollon Rim running east and west through central Arizona.

(See Figure 4.)

At about the same time, in southern Arizona the plates were pulling apart and forming the Southern Deserts Province. Between the eroding Northern Plateau Province to the north and the expanding plates of the Southern Deserts, the uplifted central mountains exposed 1.7-billion-year-old metamorphosed rock forms. This, the Central Mountains Province, remains today the most mountainous segment of the state—with drainages that flow to the lower deserts providing the basis of desert agriculture and subsequent population densities.

(See Figure 5.)

The present-day geologic landscape changes imperceptibly in one human lifetime. In our short adventure on this geologic canvas we pretty much get what we see. Were we to come back in a million years we would see a few changes—but not as much as you might think.

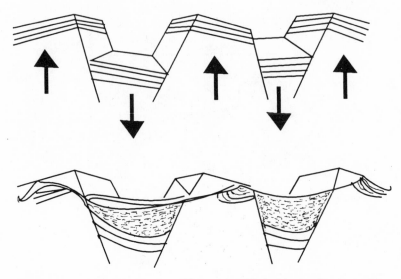

Figure 5. Geologic action created basins that filled with gravel as mountains eroded.

Ten million or 100 million years would make a difference. But that also is short in geologic time, a difficult concept for humans to grasp because we tend to think in terms of a hundred or maybe a thousand years. These timeframes are so short in the big geologic picture as to become almost meaningless.

The important concept is that the beauty and satisfaction we gain from the outdoor hiking experience can be further enhanced by the realization of how much time and cosmic effort went into creating this thing called earth-life.

Climate and Weather

This section provides an overview of the climate of the provinces; the following chapters will focus on local weather.

Arizona is truly a state for all seasons. Usually, when it's raining in one part, it's clear in another. When it's cold in one part, it's warm in another. Windy in one part, calm in another. This presents an unpredictability factor that forces the outdoor person to plan for changing circumstances. It also allows for a host of choices within a short driving distance. For example, if it's raining in Prescott, you may be able to hike under clear, cloudless skies in the McDowell Mountains, just a couple of hours to the south.

Climate is defined as the long-term averages of high and low temperatures, winds, humidity, and precipitation (rain, snow, sleet, hail). It is the Chamber of Commerce description of an area. Weather is the day-to-day variation within the overall climatic picture, including all the unpredictable events and surprises inherent in the ever-changing cycles of sun, snow, and storm.

Paleobotanists agree, based on prehistoric plant fossils, that the climate of Arizona has fluctuated between cool/wet and hot/dry for a period of about 3 million years. About 200,000 years ago, the climate got cooler and wetter as mountain glaciation ushered in the first of four ice ages.

This glaciation took place on the San Francisco Peaks near Flagstaff and on Mount Baldy in the White Mountains of east-central Arizona. These glaciers—and hence the cold/wet weather—advanced and receded four times, each followed by a hot/dry trend. The last cool/wet period ended about 12,000 years ago. As the climate dried and warmed, wetter vegetation zones moved up to higher elevations throughout the state. Lakes dried up and most streams changed from permanent to seasonal—as they remain today. The present-day climate finds us in this generally hot/dry stage, and it's much the same as it was a few thousand years ago—with small, yearly fluctuations of precipitation and temperature.

Today, as we travel from Yuma in the southwest corner of the state, heading north and east up through the deserts to the central mountains and then to the plateaus, we gain altitude and usually get wetter and colder weather.

The Southern Deserts Province receives from 3 inches of rain along the Colorado River to between 11 and 13 inches in the lusher Sonora Desert around Phoenix and Tucson. Winter temperatures average 53 degrees Fahrenheit and summers average around 85 degrees Fahrenheit. However, summer days can reach 115 degrees Fahrenheit with nights getting as low as 70 degrees Fahrenheit. Winter nights can drop below freezing.

Central Mountains Province's seasonal fluctuations are awesome due to the local weather created by mountain massifs. In elevations over 5,000 feet, average rainfall is between 17 and 20 inches, with some mountains receiving 25 or more inches.

The Northern Plateau Province also creates great weather variations, with winter temperatures dipping below freezing, accompanied by harsh winds blowing across the flat plateaus and forcing the wind-chill factor down to paralyzing temperatures. Even with higher elevation, summers can be blazing hot in the desolate high desert of this landscape.

Arizona climate is influenced by two major geographic areas outside the state: (1) the gulfs of California and Mexico, which create heavy moist marine air that comes up to the deserts from the south in mid-summer and (2) Utah and Colorado mountain-range weather, which comes into the plateau and canyonlands landscape from the north in the winter months. These two influences shift back and forth across the state, creating another variable in the overall weather picture.

Yet another major climatic influence is that of the unpredictable high-altitude jet stream that fluctuates north and south across Arizona. In the winter, that stream can move south, bringing snow and rain to the state, or it can stay north and bring a drier winter. There is little pattern to this movement, and it's anybody's guess what it will do from year to year.

The best way to appreciate the great variety of Arizona climate and the subsequent local weather patterns is to watch the weather channel on cable television or read the weather page in *USA Today*. You will see that Arizona and California have the most color bands—which represent different temperature ranges—of any states in the Union. In Arizona those bands follow the general northwest/southeast directions of the prevailing geographic provinces we have been talking about.

Compared to places like the Midwest, where you must travel hundreds of miles to see a climate change, in Arizona you can travel as little as 10 miles and experience dramatic changes—say from 70 degrees Fahrenheit in the Sonora Desert around Tucson to almost freezing on top of Mt. Lemmon, just a short drive north of Tucson.

Arizona can have both the hottest and coldest temperatures in the nation on the same day when a cold front moves into the White Mountains, creating subfreezing weather at Hawley Lake, while in the lower deserts around Phoenix a high-pressure weather system brings the thermometer up into the 70s.

This author has been in the middle of the Grand Canyon on a day in May when the noontime temperature was 85 degrees Fahrenheit under clear skies—only to find himself crouched under a rock in late afternoon as wind, rain, hail, and snow dumped during a plateau storm that dipped over the rim from the north.

Figure 6a. Average annual precipitation.

(See Figures 6a,b,c.)

The amount of yearly rain is always a critical issue in Arizona. It is never enough, and because of this, water is always taken on all hikes, not just those in the deserts. The Central Mountains and Northern Plateau provinces can be just as dry out on the trail. Many a hiker has been fooled by the cattle tank, pond, well, stream, lake, spring, and other bright-blue dots on topographic maps that indicate water— only to discover the sources were dry or nonexistent.

Plant Life

Plant ecologists recognize that Arizona is a meeting place for many of the major plant communities in the United States. This great va-

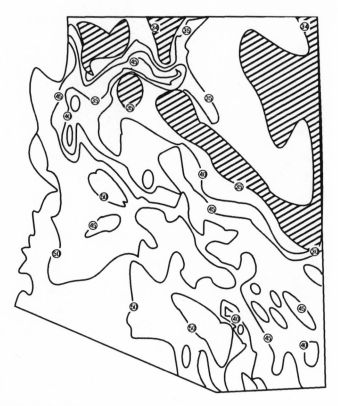

Figure 6b. Average January temperatures.

riety and complexity falls in line with the geologic, climatic, and elevation diversity. These plant communities overlap due to local
weather variations, north/south slope orientation, and east- or west-
facing valleys and canyons.

Interdependence is a major factor in plant diversity. This is man-
ifest in the many symbiotic relationships between insects and plants.
Bees need flowering plants for food, and plants need bees for polli-
nation. Moths need yucca blossoms for food, and, in turn, they pol-
linate the yucca. Fungi and algae need each other to form lichens. In
reality, interdependence is true for all living species. Intense competition is also. We are all part of similar food, water, shelter, space,
and reproductive interactions and competitions.

Interaction promotes change, and everything changes over time.

Figure 6c. Average July temperatures.

Plant life is no exception, but it often takes a long time—in some cases, millions of years. The last ice age episode occurred about 12,000 years ago, and the plant-life environment has changed steadily from wet/cool to hot/dry since then. Old-growth forests have moved up mountainsides and have been replaced by chaparral and woodlands. Grasslands have replaced woodlands at higher elevations, and deserts have replaced grasslands in lower elevations. Forest remnants occur along perennial streamsides (riparian habitats), reminding us of once-dominant plant species that have now been relegated to wetter, cooler microhabitats.

North- and south-facing slopes can demonstrate widely different vegetative cover—with many overlapping communities on both sides. This becomes evident in the spring when desert wildflowers, which are especially sensitive to moisture and temperature, bloom on southern slopes but not on northern ones. The reverse is true for mosses and ferns, which need cooler, wetter temperatures and grow on northern slopes but not on southern ones.

Since there are so many elevation differences within Arizona's three provinces, plant varieties change before our very eyes when ascending a 2,000-foot day-hike trail on Mt. Wrightson in the Santa Rita Mountains south of Tucson, or when hiking up the 1,000-foot Brown's Peak Trail in the Four Peaks Range east of Phoenix in the Central Mountains—we climb from desert up to pine trees on both peaks.

Following is an overview of the plant communities we'll be discussing in later chapters. All the plants within a community have adapted over the years to their own niche in the local climate and elevation.

As mentioned, elevation plays a critical role in plant habitat. In general, temperatures drop 1 degree Fahrenheit for every 300 feet in elevation. This is modified by local weather, but over the long run remains quite consistent. That's why we find similar plants at the same elevations in quite different geographic locations.

Common Arizona Plant Communities Although plant zones overlap and mix and change with altitude and slope variations, we can still discuss Arizona plant communities in terms of the following categories:

Desertshrub Covers the Southern Deserts Province and is found again in lower areas of the Northern Plateau Province.

Desert Grassland Lower and higher desert areas in central and eastern parts of the state between 3,000 and 5,000 feet.

Chaparral Found in the Central Mountains Province between 4,000 and 6,000 feet.

Oak-Pine Woodland Found in the Central Mountains Province between 4,000 and 7,000 feet.

Pinyon-Juniper Woodland Found in the Central Mountains Province between 5,500 and 7,500 feet.

Ponderosa Pine Found between 5,000 and 8,500 feet.

Spruce-Fir-Aspen Found between 8,000 and 11,000 feet.

Alpine Tundra Found above timberline or above 11,000 feet.

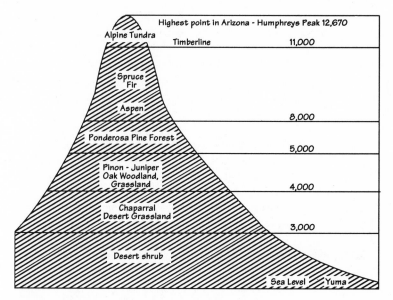

Figure 7. Common Arizona plant communities.

Riparian Habitat Includes plant microhabitats that exist along perennial waterways—be they rivers, streams, springs, or lakes. (See Figure 7.)

Most of the plants in the riparian habitats need water close to the surface to survive. The vegetation is luxurious and broadleafed. The trees are usually deciduous and many are mostly remnants from a wetter, cooler time when the surrounding area also contained these plants.

Riparian habitats reduce floods by slowing the waterflow with their thick streamside vegetation. They improve water quality by balancing water nutrients. They store groundwater supplies that end up in wells and other runoff areas. They cool and shade animals in hot weather and provide them with a reliable water supply. They provide breeding and nesting habitats for birds, animals, and fish that don't exist outside the riparian zone.

A sampling of riparian trees, in order of descending elevation down to desert level, include maples, alders, oaks, willows, cottonwoods, sycamores, black walnuts, tamarisk, and the mesquite/palo verde community.

Animal Life

The great variety of animal life follows the great variety of plant life throughout Arizona's provinces.

The Southern Deserts community houses many more species than meets the daytime eye because most animals living in this province make their living at night—at least for six months of the year, when the ground and air temperatures are too hot for daytime activity.

At first, you might think animal life is sparse on the desert. Not so. Due to the lack of vegetative cover on the desert floor, a lot of it can be seen—but, you must get into the backcountry where the animals live. You should get on the trail before dawn. And stop long enough along the trail to observe animal movement. If you do, you might see such creatures as mule deer, jackrabbit and cottontail, white-tailed deer, javelina, desert bighorn sheep, skunks, coyotes, bobcats, badgers, foxes, and—if you're really lucky—mountain lion.

To the careful observer, bird life abounds in the desert. The cactus wren, Gambel's quail, mockingbird, flicker, thrasher, Gila woodpecker, and bright red cardinal flash through the desert brush, while hawks, eagles, owls, ravens, and vultures float above the desert basins and ranges looking for rock squirrels, woodrats, kangaroo rats, gophers, and mice. The famous roadrunner, seemingly afraid of nothing, zips along the ground, grabbing anything that suits its taste.

Deserts are known for their reptiles. They include lizard species such as chuckwallas, swifts, geckos, and whiptails. Among these reptiles are the poisonous snakes—the most visible being the western diamondback and the Mojave.

The Central Mountains Province hosts many of the Southern Deserts animals plus larger mammals, fishes, tree dwellers, and quite a few more birds. The higher, wetter elevations—along with increased vegetative cover—allow for spotted and striped skunks, red foxes, beaver, black bear, wild turkey, porcupine, bobcat, mountain lion, white-tailed deer, raccoon, red squirrel, deer mouse, western bluebird, Steller's jay, common flicker, and bald eagle.

The Northern Plateau Province contains a range of animals common to the Mojave Desert on the western end, and common to the ponderosa pine communities on the higher plateaus. Wyoming elk live on both rims of the Grand Canyon.

Some animals live in narrow habitat ranges and survive in fairly limited areas. The sidewinder rattlesnake (cold blooded) is an example. Other animals are quite mobile. They have range limits but can adapt behaviorally to changing circumstances as they go—especially the mammals, since they are warm blooded and can adjust their body temperatures. Some creatures, like coyotes, rabbits, and other rodents, roam the entire state.

PART ONE

SOUTHERN DESERTS PROVINCE

CHAPTER 3

Forming the Southern Deserts Province

Geology

Southern Deserts history goes back 1.7 billion years, to when the Pacific plate collided with the North American plate—pushing mountain ranges into the air and causing vast changes in the western landscape of the continent. As the ranges rose, the Pacific plate slanted under the North American plate, causing great friction and melting of rock. This melted rock (magma), being lighter than the surrounding hard rock, rose up through the mantle into vast domes—some not quite reaching the surface, some erupting in volcanic explosions.

For millions of years, seas advanced and receded over the landscape—laying down layers of sedimentary limestone, sandstone, siltstone, and conglomerates. Then more crustal lifting, bending, and erosion took place. More seas advanced and receded. A long period of geologic stability followed during which erosion leveled the land. It stayed that way until the Mesozoic Era, which occurred between 250 and 65 million years ago.

During the Mesozoic, great volcanic explosions occurred, and crustal collisions pushed up more mountain ranges while more intrusions came up from the mantle to the surface. This lasted for about 25 million years, and is known as the Laramide Orogeny (orogeny means "mountain-building event").

Another geologically quiet time followed (50 to 28 million years ago) and lasted until another mountain-building event started, the Mid-tertiary Orogeny (28 to 15 million years ago). This episode involved the pulling apart of the crustal plates and formed the now-characteristic northwest-southeast mountain ranges that spread out in southern Arizona, California, and Nevada. As the crust pulled apart, it broke up into fault blocks that resulted in the tilting of many of the chunks. Erosion gradually wore away the edges of the chunks and filled the areas between them with its own refuse.

In some areas, lava flows formed closed basins that river drainages filled to form lakes. Sedimentary strata piled up at their bottoms. Then the lakes dried up, leaving still more sediment. The combination of erosion and sediment provides the basin part of the Southern Deserts we see today.

In most of western and southern Arizona, fault-block sinking went on from about 15 to 7 million years ago. It is still going on in the eastern corner of the state.

Today's uplifted—or range—part of the Southern Deserts is the remaining tops of the blocks. These tops are a series of jagged, tilted desert mountain ranges that when viewed from above look like giant lizards inching northwest across the desert lands—their exposed backs made up of ancient rocks with names like gneiss, schist, granite, basalt, rhyolite, and andesite.

As erosion continued on these uplifts, streams coalesced and formed rivers. The Salt River drained down from the northeastern mountains. The Gila came in from the east and south, captured the Salt, and continued on through the desert basins to dump its contents into the Colorado River—which in turn dumps into the Sea of Cortez at Yuma. The Verde River drained the northern and central mountains, dumping into the Salt.

The Colorado River became the main western river about 5 million years ago when it captured north-flowing streams and cut down through the uplifting Northern Plateau Province to form the Grand Canyon. Relatively young in geologic time, the Grand Canyon is the finest and grandest display of Northern Plateau Province geologic history. The Grand Canyon also displays Southern Deserts topography along the Colorado River, where a mixture of Sonoran and Mojave deserts exists at an elevation of 1,500 to 2,500 feet—the same kind of Sonoran and Mojave deserts that exist in southern and western Arizona.

Mineralization is evident in the southern deserts because it's adjacent to the subduction of the North American and Pacific plates. At this location, three episodes of crustal collision caused mountain building and the subsequent melting of crust beneath the surface. When the hot subsurface solutions were forced up into cracks and fissures in the overlying strata, they cooled and mineralized at dif-

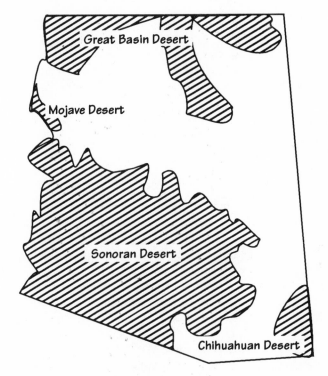

Figure 8. The deserts of Arizona.

ferent rates, forming copper, silver, and gold mineral deposits. This is evident in the ore-rich areas of Bisbee, San Manuel, Globe-Miami, and Pima.

Climate

The Southern Deserts Province is especially arid. It's made up of four deserts: the Mojave, Great Basin, Sonora, and Chihuahua. But what defines these deserts?
(See Figure 8.)

Southern Deserts characteristics include the following:

1. Less than 11 inches of rainfall annually—from 3 inches along the Colorado River to around 11 inches in Phoenix and Tucson (on the average). This means little surface water.

2. High rates of evaporation—rainfall is subject to quick return to the atmosphere.
3. High winds—summer and winter storm winds roar across the sparsely vegetated deserts.
4. High daytime temperatures—due to continental positioning and intense sunlight.
5. Wide range of air temperatures between day and night—due to lack of vegetation and cloud cover that would normally hold in nighttime temperatures.
6. High solar radiation—lots of sunny days—due to minimal cloud cover and clean air that lets sun rays through.

Southern Deserts summer months are June through September. This is 100+ degrees Fahrenheit weather, when most animals (including humans) don't go out on the trail during the day. It's simply too hot and dehydrating to do anything except escape the heat by finding shade or water. That's what most of the animals are doing up in treetops, inside cacti, or underground.

Fall months are October through November. Days are still hot but nights cool off. This is usually a dry time on the desert—between rainy seasons. Winter lasts from December through February and spring runs from March through May.

Rains fall during the winter months when northwest storms blow in from the Pacific Ocean and cross the continent. These are usually undramatic, low, lingering storms that soak the ground, preparing it for the spring growth to come.

Summer rainfall occurs when the moist air from the gulfs of California and Mexico come into the deserts. Hot ground and air temperatures combine with the moist air to form subtropical (monsoon) weather—creating dramatic thunderstorms of wind, thunder, lightning, and pounding rain. These ferocious storm cells come and go in a matter of hours, dissipating their enormous energy on the overheated desert ground below. Their intensity and frequency diminish in a westerly direction, dropping less and less moisture on the deserts closest to the Colorado River.

Plant Life

The Southern Deserts plant community is called desertshrub. Much of this desert vegetation has evolved from plants that once lived in a subtropical climate. Over millions of years they adapted and changed to a slowly drying and warming climate.

Most of the plants that live under the present arid conditions have adapted to the climate using the following strategies:

1. Specialized leaves—waxy or leathery covering to reduce water loss.
2. Reduced leaf area—smaller-sized leaves to reduce evaporative area and water loss.
3. Leaves replaced with spines—applying mostly to the cacti where the trunk of the plant replaces the leaves for photosynthesis, and the original leaves have been reduced to spines that both shade and protect the plant.
4. Deciduous leaves—drop during dry spells to conserve water.
5. Shortened life cycle—those ephemeral desert plants that grow quickly with the spring or summer rains, blossom, breed, and go to seed before the hot, dry summer kills them. Seeds may lie in the ground for years, awaiting the right combination of rain and temperature that allows them to sprout. Some botanists still look at ephemerals as subtropical plants, actually growing during the subtropical spring climate of the desert year.

Plant-life volume and variety slowly increases from the Colorado River eastward due to the increase in the summer rains that reach up into the Sonoran Desert.

Animal Life

There is more animal life in the Southern Deserts region than meets the untrained eye. Its variety increases from the Lower Colorado River desert eastward, just as the rainfall and plant life increase. This becomes visible to those hikers who take the time to stop and observe. The sparse plant life allows open fields of vision for observation.

Most of the insect orders are represented, and they fit into the desert pretty much as they fit in everywhere—without special modification to the heat.

The rodents (rabbits, ground squirrels, packrats)—which form the main food link between plant and predaceous animals—occupy a huge niche and have adapted to the arid lands mostly through behavior modifications such as sleeping during the hot days and working at night and extracting precious water from plants and seeds.

There are many predatory mammals such as skunks, badgers, foxes, ringtail cats, coyotes, and bobcats that prey on the rodents. They too have adapted to the summer heat by working at night and sleeping during the heat of the day.

There is an amazingly rich bird variety on the desert lands, from ground-dwelling quail to high-flying buzzards. They adapt to summer by living inside saguaro cactus stems where the temperatures are modified by internal water storage or in the shaded branches of desert trees.

Large mammals such as mule deer and javelina (wild peccaries) have wide ranges and may come onto desert lands to feed and breed.

Reptiles occupy a large niche, with the lizards and snakes being most visible.

MOJAVE DESERT

Climate

The Mojave Desert—its name is taken from the Mojave Indian tribe that lived along the Colorado River in the 1800s—occupies an area in the northwest corner of Arizona, bordering the Colorado River on the west, extending east to Kingman and south to Wickiup, with a small area concentrated west of Congress along Highway 93 northwest of Wickenburg (designated the Joshua Tree Parkway by the State Department of Transportation). Annual rainfall is between 5 and 11 inches. Mojave Desert elevations range from 800 feet along the Colorado River up to 3,000 feet on top of some desert peaks.

In the summer, daytime temperatures can reach 120+ degrees Fahrenheit, cooling to the 70s at night. The air is so dry that perspiration evaporates before it is noticeable on the skin; dehydration takes place rapidly. Because monsoon rains from the south barely reach the Mojave, there is little relief from summer heat.

October starts a cooling trend, but days can still be hot. They are definitely dry. In the fall, desert plants start drying up and flowers bear fruits and seeds. Occasionally, an early winter storm moves into the area, changing the desert from fall to winter overnight.

Winter is the rainy season for the Mojave. It's when Pacific storms move across the state, bringing much-needed moisture to plants, animals, and humans. This provides water for the fast-growing (and fast-dying) spring wildflowers and for the desert plants that have adapted over the long term to store the precious liquid until the next rain.

Winter nights can be downright cold, with the daytime heat re-radiating back into the atmosphere after the sun goes down. Spring is magic time on the Mojave as the combination of winter rains and spring warmth brings plants to bloom. Spring is the plant-life mating season, when pollen dust mixes with stigmas to create the buds and flowers that will ensure the next year's crop. This magic dust is trans-ported to its recipients by wind, insects, and other creatures.

Remember, these seasons are variable and determined by precip-itation and air temperatures. Winter storms can arrive early and/or late, causing all kinds of variations in the "normal" patterns. Rainfalls can occasionally be so abundant (1973, 1980, 1992–93) that the sea-sons blend, creating off-season plant flowering, explosive animal (es-pecially rodent) populations, and flash flooding all over the deserts.

Plant Life

The range of the Joshua Tree corresponds quite precisely to the range of the Mojave Desert in Arizona. Other dominant species in this range include creosote bush, all-scale, brittlebush, desert holly, white burro bush, shadscale, and blackbrush. The sparse foliage on these plants is an adaptation to the hottest, driest desert in North America.

The Mojave desertshrub evolves into the Great Basin desertshrub in the Northern Plateau Province and into the Sonoran desertshrub to the south and east. When saguaro cactus, palo verde, and ironwood trees become visible, you leave the Mojave and enter the Sonoran desert.

Various cacti are found in the Mojave, including Engelmann hedgehog, silver cholla, Mojave prickly pear, beavertail cactus, barrel cactus, and buckhorn cholla.

There are over 250 species of annuals in the Mojave—those once-a-year blooms that carpet the spring desert floor with spectacular color. February through May are the best wildflower months. The cactus blooms come out in May, June, and July, requiring humans to suffer the heat to see most of them, but it's worth the effort.

One other factor affects plant life—elevation. Even in the desert mountains, elevation means a cooling rate of about 1 degree Fahrenheit for every 300 feet increase in elevation. That means the higher the elevation, the later the plants bloom. As a matter of fact, you can hike up through many different levels of budding, blossoming, fruiting, and seeding plants in one desert day hiking afternoon.

Animal Life

Rodents make up the majority of animals that populate the Mojave Desert. They include desert woodrat, Merriam kangaroo rat, long-tailed pocket mouse, little pocket mouse, white-tailed antelope squirrel, cactus mouse, and canyon mouse.

Lizards include banded gecko, chuckwalla, desert iguana, zebra-tail lizard, leopard lizard, banded Gila monster, and regal horned lizard.

A great variety of snakes inhabit the Mojave, including western leafnose, desert rosy boa, striped whipsnake, California kingsnake, sidewinder rattlesnake, Mojave rattlesnake, and speckled rattlesnake.

Mammals are represented by the desert bighorn sheep, coyote, mule deer, javelina, coyote, and pronghorn antelope.

The best time for sighting wildlife in the desert is early morning, late evening, and nighttime. That's when most animals go about their business of hunting, gathering, mating, building, and socializing. The best way to see these types of activities is to slow down your pace—stop for a while to look and listen. Binoculars are a necessity; they expand your wildlife viewing potential beyond measure.

SONORA DESERT

The Sonora Desert covers west-central and southern Arizona. It takes its name from the state of Sonora, Mexico, where the largest extension of its landscape lies.

It is divided into two sections in Arizona: (1) Lower Colorado River Division, along the lower Colorado River Valley and east to parts of the Salt River Valley (Phoenix area) and (2) Arizona Uplands Division, the higher desert elevations surrounding Tucson and parts of Phoenix.

LOWER COLORADO RIVER DIVISION

Climate

This division is almost as hot and dry as the Mojave, resulting in a landscape with minimum plant and animal life. Its western boundary is the riparian (streamside) habitat of the Colorado River as it flows into the Gulf of California. The eastern boundary is approximately the western edge of Phoenix.

Annual rainfall is 3 to 10 inches, increasing from west to east, most of it falling during winter storms. Elevations range from 100 feet near Yuma to 3,000-foot desert peaks. The biggest sand dunes in Arizona exist in this division. Most of them lie just outside Yuma, although there are a few near Bouse on the border of the Mojave Desert.

Summers are similar to the Mojave Desert with daytime temperatures that can reach 120 + degrees Fahrenheit. Shade and water are hard to come by. Some areas resemble Middle Eastern deserts. The skies are bright and glaring, with high-intensity light and heat radiating off the bare ground.

Fall and winter are pleasant and bring what little rain the Pacific Ocean gods send over. Nights cool off into the 60s and 70s. The Lower Colorado River Division grades up into the adjacent Uplands Division, where elevations are higher and there is more rain and plant life.

Plant Life

Predominant vegetation in the Lower Colorado River Division is creosote bush, white bursage, burro bush, desert broom, Anderson thornbush, and brittlebush. Desert trees include foothill palo verde, ironwood, smoketree, and honey mesquite.

There are large areas of open landscape that look barren but contain small groundcover plants. A phenomenon called "desert pavement" covers large unvegetated areas. This hard-surfaced landscape consists of small rocks cemented together by thousands of years of erosion and weathering.

A few cacti live in this dry desert, notably the saguaro, prickly pear, and staghorn cholla. They are on the edge of their liveable range, however, and of questionable health during the summer months. The climatic harshness of this desert stresses all plant, animal, and human life.

Animal Life

Characteristic rodents in this division include round-tailed ground squirrel, white-tailed antelope squirrel, long-tailed pocket mouse, and desert and Merriam kangaroo rats.

Lizards include fringe-toed lizard, flat-tailed horned lizard, chuckwalla, and desert spiny lizard.

Snakes include banded sand snake and the sidewinder.

Many birds survive in this barren landscape, including buzzards and hawks that soar overhead. LeConte's thrasher frequents the area, along with cactus wrens and roadrunners.

The animal most known for its adaptation to this hard land is the desert bighorn sheep, which frequents the lonely desert mountains and bajadas (sloping foothills). Coyote? He's everywhere. Even the burro is here, introduced by miners from the past.

ARIZONA UPLANDS DIVISION

Climate

As the Lower Colorado River Division extends eastward and up in elevation across the state, it changes gradually into the Arizona Uplands Division, which is notable for its gradual west-to-east increase in plant life. This division occupies the higher desert foothills and ranges around Phoenix and Tucson, along with the sloping alluvial foothills (bajadas) off those same mountains.

The farther east one goes from the Colorado River, the more chance there is of encountering the summer rains that come up from the Gulf of California and Gulf of Mexico. These rains increase as one gets closer to Phoenix and Tucson, creating the lushest of all deserts—the Uplands Division of the Sonora Desert. This is the picture-postcard desert, with its stately saguaros, palo verde and mesquite trees, and dramatic cacti. It is an example of the finely tuned, minutely specialized, and sensitive character of Mother Nature. With just a little more elevation and a little more rain, Arizona Uplands Division plant life is significantly more abundant than that of the Lower Colorado River Division.

Summer temperatures range from 115 + degrees Fahrenheit during the days to the 70s at night. Awesome summer thunderstorms build up from the superheated desert surface during August and September, dropping sheets of water and blowing tremendous wind gusts across the land.

Fall is dry and cool (especially at night), while winter storm patterns build up in the Pacific. When those first storms usher in winter, temperatures can get down to freezing at night and average in the 60s during the day. This can change unpredictably with the movement of the high-altitude jet stream. These storms can last a few days (normal) or a couple of weeks (abnormal), raining and drizzling onto the desert floor while dropping snow onto the higher mountains in the Central Mountains and Northern Plateau provinces. The snow can get low enough to dust desert peaks.

Spring ushers in the blooming time, which depends on the previous winter rains. It usually means a dry time also, unless late winter storms linger over the desert.

Plant Life

The Sonoran desertshrub environment, as we see it today, became established about 8,000 to 9,000 years ago—very recent in geologic time. The rainfall patterns of winter and summer allow a greater diversity of vegetation than in any other desert.

One of the differences most visible in the Sonoran desert is the presence of taller shrubs, trees, and an abundance of cacti (this desert is sometimes referred to as the Palo Verde, Saguaro, Cacti Desert due to the abundance of these plants), along with the prevailing desertshrub. This provides a huge diversity of form, color, shade, and texture, especially during the spring wildflower season when fragile, round annuals blend with massive, sharp cacti to provide the viewer with unparalleled visual and tactile contrasts.

All the species that appear in the Lower Colorado River Division appear in the Arizona Uplands Division with the addition of cane cholla, chain-fruit cholla, teddy bear cholla, desert Christmas cholla, pencil cholla, organ pipe, senita, night-blooming cereus, pincushion cactus, barrel cactus, jojoba bush, desert hackberry, fairy duster, crucifixion thorn, Engelmann prickly pear, palo verde, ironwood, and mesquite.

In wet years this desert displays an overpowering spring wildflower bloom. Photographers come from around the world to record these short-lived spectacles. The Desert Botanical Garden in Phoenix and the Tucson Botanical Garden have spring wildflower hotlines that tell callers where the flowers are blooming around the state.

Animal Life

In addition to the same animals that live in the Lower Colorado River Division, the Arizona Uplands Division supports a population of desert mule deer, javelina, black-tailed jackrabbit, desert cottontail, gray fox, woodrat, mouse, ground squirrel, Harris hawk, white-winged dove, elf owl, crested flycatcher, curved-bill thrasher, cactus wren (the official state bird), horned lizard, Gila monster, western diamondback rattlesnake, Mojave rattlesnake, and black rattlesnake.

CHIHUAHUA DESERT

Climate

This desert is named for another state in Mexico—Chihuahua. It is Southern Deserts landscape, but with higher basins and much higher ranges. It covers parts of southeast Arizona and gradually evolves into the Sonora Desert west of Tucson. The basins, which can extend up to 3,500 feet in elevation, consist of rain-shadow valleys, outwash plains, low hills, and bajadas. Some geographers consider this area a grassland and put it into the Central Mountains Province; others consider it a part of the Sonora Desert.

Mountain ranges shoot up to 9,700 feet in their "sky island" configurations. ("Sky island" refers to mountain ranges that rise off the desert and grassland floors into higher plant and animal communities, like "islands" in a sea of desert.) Known locally as "jewels in the desert" they provide hikers with a vertical life-zone variation unequalled anywhere in the United States. Ranges like the Santa Ritas, Chiricahuas, Dragoons, and Huachucas angle up from the desert floor into cooler, wetter temperatures that provide habitat for overlapping zones of vegetation and wildlife. Ninety percent of this desert land mass spreads south into Mexico. A small portion of it extends up into southeast Arizona, where it mixes with the Arizona Uplands Division and desert grassland.

A colder desert than the Sonoran, the Chihuahua Desert receives from 7 to 12 inches of rain annually, most coming in the summer months with the arrival of the monsoon rains. It gets hot in those summer months (over 100 degrees Fahrenheit), but cools off at night. A few Pacific storms move over the Chihuahua Desert during the winter months, especially when the jet stream moves south. Winters can dip below the freezing level, and can stay below that level day and night.

Plant Life

Thorny, spiny plants characterize Chihuahuan desertshrub. There are few desert trees. Creosote bush, along with whitethorn acacia, tar bush, and sandpaperbush, dominate the valleys and low slopes. Ocotillo, nolina, agave, sotol, shrubby senna, and desert zinnia occur occasionally in pure stands. With a gain in elevation, the vegetation changes to various succulent-shrub species, such as lechugilla (shin daggers), dogweed, candelilla, and yucca.

Small cacti grow in separate, cohesive areas but are not common. Prominent types include prickly pear, cane cholla, and hedgehogs.

Animal Life

Typical rodents of the Chihuahua Desert include the kangaroo rat, pocket mouse, desert shrew, and Texas antelope squirrel. Bird life includes the scaled quail, mourning dove, roadrunner, nighthawk, and cactus wren. Desert bighorn sheep occupy areas in the mountain chains. Antelope frequent the grassy valleys.

Reptiles include the round-tail horned lizard, fringe-toed lizard, whiptail lizard, gecko, Mojave rattlesnake, and diamondback rattlesnake, trans-Pecos ratsnake, and Texas black-headed snake. The Bolson tortoise is a holdover from past grassland habitats.

COMMON DESERTSHRUB/ DESERT GRASSLAND PLANTS

Reduced Leaf Types

Palo Verde (green stick) This deciduous tree has small leaves and thorns. The small leaves don't provide much protection from the

Mesquite

sun but also don't use much water during photosynthesis. The tree also minimizes water use by dropping its leaves during drought. The bark itself produces photosynthesis—therefore its "green stick" color.

Three types of palo verde inhabit the desertshrub: (1) blue palo verde, with a bluish tint to the leaves and bark, (2) standard palo verde, with green bark and leaves, and (3) little leaf palo verde, which has a yellowish tint to it. All three trees bear an explosion of yellow blossoms in the spring. These blossoms turn to sweet, green peas around June and are delicious. You'll see them all over the ground in the summer because animals think they're delicious too.

Mesquite Tree Mesquites are similar in appearance to the palo verde but have dark, rough bark and very small yellow-green leaves. They blossom in the spring and bear seed pods that become edible in the fall when they dry out. The pod tastes sugary and contains carbohydrates. This was a most important tree for early Americans because it produces food, fuel, fiber, and shade.

In the drier deserts, this tree grows in dry washes with tap roots that can reach 50 feet or more to the water table.

Ironwood Tree Leaves of the ironwood tree are similar to those of the mesquite but are larger, as is the tree itself. The bark is dark and smooth. Spring blossoms are lavender in color. Fruits turn to edible nuts that resemble peanuts. The extremely hard wood is used for carving and long-burning firewood.

Catclaw This bush with its cat's-claw-shaped spines will stop you in your tracks if you brush against it. Leaves are similar to those of ironwood, but the plant is a shrub. It produces an edible bean in the spring. It is found frequently in drainages.

Bursage This small, abundant, triangular-leaved shrub is frequently associated with the creosote bush. The two often dominate dry desert landscapes. Flowers appear March through May.

Deciduous Plant Types

Ocotillo This plant looks like a cactus but is actually a member of the lily family. It leafs out and blossoms strictly according to the availability of water from March through July.

This plant was used for corral fencing—live stalks stuck into the ground grow easily into a barbed fence. The flowers are edible and contain a sweet nectar at their base.

Brittlebush This true shrub with bright yellow spring flowers blooms from February through June. Leaves are silver-green, triangular, and 1 to 2 inches long. In the winter, the plant drops most of its leaves and assumes a brittle brown-gray appearance. Broken stems exude a resin that was used by American Indians as a glue, an external pain reliever, and a chewable remedy for tooth pain. Spanish missionaries burned this resin in their churches as incense.

Specialized Leaf Types

Creosote Bush Probably the most successful desertshrub plant, creosote bush grows in a bushy form with very small resinous leaves that exude a creosote odor when wet. The coated leaves

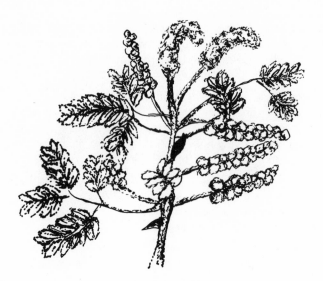

Catclaw

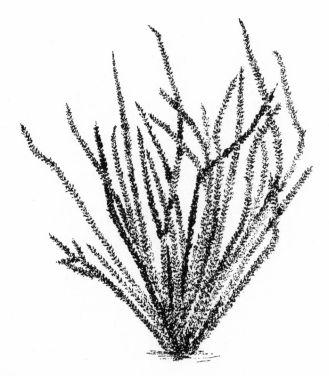

Ocotillo

Creosote bush

Jojoba

reduce water evaporation. The plant can withstand almost 50 percent water loss and still survive. Living specimens as old as 11,700 years have been found. Yellow flowers appear from February through August. Fuzzy, silver seed balls appear later.

Leaves are dried, put into a box with a label, sold as chaparral tea in food stores, and touted to cure everything from gout to cancer. The resin is also used as an insect repellent. The bottom 12 inches of the branches are usually very dry and provide good tinder.

Jojoba A very conspicuous shrub with large, gray-green leaves that have leathery surfaces that reduce transpiration. The nuts are edible but bitter and can make you sick because of the oils and acids. The oil has industrial applications and is also used in cosmetics.

Replaced Leaf Types

Barrel Cactus A fleshy cactus, sometimes mistaken for a saguaro. The barrel has flat, broad, curved spines that grow in denser patterns than those of the saguaro. Yellow-orange flowers blossom from July to September and are edible. The seeds from the fruit are also edible. When the fruit dries into a buff-colored fluff, it's perfect for fire tinder. The strong, curved spines were used by early Americans as sewing needles.

The barrel's crown often curves and points to the southwest, earning the cactus the nickname of "compass barrel."

Pincushion Cactus One of the smallest cacti, produces pink, red, and lavender flowers in spring and early summer. The flowers produce a tiny edible fruit resembling a chili pepper.

Saguaro Cactus This Sonora Desert plant can grow to over 50 feet, can weigh 10 tons, and may live 200 years. It blooms May through June with the white Arizona state flower. Ripened fruits provide food for many animals and are still used by some people for fresh fruit, jelly, and alcoholic beverages. The skeletal remains of the woody stalks are used for walking sticks, fencing, and wickiups. The spines are dark and straight as opposed to the barrel cactus's reddish and curved spines.

Hedgehog Cactus Grows in clumps of 5 to 20 stems, covered with long, straight spines. Purple or magenta flowers—a few gold— bloom February through May. Fruit is eaten by animals.

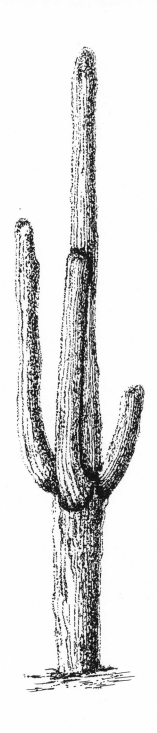

Saguaro cactus

Staghorn Cholla Cactus Treelike cactus with antlerlike branches of green to purple color. Multicolored flowers bloom in May. The yellowish fruit is eaten by animals and humans.

Prickly Pear Cactus Flat, oval joints characterize this widely distributed cactus. In May, yellow, orange, or magenta flowers bloom, producing a sweet, fleshy, red fruit by July that was used by early Americans to make muffins, jelly, and wine. Various species of prickly pear inhabit elevations from the deserts up to the pines.

Teddy Bear Cholla Cactus Known as "jumping cholla" because its stems break off easily and stick to hikers' boots, pants, and shirts. Branches are densely covered with spines. Produces a yellow flower and a green, edible fruit. Many times, bird nests can be seen in teddy bears. You're not a real desert hiker until you have picked up a teddy bear segment on your boot while hiking.

Chain-fruit Cholla Cactus Treelike cactus, resembling staghorn cholla, that blossoms with small, pink flowers. Green fruit is edible and hangs down in long chains from branches.

Christmas Cholla Cactus Inconspicuous, slender branches often hide this small bush, but in the winter it produces a bright red fruit that looks much like a tiny Christmas ball.

Mojave Thorn Shrublike plant that resembles palo verde. Has tiny leaves, but many gray-green thorns. Occupies a narrow elevation band between 3,000 and 4,000 feet.

COMMON DESERT ANIMALS

Insects

Spiders The black widow and brown recluse are the main poisonous spiders in Arizona, but they pose little harm to hikers. They both live in woodpiles, homes, and other places where they can "hide."

Scorpions Live under dead cactus skeletons, under rocks, and underground. You'll see one occasionally, but like most other desert animals, scorpions do their business at night.

Centipedes Rarely seen in the desert.

Prickly pear cactus

Chain-fruit cholla

Scorpion

Others Beetles, grasshoppers, butterflies, termites, crickets, ants, and bees. Also, little black ants are everywhere!

Tarantulas Summer is their most active time, especially at night. However, they live in burrows and are rarely observed.

Many of the common insects get moisture from the plant life and other insect life they consume. While the sun is up, they escape the daytime desert heat by going underground, into other plant life, under rocks, and into shady areas.

Rodents

Kangaroo Rat This little hand-size jumper is the best adapted of all desert animals in that it never has to drink water. It secures water through an efficient kidney that extracts what it needs from the food it eats. This character can gather a phenomenal amount of seeds in its cheek pouches as it hunts.

Harris's Antelope Squirrel Also well adapted to the desert, this chipmunklike rodent is identified by white stripes along each side of its body. It too secures most of its water from the food it eats.

Tarantula

Black-tailed Jackrabbit This fast-moving gray-brown jumper stays in the shade or hunkers down in cooler soil during the summer. It can grow to the size of a small coyote and is extremely fast. Desert hikers often scare it into movement.

Desert Cottontail Rabbit These gray-brown, domestic, cat-size rodents are smaller and slower than jackrabbits but can still be seen scurrying along the desert floor when spooked. They seek shade in holes and brush and provide food for many predators, including hawks.

White-throated Woodrat This double-hand-span-size "packrat" trades sticks and stones for trinkets it finds. It builds its apartmentlike home out of dried cholla cactus segments, which blend in with its own color. These "apartments" can be seen on the desert floor in huge piles.

Cottontail rabbit

Reptiles

Chuckwalla This large lizard found on rocky hillsides inflates itself in rock crevices for protection. Dark in color with an orange back and beige tail. Early American Indians would deflate them with a sharp stick and eat them.

Gila Monster A large venomous lizard with black, yellow, orange, and pink beadlike scales, can grow to 12 to 18 inches in length. Mostly nocturnal, lives in holes, and is quite secretive. You'll be lucky to see one and won't forget it when you do.

Desert Tortoise These animals are sometimes seen feeding in the early morning or evening. They live in burrows. You might find the shell of a deceased tortoise.

Horned Lizard Famous for its miniature dinosaur profile, this popular palm-size animal takes on the color of its surroundings—you

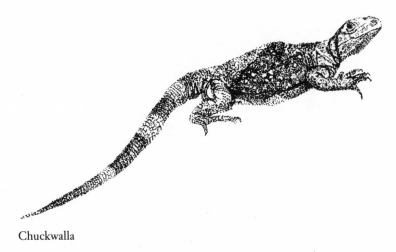

Chuckwalla

may see brown and tan, gray and blue, or reddish-rust horned lizards scampering over the terrain.

Snakes These much maligned animals inhabit all areas of Arizona but are mostly nocturnal and hide underground during the day. Most common are gopher snakes (resemble rattlers), king snakes (eat rattlers), garter snakes, and whiptail snakes.

The most common venomous snakes are the western diamondback and Mojave. They are usually heard before they're seen and will usually curl around the closest bush and rattle their warning when threatened.

Birds

Birds are the most mobile of all animals and can flit and fly back and forth between life zones and provinces. Some of those common to desert areas include the following:

Seed- and Insect-eating cactus wren, quail, thrasher, flicker, kingbird, hummingbird, mockingbird, flycatcher, and cardinal.

Predatory birds include red-tail hawk, bald eagle, great horned owl, roadrunner, raven, and vulture. The reddish-rust color of the large red-tail hawk distinguishes it as it floats on afternoon thermals, peering down for its rodent prey. The secretive bald eagle frequents waterways and is easily identified by its white head feath-

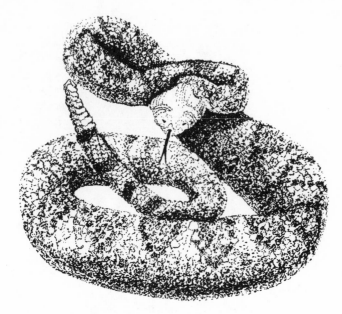

Western diamondback

ers. The grayish-colored great horned owl—one of the largest owls—hunts rodents at night. The brown-and-tan roadrunner chases just about everything across the desert floor. The jet-black raven is a scavenger, and the vulture lives off field carcasses and road kills.

Mammals

Coyote Song Dog of the West, Trickster, God's Dog—there are many names for this most adaptable canine. It eats almost anything and its range extends from Alaska to South America.

Gray Fox Smaller than the coyote, this nocturnal animal has a long tail, often striped down the back and black-tipped. Good tree-climber.

Ring-tail Cat Looks like a small raccoon. Inhabits rocky areas and can become a camp pet—or pest.

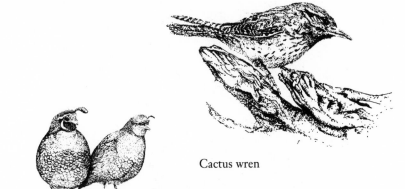

Cactus wren

Gamble quail

Roadrunner

Great horned owl

Coyote

Venomous Creatures

Concern for poisonous animals has been addressed in Chapter 1. Following is a more in-depth discussion of these creatures and how they fit into the natural history of this state.

Rattlesnakes These animals are called "pit" vipers in that they have a "pit" between the nostril and eye that serves as a heat-sensing device to help determine location and size of prey—especially at night, when they do most of their hunting.

Twenty-five percent of all poisonous snake bites are "dry" in that there is no envenomation. Every bite varies in the amount of venom injected, exact location of the venom, how toxic the venom is at the time of the bite, condition of the bite, and immune-system response.

Signs and symptoms of envenomation are metallic or rubbery taste in the mouth several minutes after bite, with tingling or numb tongue; swelling within ten minutes of bite; nausea, weakness, and temperature change; possible black and blue discoloration within three to six hours.

First Aid for Snakebites Get calm and let the anxiety level decrease before making any decisions. Get the victim to medical help. Don't try to treat the wound or catch the snake. Just proceed at your normal pace back to the vehicle, get to a ranger station or telephone, and advise the nearest hospital or clinic that you are headed there.

Scorpions Like most wild animals, scorpions have no use for humans—unless they get sat upon, grabbed by accident, or have their immediate territory invaded. They will sting out of defense, which results in numbness or swelling that is usually not any more of a problem than a bee sting.

One scorpion has the most potent venom—the bark scorpion, a small, delicate, slightly translucent animal. The great big scorpions you see in zoos and collections have big stingers but only average venom potency. Desert bare-ground campers are the most likely to get stung, especially if they don't make camp until after sundown.

Paper Wasps Commonly build nests in rock crevices and trees. May sting repeatedly.

Bees If you get stung and see the tiny stinger, don't pull it out. Instead, scrape the surface of your skin with a knife or smooth, straight object to dislodge the poison sack.

Velvet Ant The female is a wingless wasp with a velvety body of varying bright colors including black, orange, red, yellow, and white. Her body is beautiful but her sting is painful, like a bad bee sting.

Tucson Day Hikes

TUCSON

Tucson, Arizona's second largest city, is home for 678,000 citizens—a blend of Indian, Spanish, Mexican, and Anglo heritage. The original inhabitants, Hohokam Indians, developed complex farm irrigation systems from nearby mountain springs. Their Indian word "Chuk-son" (village of the dark spring at the foot of the mountains) was turned into "Tucson" by the Spanish and the name stuck. In 1775, the Spanish established the city as a walled presidio—the Presidio of San Augustine de Tucson.

The city became part of Mexico in 1821 when Mexico won its independence from Spain. In 1854 it became part of the United States as part of the Gadsden Purchase. Today, Tucson is a cosmopolitan city and one of the fastest growing in the United States. Population is expected to reach 1 million by the year 2000. Generally speaking, Tucson citizens are environmentally aware folks who are monitoring change in the "Old Pueblo" so that the city keeps its Southwest flavor.

At 2,548 feet, Tucson lies in the middle of the lushest desert in North America. To either side of the city lie the thickest stands of saguaro cactus anywhere—represented in Saguaro National Parks East and West. Adjacent to Saguaro National Park West is Tucson Mountain County Park, which comprises 17,000 acres of desert recreation area.

Just north of the city, the "sky island" Santa Catalina Mountains jut up into ponderosa pine and spruce-fir-aspen plant communities, making Mt. Lemmon (at 9,100 feet) the southernmost ski area in the nation—that is, when the winter jet stream drops far enough south to dump snow on it. About 40 miles south of Tucson lie the Santa Rita Mountains with the summit of Mt. Wrightson shooting up to 9,453 feet.

In one long day you can hike from Tucson's Sonora Desert up through five life zones to the top of Mt. Lemmon or Mt. Wrightson. No other place in the United States offers that much vertical hiking diversity in that short a time.

Directions to all Area Day Hike Takeoff Points around Tucson will start from I-10, which runs north and south through the city.

When to Go

Day hiking is done year-round in Tucson. During fall, winter, and spring, hikers have a choice of all the desert trails and some of the mountain trails (depending on snow). During summer, wise hikers start early in the morning on the mountain trails and get up into cooler temperatures by midday.

Places to Visit

The *Arizona-Sonora Desert Museum* is one of the most distinctive zoos in the United States because of its animal enclosures that look and feel like stone and earth, but are constructed with wood, wire mesh, and stucco—a pioneering technique copied around the world. Housing over 200 animal species, this living museum has been built with both humans and animals in mind.

Reptiles, invertebrates, and insects from the desert, along with Gila monsters, snakes, and endangered chuckwallas are on display. Mountain lions, black bears, and Mexican wolves are displayed in the Mountain Habitat exhibit. Bird exhibits include over 300 individuals, with an enclosed aviary and hummingbird sanctuary. A Riparian Habitat exhibits river otters and beavers.

But this is more than a zoo. It is a desert garden and a treasureland of Arizona natural history. More than 1,200 plant species are scattered throughout the grounds, including an area that displays natural vegetation from the Sonora Desert up to the fir-spruce-aspen community. Sonora Desert cactus are displayed throughout the museum.

This is one of the best places to start your Tucson day-hiking experience. After visiting this world-renowned zoo and garden, take a few hikes in the area—using this book—and you'll develop a much greater appreciation for the "lands of little water" and the plants and animals who live in it.

For more information, call or write the Arizona-Sonora Desert Museum, 2021 North Kinney Road, Tucson, AZ 85743, (602) 883-1380.

Tucson Botanical Gardens is located on five acres of landscaped desert grounds, herb gardens, native Southwest crops, and a tropical greenhouse. The garden offers tours, birding, horticulture, and plant identification classes for children, adults, and disabled persons, and an annual spring plant sale. For more information, contact Tucson Botanical Gardens, 2150 N. Alvernon Way, Tucson, AZ 85712, (602) 326-9686.

Saguaro National Park West Area

Saguaro National Park West contains the Tucson Mountains. It encompasses a series of desert peaks that go as high as the summit of Wasson Peak at 4,687 feet. This is a great winter and spring hiking region, giving the desert hiker a wilderness experience just outside the city limits. It has an excellent information center and three signed natural-history trails.

The 6-mile Bajada Loop Drive takes you on a dirt road through the most dense saguaro forest in the world. It also provides access to three of the best day hikes in the area.

Day Hike Area Takeoff Point Red Hills Information Center: Turn west off I-10 on Speedway Boulevard, which turns into Gates Pass Road and heads toward the Arizona-Sonora Desert Museum. Drive up and over Gates Pass, then down into the lower desert, where the road

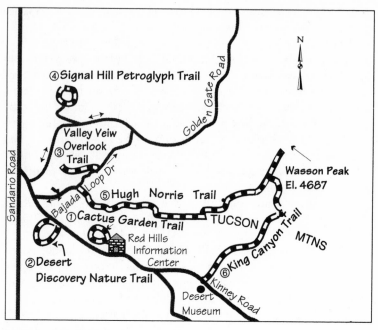

Saguaro National Park West Area

turns into Kinney Road at an intersection. Follow Kinney Road past the Arizona-Sonora Desert Museum and go to the Red Hills Information Center.

Campgrounds Gilbert Ray Campground located on the McCain Loop Road just off Kinney Road in Tucson Mountain County Park.

1. Cactus Garden Trail

Time: .5 hour. *Distance:* 100 yards. *Elevation Gain:* Level. *Rating:* Easy.

Trailhead: Just left of the Information Center entrance is the trailhead sign.

High Points: Interpretive signs provide information about the various water-adaptive mechanisms of desert plants. A good introduction to the local plant life.

Hiking the Trail: The path is wheelchair accessible and does a 100-yard loop through signed examples of the lush Sonora Desert Uplands Division plant life. Take the time to read the signs and you will gain a greater appreciation of the amazing adaptations and struggles that all life goes through to exist in this harsh environment.

2. Desert Discovery Nature Trail

Time: .5 hour. *Distance:* .5 mile. *Elevation Gain:* Level. *Rating:* Easy.

Trailhead: From Red Hills Information Center, drive northwest about 1 mile on Kinney Road to the sign that directs you to the vehicle pullout area. The trailhead is here.

High Points: Interpretive signs, describing features of the desert plants. A good trail for getting familiar with the Sonora Desert Uplands Division vegetation.

Hiking the Trail: This paved, wheelchair-accessible path offers shaded ramadas along the route. Many desert birds flit in and out of the ramadas and the surrounding brush. Take time to digest the information along this trail and the desert day hikes will have much more meaning for you. These interpretive signs explain how the web of life is formed in the desert areas.

3. Valley View Overlook Trail

Time: 1 hour. *Distance:* 1.5 miles roundtrip. *Elevation Gain:* Level. *Rating:* Easy.

Trailhead: From Red Hills Information Center, drive 1.5 miles northwest on Kinney Road to Bajada Loop Drive. Turn right on Bajada Loop Drive and drive past the Hugh Norris Trailhead for another .3 mile to the Valley View Overlook Trail sign. This is the trailhead.

High Points: Overlook of Avra Valley and the western horizon of the Coyote Mountains, Kitt Peak, and Baboquivari Peak.

Hiking the Trail: This trail provides a good opportunity to become familiar with the area bajada (floodplain) plant and animal life. The trail was built in the 1930s by the Civilian Conservation Corps.

Lots of bird and packrat nests can be seen in the cacti along this path. Packrats build huge mounds of cholla stems around their dugouts to ward off predators. Thrashers and cactus wrens build in the middle of chain-fruit and teddy bear cholla for the same reasons. It is fascinating to watch them flit in and out among the spines without getting spiked. You pass through a mini-forest of pencil cholla intermingled with the saguaro forest.

The path goes down and out of a large wash that displays the desert-wash runoff vegetation of giant bursage, more abundant mesquite, and larger palo verde trees. The path ends at the granite boulder overlook of Avra Valley and the far western skyline of Kitt Peak, Baboquivari Peak, and the Coyote Mountains. Picacho Peak is visible to the northwest. Return by the same route.

4. Signal Hill Petroglyph Trail

Time: .25 hour. *Distance:* .25 mile. *Elevation Gain:* 50 feet. *Rating:* Easy.

Trailhead: From Bajada Loop Drive, continue along the one-way route to Golden Gate Road. Turn left on Golden Gate and drive about a mile to the Signal Hill picnic area turnoff. Turn right onto the dirt road leading to the picnic area. The trailhead is immediately to the north of the picnic area.

High Points: Petroglyphs in profusion among the rock pile that overlooks the picnic area.

Hiking the Trail: Follow the path over the bridge to the huge boulder pile. Notice the picnic benches, fire pits, barbecue pits, and ramadas that are made out of local rock. The trail stops at the top of the rock pile, but you can climb around the jumbled mass of black boulders, discovering new spiral- and animal-shaped petroglyphs around each turn. These images were chipped out of the patina on the rocks with harder chisel rocks by early Hohokam Indians between 1400 and 900 A.D. Return the same way.

5. Hugh Norris Trail

Time: 6 hours. *Distance:* 6 miles roundtrip. *Elevation Gain:* 1,000 feet. *Rating:* Moderate.

Trailhead: From Red Hills Information Center, drive northwest on Kinney Road about a mile and a half to Bajada Loop Drive. Turn right on this road and drive another three-quarters of a mile to the Hugh Norris Trail sign. The trailhead is here.

High Points: Spectacular views of Tucson, the surrounding "sky island" mountain chains, and the Sonora Desert into Mexico.

Hiking the Trail: The first part of the route is constructed with rock steps to help control erosion. The Avra Valley, Kitt Peak, the Coyote Mountains, and Baboquivari Peak—the large nipple on the southwest horizon—come into view as the trail ascends. About .25 mile along, you cross a sandy wash and climb back out, gaining elevation. You are walking on decomposed granite, with its crumbly trail surface. Palo verde, mesquite, acacia, squaw berry, turpentine bush, and globe mallow line the path. Resurrection plant comes into view as the trail approaches the ridgeline. Various small saddles are reached that have side trails going to lookout points. Large granite boulders are exposed along the route, evidence that weathering from rain, ice, and wind grinds everything down in time.

The path reaches a ridge and crosses back and forth on the north and south slopes. From the north side, views of the Santa Catalinas, Picacho Peak, and the western part of Tucson open up. From the southern ridgeline, the Santa Ritas and Rincons show their "sky island" profiles. Yucca, agave, resurrection plant, chain-fruit cholla, and, of course, saguaro cactus show up along the ridge. Looking back to the Avra Valley, you can see thousands of saguaros dominating the landscape within the park. This is part of the largest concentration of saguaro cacti in the world.

The rock surface changes from granite into an older metamorphic core. As the trail traverses the north slope, a view of Wasson Peak to the east is seen with parts of the trail angling up it. You will pass some old mine diggings before reaching the junction of the Sendero Esperanza Trail coming in from the right and left. You have walked 2.7 miles. You can see the Arizona-Sonora Desert Museum to the southeast. Be on the watch for red-tail hawks and turkey vultures.

From here you can return by the same route or continue on to Wasson Peak—2.7 more miles of hiking.

6. King Canyon Trail

Time: 7 hours. *Distance:* 7 miles roundtrip. *Elevation Gain:* 1,900 feet. *Rating:* Challenging.

Trailhead: From Red Hills Information Center, travel southeast along Kinney Road to the Arizona-Sonora Desert Museum. The trailhead is just across the street from the museum entrance.

High Points: Wasson Peak, at 4,687 feet, is the highest point in the Tucson Mountains, with fantastic views of the Tucson basin and surrounding mountain "islands." Exhilarating hiking with continual views. Petroglyphs in the main wash.

Hiking the Trail: This path is the shortest route to the summit of Wasson Peak. It travels through an old copper mining area with evidence of mine shafts on steep hillsides. It starts as an old jeep road and gradually climbs along a drainage with exposed areas of a metamorphic core exhibited along the route. This core was lifted up and over the younger rocks by plate-tectonic pressures millions of years ago. There is a dramatic dropoff to the left into the wash that roars with spring runoff water.

Bedrock is exposed and bird life can be seen and heard down in this wash. The trail drops down and crosses the wash. A .25-mile side hike down the wash takes you past a small dam and to an area with many petroglyphs along both sides of the drainage. Linger in the streambed a bit to observe the plant life that is different and thicker here than in most other desert washes you encounter. Water lingers longer in washes due to the bedrock that pushes it to the surface. It stays longer into the summer and provides riparian habitat for animals and plants.

To continue on the King Canyon Trail, turn right at the Mam-a-gah sign and go past the old stone restrooms. You'll find another metal trail sign, directing you along the King Canyon Trail. This is the junction with the Sendero Esperanza Trail that comes in from the left. Stay right and head up the canyon. It is 2.7 miles to Wasson Peak from this point. The route continues up the ridges with ever-increasing views of the surrounding desert. An old mine road parallels the wash on the opposite side of the drainage. This climb continues up to a ridge that once again becomes an old jeep trail. Follow the trail until the road connects with the Sweetwater Trail. It is now a steep 1.2 miles to the summit of Wasson Peak. Turn left at this junction and switchback up to the junction of the Hugh Norris Trail. A short, level open path leads you to the summit trail and the top of Wasson Peak. Return by the same route.

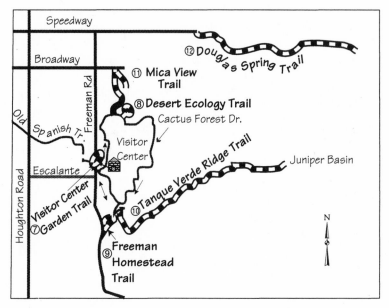

Saguaro National Park East Area

Saguaro National Park East Area

Saguaro National Park East is also called the Rincon Mountain District.

Evidence of early Hohokam occupation is found in these mountains in the form of petroglyphs and rock-grinding holes (holes shaped out of flat rock surfaces and used for grinding corn in combination with a rounded grinding rock).

The range is made up of ancient metamorphic rock complexes over a billion years old that were thrust up over younger layers. There is a predominance of black, white, and gray bedrock throughout the range and park.

Plant communities within the park include desertshrub, desert grassland, chaparral, oak-pine woodland, ponderosa pine, and spruce-fir-aspen zones. The Rincons are truly a "sky island" chain of mountains.

Animal life runs the gamut for all these communities. Since there are so many varied life zones within such a short vertical distance, many birds live on the sides of the mountain in the summer and down in surrounding desert in the winter.

There are over 128 miles of trails in the park. The highest destinations and life zones are best reached by overnight backpacks because they require long hikes up into the foothills. However, day hikers can reach the oak-pine woodland and even the ponderosa pine forests in a long, full-day hike.

Day Hike Area Takeoff Point Saguaro National Park East Visitor Center: From I-10, turn east on Broadway and go all the way to Freeman Road, which skirts the western boundary of the park. Drive south on Freeman Road to the intersection of Old Spanish Trail. Look for the park sign and turn into the park. The Visitor Center is just inside the boundary.

Campgrounds There are no vehicle access campgrounds in the east end of the park—there are only backcountry campgrounds. Use Gilbert Ray Campground in the Tucson Mountains (see Saguaro National Park West). You can also use campgrounds in the Coronado National Forest.

7. Visitor Center Garden Trail

Time: .5 hour. *Distance:* 50 yards. *Elevation Gain:* Level. *Rating:* Easy.

Trailhead: Next to Visitor Center.

High Points: Interpretive trail with plant identification signs.

Hiking the Trail: This is a short, paved path right next to the Visitor Center but well worth spending some time on, for it introduces the hiker to the vegetation of the area. It also houses a variety of bird life that flits in and out of the trees and shrubs, unconcerned with the human visitors who frequent this path.

8. Desert Ecology Trail

Time: 30 minutes. *Distance:* .25 mile. *Elevation Gain:* Level. *Rating:* Easy.

Trailhead: From the Visitor Center, follow the one-way Cactus Forest Drive past the Mica View picnic area and look for the Nature Trail sign where you can turn off and park. The trailhead is by the turnoff.

High Points: Interpretive signs describing the seasons in the Sonora Desert and water use by plants, animals, and humans.

Hiking the Trail: This is an excellent introduction to the Cactus Forest area and Sonora Desert weather patterns. When you hike this path, you are walking through the most lush desert in the world. At times, it almost seems like you are in a jungle—a jungle of spiny plants. The barrel cactus, acacia, mesquite, and staghorn cactus are huge along this path. The path winds by a streambed. Notice the heavier vegetation next to the wash—even though it is dry 95 percent of the year.

9. Freeman Homestead Trail

Time: 1 hour. *Distance:* 1 mile. *Elevation Gain:* 100 feet. *Rating:* Easy.

Trailhead: From the Visitor Center, turn right on the two-way drive that takes you to the Javelina picnic area. Look for the Freeman Homestead Trail sign. This is the trailhead.

High Points: A huge, eroded wash that once provided water for the early homestead. Site of the homestead cabin.

Hiking the Trail: Follow the arrows painted on the concrete triangles that lie at the trail junction. They lead you down into what remains of the homestead site alongside a huge arroyo, or desert wash. The path circles the site and heads back along the wash to the starting point. Even though the wash is dry most of the year, there is a difference in the vegetation along the streambed. Giant bursage is typical along the wash, as are mesquite and acacia. Look for the arrow that leads you out of the wash and back onto the original trail.

10. Tanque Verde Ridge Trail

Time: 9 hours. *Distance:* 12 miles roundtrip. *Elevation Gain:* 2,900 feet. *Rating:* Challenging.

Trailhead: From the Visitor Center, turn right on the two-way road that leads to the Javelina picnic area. Drive all the way to the picnic spot and look for the Tanque Verde trailhead at the edge of the turnaround.

High Points: Spectacular views of the Tucson basin and surrounding "sky island" mountain chains. The great variety in the plant community changes as you gain elevation. This trail is great for anything from a half-hour hike to the ridgeline, to a full day's hike to Juniper Basin—and everything in between. There are many vistas and lunch spots along this route, so you can make it as long as you want.

Hiking the Trail: After crossing a couple of small washes, you come to a post that holds a sign-in trail register. The path gets steeper as you climb up to the ridgeline. You are hiking on the crumbly erosion of uplifted ancient metamorphic rock. This black-and-white striated rock is pretty much the same bedrock you walk on for the entire hike. The path climbs to a couple of lookout points with side paths leading to overlooks of the bajadas that slope down from the main mountain. Bajada plant life includes prickly pear, teddy bear cholla, chain-fruit cholla, saguaro, ocotillo, hedgehog cactus, acacia, barrel cactus, palo verde, fairy duster, and desert hackberry. In summer and fall, the orange berries of the hackberry are favorite foods for animals, especially birds, but humans can eat them too. As the trail turns northeast along the ridgeline, grasses appear and the vegetation transitions from desertshrub to desert grassland. You pass through a mini-forest of prickly pear. Amole (shin dagger)—a small, clumplike succulent plant with sharp upward-pointing spines—begins to appear. Beargrass, agave, and sotol also appear, as you near the 4,000-foot level. The path crosses much flat bedrock. Look for the cairns.

Just past the 4,000-foot sign, there is a shady spot. Shade is scarce on this trail. At about 4,500 feet, you find the first scrub oak trees. Since this trail is long and gradual, you can see all the way up to the pines. A few more shady spots are found under the oaks. To the south, the point of Mt. Wrightson and the accompanying peak of Mt. Hopkins outline the Santa Ritas. To the west are the dark shadows of Kitt Peak, the Coyote Mountains, and the brooding, rounded summit of Baboquivari Peak. The sharp profile of Picacho Peak is seen in the haze to the northwest. The Santa Catalinas loom directly north. The long ridgeline you are on leads to Mica Mountain—at 8,666 feet the highest point in the park.

Junipers appear, along with manzanita, shortly before you reach the 5,000-foot elevation sign. Past the sign, the trail drops down into a large drainage. Pinyon is found along the route now. The climb back out of the wash leads to a hilltop where large oak trees make a good rest and snack spot with 270-degree vistas.

Reference to the city disappears as you continue on to Juniper Campground. You feel you are out of the desert and into a completely new environment. You cross a sandy streambed and climb up an area of loose rocks. Follow the red metal strips on the trees. After crossing a flat, rocky area and another streambed, hike another half mile to the Juniper Basin Campground. You'll find picnic tables, a toilet, and cooking grills.

Return by the same route.

11. Mica View Trail

Time: 2 hours. *Distance:* 1.5-mile loop. *Elevation Gain:* Level. *Rating:* Easy.

Trailhead: From the Visitor Center, go left through the fee station and onto the one-way Cactus Forest Drive. Follow this to the Mica View picnic area turnoff. Follow the dirt road for about .5 mile to the small picnic area. The trailhead starts here.

High Points: Great introduction to the Uplands Division of the Sonora Desert. Look for cactus wrens, roadrunners, doves, red-tail hawks, and various lizards.

Hiking the Trail: This is one of many loops possible in the Cactus Forest area. It is quite popular and easy to follow, with metal trail signs along the route. The first .7 mile is pretty much straight ahead and level to the Cactus Forest trailhead at Broadway Boulevard. It is a true wilderness experience, even though you are right next to the city.

Typical Uplands vegetation surrounds you with palo verde, mesquite, whitethorn acacia, creosote bush, desert hackberry, bursage, and chain-fruit cholla all around. This is a "dry" outwash area. These "dry" washes contain some moisture in the form of lusher plants and a corresponding increase in insect life. Birds and reptiles eat these small animals and the surrounding plant life, gaining food and water by doing so.

A large trail sign is located at the Broadway trailhead. Go east from the trail sign for a few yards until you find another metal trail sign pointing you back to the Mica View Campground at .9 mile. Follow this for a little over a half mile until you find another trail sign that directs you back to the picnic area—about .3 mile.

12. Douglas Spring Trail

Time: 8 hours. *Distance:* 12 miles roundtrip. *Elevation Gain:* 2,000 feet. *Rating:* Challenging.

Trailhead: From the Visitor Center, go back out of the park and turn right on Freeman Road. Follow Freeman to Speedway Boulevard. Turn right on Speedway and follow it to the end where the Douglas Spring trailhead is located.

High Points: Great views of the Tucson basin and the Santa Catalina Mountains. The juxtaposition of revegetation over an old burned area. Unusual bedrock streambed surfaces surrounded by mesquite bosques.

Hiking the Trail: This trail can be enjoyed for short or long distances, since there are great vistas and lunch spots all along the route. Most of this trail was burned over in a fire during July of 1989. It has revegetated remarkably and provides a visual juxtaposition of the old fire and the new growth. The trail starts by a shaded ramada and is level for the first .25 mile, going through a creosote bush forest. You are in the wilderness from the minute you step out onto the trail, with no reference to Tucson until you climb higher. The path angles up into the foothills with a steep drainage on the left. There are several view spots with side trails leading to them.

Looking back, the Tucson basin starts to appear over the foothills. You notice the blackened stalks of burned vegetation and the new, green growth surrounding them. After a couple of miles, you cross a large wash with lots of exposed bedrock. The trail continues to angle up with the drainage on the right. Large stands of mesquite trees are visible in the drainage, evidence of a good deal of water that stays in the soil most of the year. Look for water pockets in the rocky streambed bottoms. Also look for deer, javelina, skunk, coyote, and fox along this drainage. The path continues to skirt this impressive streambed that invites you to explore its many pools and clusters of vegetation. Local hikers frequently swim in the many pools during the summer months, but you do so at your own risk because there is no assurance of safety. The route turns left away from the drainage and continues on to Douglas Spring. A large outcropping of rocks straight ahead is Helen's Dome. Further east is Spud Rock, named

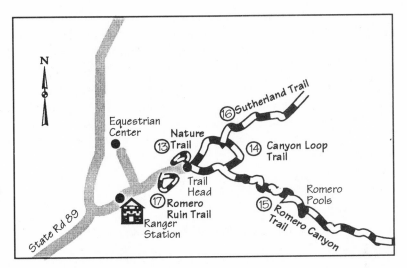

Catalina State Park Area

after a man who grew potatoes near the rock in 1890. The trail now descends to the campground. The campground contains a restroom and horse hitching post. Return by the same route.

Catalina State Park Area

Catalina State Park has one of the most dramatic backdrops in the state—that of the northwest escarpment of the Catalina Mountains. The escarpment looks like a Yosemite Valley of the desert as it slopes down from ponderosa pines through chaparral, pinyons, and junipers and into the desert canyons and foothills where the park lies.

Early Hohokam Indians farmed and hunted this area, with its year-round water, mixed vegetation, and variety of animal life. Gold seekers traveled the valley below the range and later cattle ranchers settled here—continually fighting off Apache Indian raids. The huge vertical walls of the escarpment are composed of metamorphosed schist and granite, providing rock climbers with myriad route opportunities.

The 5,500-acre Catalina State Park sits at the base of a true "sky island" with its mixed vegetation and animal life combinations overlapping in vertical zones of biotic diversity. A strong hiker can trek up through five life zones in one long day. We won't go that far in this book, but we'll go partway up into the rugged range, enticing you to further explore its remote wilderness trail system.

Day Hike Area Takeoff Point Catalina State Park Trailhead Parking Area: From I-10, turn east onto Tangerine Road and follow it to 1st Avenue. Turn south on 1st Avenue, driving past Nariana Road to Oracle Road. Turn northeast on Oracle Road and drive to the park entrance.

Campgrounds Catalina State Park Campgrounds.

13. Nature Trail

Time: 1 hour. *Distance:* .75 mile. *Elevation Gain:* 50 feet. *Rating:* Easy.

Trailhead: At the northwest end of the trailhead parking area.

High Points: Signed plant posts for desert plant identification. Overviews of the Santa Catalina escarpment.

Hiking the Trail: Follow the trail sign at the end of the parking area. The path leads to a series of steps, formed by railroad ties. The path levels out and travels along an outwash bajada, created by millions of years of erosion from the steep escarpment of the Santa Catalina range. This escarpment is formed by Yosemite-Valley-like walls jutting up in the middle of the Sonora Desert. Wooden benches allow 360-degree views of the range, the city of Tucson, and the Oro Valley, which runs along the base of the range. The blackened vegetation is evidence that you are passing through a previous burn area. The path loops around and back to the parking area.

14. Canyon Loop Trail

Time: 2 hours. *Distance:* 2 miles. *Elevation Gain:* Level. *Rating:* Easy.

Trailhead: Look for the trailhead sign just to the left of the portable toilets at the end of the trailhead parking area.

High Points: A great, short trail that includes a watered desert wash, a sandy bench, and a park that leads up a bajada.

Hiking the Trail: This path connects with both the Romero Canyon and Sutherland trails and forms a delightful loop for a short,

2-hour day hike. Follow the route along Sutherland Wash, which displays huge sotol plants, barrel cactus, and giant bursage. Quail, roadrunners, doves, cactus wrens, and thrashers abound. A sandy bench and bajada section takes you right up to the edge of the range with fantastic views of the escarpment walls.

15. Romero Canyon Trail

Time: 5 hours. *Distance:* 6 miles roundtrip. *Elevation Gain:* 1,000 feet. *Rating:* Challenging.

Trailhead: A large trail sign is located just past the portable toilets across from the trailhead parking area. The trailhead starts here.

High Points: This is one of the state's most beautiful and remote hiking areas located close to an urban center, with spectacular canyon and escarpment vistas. Changing vegetation zones. Beautiful swimming pools in Romero Canyon.

Hiking the Trail: The path crosses Sutherland Wash and follows a roadbed, slowly climbing to an intersection of the Canyon Loop Trail. The path is sandy, surrounded with mesquite trees, and proceeds along a foothill. You next come across the intersection of the Romero and Montrose Canyon trails. Montrose Canyon slopes off to the right where bedrock pools are visible down in the canyon. The easy, sandy roadbed trail ends here and the rocky, rough ridgeline trail begins. Stay left past the intersection sign and follow the well-used trail as it angles up the left side of Montrose Canyon. Various side trails lead down to the canyon, but you must stay left in the main path. The angle steepens and the Tucson skyline becomes visible. You are now in wild country, surrounded by decomposed granite and gneiss, providing views of the great faces, domes, and walls of the Catalina escarpment.

The trail continues to climb up above Montrose Canyon and reaches the top of a ridge where the path crosses over to Romero Canyon. You have been climbing up the raised edge of a fault-block mountain range—a piece of the earth's crust that was cracked and broken and tilted millions of years ago. As you look down into Romero Canyon, you can hear the waterfalls and see the bedrock pools, formed from rainwater and snowmelt runoff. They are inviting in the warm months, and the water is not that cold. Continue along the main path until you come to the canyon crossing. Side paths along the pool edges take you to various swimming holes.

Return by the same route.

16. Sutherland Trail

Time: 4 hours. *Distance:* 4 miles roundtrip. *Elevation Gain:* 400 feet. *Rating:* Easy.

Trailhead: A large trail sign is located left of the portable toilets and left of the Romero Canyon Trail sign at the Trailhead Parking Area.

High Points: Easy, gentle trail that offers unparalleled views of the Santa Catalina range escarpment.

Hiking the Trail: The path follows along Sutherland Wash before intersecting the junction of the Canyon Loop Trail at the edge of the wash. The wash generally has water running in it. The route angles up out of the wash and proceeds along a level, sandy bench with spectacular views of the Catalina escarpment to the east, greater Tucson to the south, and the Tucson Mountains to the west. This very pleasant path winds slightly uphill along the bench to give you even greater views of the granite and gneiss domes and walls of the range. At about the 2-mile mark, the trail becomes overgrown with brush and somewhat difficult to follow beyond Cargodera Canyon. Return by the same route.

17. Romero Ruin Trail

Time: .5 hour. *Distance:* .5 mile. *Elevation Gain:* Level. *Rating:* Easy.

Trailhead: From the trailhead parking area, drive back toward the park entrance. You will see the Romero Ruin Trail sign on the left. Pull off into the parking area on the right. The trailhead is across the street.

High Points: Interpretive signs that point out the remains of early Hohokam habitation and the remains of the Romero Ranch—a pioneering effort to raise cattle in the area.

Hiking the Trail: Take the loop path up the slightly elevated ridgeline and follow the interpretive signs. With plenty of water, game, and an abundance of plant life, this spot was ideal for early habitation.

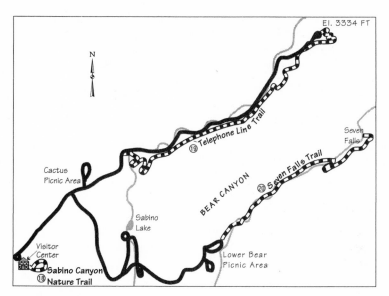

Sabino Canyon Area

Add to that the fact that the inhabitants could easily go up the mountain in the hot summer months to escape the desert sun, and this spot is hard to beat.

Sabino Canyon Area

Sabino Canyon is one of the most beautiful desert canyons in Arizona. Sabino Creek drains from the southern slopes of the Catalina Mountains, eroding the steep, striated, metamorphosed gneiss walls into the drainage, slowly grinding the large streambed stones to particles that will eventually find their way to the desert bajadas below. Water means wildlife in the desert. Early Native Americans settled the area due to the bountiful water and mammoths, bison, and other large animals to hunt. Later Native American cultures hunted deer, antelope, bighorn sheep, and rabbit. The canyon provided access to higher, cooler areas during summer migrations. The year-round water also provided nourishment for corn, squash, and beans on the floodplain.

In the 1930s, the Civilian Conservation Corps helped build a road, bridges, picnic areas, toilet facilities, and retaining walls in the canyon. Today, access is possible only by foot, bicycle, and motorized tram. The tram takes visitors up the old Sabino Canyon Road, stopping along the way at scenic spots. It's an hour roundtrip. Hikers sometimes take the train up and hike back down the road.

Day Hike Area Takeoff Point Sabino Canyon Visitor Center: From I-10, turn east onto Orange Grove Road. Follow Orange Grove to Sunrise Drive. Follow Sunrise Drive to the end where signs direct you to the Sabino Canyon Recreation Area parking lot and visitor center.

Campgrounds Catalina State Park Campground and open camping in the Coronado National Forest.

18. Sabino Canyon Nature Trail

Time: .25 hour. *Distance:* .5 mile. *Elevation Gain:* Level. *Rating:* Easy.

Trailhead: Located next to the Sabino Canyon Visitor Center.

High Points: Signage that introduces vegetation of the surrounding desert.

Hiking the Trail: This delightful walk introduces you to the foothill vegetation surrounding the Santa Catalina Mountains. If you can pick these out on the trail, you are on your way to becoming an amateur naturalist. You might even walk this path twice to remember the plant names.

19. Telephone Line Trail

Time: 3 hours. *Distance:* 4 miles. *Elevation Gain:* Drops 300 feet. *Rating:* Moderate.

Trailhead: From the Visitor Center, take the hourly narrated tram ride up the paved road to the turnaround at the head of Sabino Canyon. Notice the huge, vertical walls of layered brown and white gneiss strata on each side of the canyon as you ride the tram up. The trailhead starts at the end of the tram ride, at the turnaround point in the road.

High Points: Great views looking down into Sabino Canyon and out to the Tucson skyline.

Hiking the Trail: A prominent trail sign indicates the Romero Pass and Palisades trails. Follow this obvious switchbacking trail for about .25 mile up to the junction of the Phoneline Trail. Turn right on the Phoneline Trail and start along the level path that takes you back down to the Visitor Center. You are walking on pieces of very friable gneiss, characterized by soft, brittle layers that break off as you walk on them. You pass a variety of vegetation that includes brittlebush, catclaw, cane cholla, desert hackberry, burro bush, fairy duster, hop bush, turpentine bush, palo verde, buckwheat, sotol, barrel cactus, desert lavender, and ocotillo. Remnants of an old telephone line are visible above the trailbed. Rock-climbing routes have been pioneered on the surrounding gneiss walls. You may see or hear climbers ascending the vertical faces. Down and to the right lies the drainage of Sabino Canyon with its riparian vegetation of willow, Arizona sycamore, box elder, Emory oak, and wildflowers. Various pools are now visible along the canyon drainage. By looking back and to the right, you can see the tops of the Catalinas, with ponderosa pine and fir communities on the highest ridgelines. In front, the Tucson skyline opens up as you gradually descend the canyon from your higher viewpoint. After a little over 3 miles along the route, you reach a sign designating a right turn down to the first tram stop on the road. Follow this to the road and follow the road another mile or so back to the Visitor Center.

20. Seven Falls Trail

Time: 2 hours. *Distance:* 2.2 miles. *Elevation Gain:* 200 feet. *Rating:* Moderate.

Trailhead: From Sabino Canyon Visitor Center, take the hourly tram to Bear Canyon picnic area. The trailhead starts near the restrooms at the end of the picnic area loop.

High Points: Seven Falls pools and waterfalls. Rich riparian vegetation along the route. Views of the upper canyon walls and domes.

Hiking the Trail: This path follows the Bear Canyon streambed and crosses the drainage at various spots, requiring boulder hopping and some rock scrambling. Flash floods have brought down large gneiss boulders that fill the drainage. Many are piled up over the path, necessitating rock hopping on some of the crossings. Remnants of old cemented rock supports show the power of the floods, as the remaining bent over .75-inch-thick steel rebar shafts show. The route is confined to the narrow canyon, and vegetation is riparian. Mesquite trees dominate the drainage with Arizona sycamore, alder and willow trees, brittlebush, and giant bursage spread throughout. About 2 miles along the route, the path starts up and climbs about 200 feet above the canyon floor. You begin to see a large pool ahead to the left. The spectacular Seven Falls drainage comes upon you suddenly, coming in at a 90-degree angle from the left. In the spring and summer, these pools are fed by upper-canyon water flow, creating a series of seven major falls and pools—favorites for summer hikers to cool off in. Return by the same route.

Santa Rita Mountains Area

The Santa Rita Mountains jut up from the desert floor to the southeast of Tucson. They are heavily mineralized and contain an historic past of both violence and riches in the efforts to extract the wealth. The gold rush is long past and the area is now sought after for its scenic and recreational values.

The day hikes on Mt. Wrightson are the southernmost hikes in this book. Views from these hikes extend south into Mexico.

Day Hike Area Takeoff Point Intersection of I-19 and Madera Canyon Road: From I-10, drive south through Tucson and get onto I-19 heading for Nogales. About 4 miles south of Green Valley, look for Madera Canyon Road.

Campgrounds Bog Springs, Coronado National Forest open camping.

21. Kent Springs—Bog Springs Loop Trail

Time: 7 hours. *Distance:* 5.5 miles. *Elevation Gain:* 1,800 feet up and 1,800 feet down. *Rating:* Challenging.

Trailhead: From the intersection of I-19 and Madera Canyon Road, follow Madera Canyon Road to Bog Springs Campground. The trailhead is located on an old road just downhill from the parking lot.

High Points: Lush riparian vegetation and the resulting bird and wildlife. Manmade spring sites.

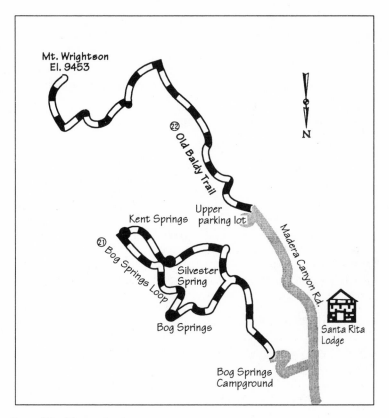

Santa Rita Mountains Area

Hiking the Trail: Follow the old road about .75 mile to the turnoff to Bog Springs. The road turns into a narrow trail and climbs for a mile until it slopes down to Bog Springs. The spring is actually a concrete tank with a drinking-water spigot close by. This bog, or wet place, attracts doves, hawks, thrashers, javelina, coyotes, and all manner of other birds and wildlife in great numbers, and it might be worthwhile to just sit here awhile—back from the spring—and watch the action. This special area contains sycamore, walnut, fir, and Arizona bamboo.

Continue climbing onto the scrub oak ridgeline and on to Kent Spring with its views southeast to Mt. Wrightson. Soon you are on top of the ridge, looking east to Kitt Peak and Baboquivari Peak. Kent Spring is another boggy area with lush riparian habitat. After a sharp right turn the trail turns into an old jeep road that skirts a small stream back down to Sylvester Spring. Follow this riparian habitat path along the lovely streambed back to Bog Springs Campground.

22. Old Baldy Trail to Josephine Saddle

Time: 5 hours. *Distance:* 5 miles roundtrip. *Elevation Gain:* 2,200 feet up and 4,000 feet back down. *Rating:* Very challenging.

Trailhead: From the intersection of I-19 and Madera Canyon Road, follow Madera Canyon Road through Continental, and on to the upper parking lot. The Old Baldy trailhead is located .3 mile down a road from the southern end of the parking lot.

High Points: This is a true wilderness day hike into a "sky island" with its inherent vertical life-zone mixtures and fantastic birding opportunities and views into Mexico.

Hiking the Trail: This is the most direct route to Josephine Saddle. An overnight at the Saddle would allow you to climb to the summit of Mt. Wrightson the next day. A short way from the trailhead, the Old Baldy Trail makes a sharp left. The trail climbs continually from here through Emory oaks, Arizona oaks, and junipers to Josephine Saddle. Stop (as you surely will) along this climb and listen for bird calls. The area is rich in bird life, and birders from all over the world come to the Santa Ritas, and other southern Arizona areas, looking for various species. You might spot sulphur-bellied flycatchers, yellow-eyed juncos, western tanagers, flickers, grosbeaks, and jays. As you reach the shoulder of Josephine Saddle, look up at the impressive summit blocks. Then look back at the Tucson basin. You are a long way up from the desert floor. Josephine Saddle is a ponderosa-pine-clad junction of many trails and a great camping spot. It's also a good lunch and rest spot for the steep climb up to the summit of Wrightson on an overnight backpack.

The climb to the summit is a real challenge, but worth the effort for the beauty of the changing vegetation and spectacular vistas from this "sky island" summit. You climb through thick brush, aspen, oak, and ponderosa pine. You'll pass by Bellows Spring with its flowing water pipe, then continue on up switchbacks to the summit. Views extend into Mexico and the surrounding peaks of Mt. Hopkins, Kitt Peak, and Baboquivari Peak. You are at the summit of one of the southernmost "sky islands" in this desert region.

Return by the same route.

CHAPTER 5

Phoenix Day Hikes

Phoenix

Phoenix Mountains Preserve Region
Squaw Peak Park Area
Lookout Mountain Area
North Mountain Park Area
Echo Canyon Area
South Mountain Park Area

Maricopa County Parks Region
Estrella Mountain Park Area
White Tank Mountains Park Area
McDowell Mountain Park Area
Usery Mountain Park Area

Superstition Mountains Region
First Water Area
Peralta Canyon Area
Lost Dutchman State Park Area

PHOENIX

Hohokam Indians were the first day hikers and settlers here, utilizing the Salt and Verde river systems for primitive agriculture. They appeared around 300 B.C. and continued farming until around the 1500s. They dug the now-famous gravity-fed irrigation canals—some 200 miles of them—with sticks and stones. These canals averaged 30 to 40 feet wide and 15 feet deep. They are still used today.

After the Hohokam left the Salt River Valley, Pima Indians, Spaniards, and Mexicans farmed along the river. In 1867, the first major irrigation project was started by an ex–Confederate soldier named Jack Swilling. He observed the original canals and got funding to improve them and open them for modern irrigation.

The valley filled with farms, and in 1870 the area was named Phoenix, for the mythical bird consumed by fire only to rise again from its own ashes—much as the valley did when the irrigation allowed the farming to flourish again.

Today, the Phoenix area is a metropolis of 2 million people, situated on the banks of the now-dry Salt River at the interface of the Southern Deserts and Central Mountains provinces. The Roosevelt Dam project—which was authorized by Teddy Roosevelt—remains the biggest stone-masonry dam in the world. The Salt River Project was constructed to regulate riverflow for both farming and flood control. A subsequent series of dams below Roosevelt created water-recreation areas that now host thousands of summer boaters, fishermen, campers, swimmers, and lake loungers.

For this book, Phoenix encompasses the entire Salt River Valley megalopolis. Somewhat like Los Angeles, many suburbs have combined to form the "Valley of the Sun." Almost 65 percent of Arizona's population lives in this valley, not counting the huge influx of winter visitors and pass-through tourists.

Phoenix embraces over 130 community, neighborhood, district, and mountain parks, with more land acquisition planned. This provides unique opportunities for city dwellers to experience the desert wilderness in their own backyards.

Directions to all Day Hike Area Takeoff Points for all three Phoenix Day Hike Regions are from I-17, which runs north and south through the center of Phoenix.

When to Go

Best Phoenix hiking weather is during the fall, winter, and spring months of October through April. The summer months of May through September are hot for day hiking, except for early morning strolls. However, in the summer you can head north in a short two-hour drive up to the Central Mountains Province for those refreshing day hikes in the greener, cooler climate of that higher, wetter elevation.

Places to Visit

The *Desert Botanical Garden* opened in 1939 on 145 acres in the Lower Colorado River Division of the Sonora Desert in Papago Park next to the Phoenix Zoo. There are over 15,000 desert plants representing over 3,500 species. One-third of these are from the Phoenix area; two-thirds are from South America, Central America, Africa, Australia, and other arid regions.

The garden contains a demonstration area with seasonal displays of landscape plants that show the grower how to cultivate desert plants in the arid Phoenix environment. A vegetable plot is displayed.

A new and still developing exhibit, called Plants and People of the Sonora Desert, incorporates three acres of saguaro forest, mesquite thicket, desert stream environment, and upland chaparral habitat. This exhibit displays prehistoric and historic living structures along the trail with interpretive settings for native plant uses. The garden holds annual plant sales in the spring and fall and has an activities calendar for year-round educational programs. It also has a gift shop with many books on desert natural history. For more information, call or write to Desert Botanical Garden, 1201 North Galvin Parkway, Phoenix, AZ 85008, (602) 941-1225.

The Phoenix Zoo is located on 125 acres of rolling desert hills, shaded paths, and natural environments, with over 1,000 animals displayed. The Arizona Trail section contains animals from this state in a special enclosure, including a walk-through aviary, reptiles, coyotes, roadrunners, javelina, pronghorn antelopes, mountain lions, bobcats, bald eagles, coati-mundi, Mexican gray wolf, and other desert dwellers.

Since animals are the most illusive components of Arizona's natural history, a visit to the zoo before heading out to the hiking areas is well worthwhile. The zoo is located right next to the Desert Botanical Garden, so you could visit both in one day. For more information, write or call The Phoenix Zoo, P.O. Box 5155, 5810 E. Van Buren, Phoenix, AZ 85010, (602) 273-1341.

The *Boyce Thompson Southwestern Arboretum* was founded in 1929 by William Boyce Thompson, a successful mining magnate who wanted to create a plant-life study facility and public display museum. It is now jointly administered by the University of Arizona and Arizona State Parks. It is situated on 1,076 acres at 2,400-foot elevation just south of Superior, 50 miles east of Phoenix on State Route 60.

This is an enchanting place for hiker/naturalists to visit because it is a composite of microhabitats. The hiker is led through a plant display of Desert Uplands vegetation, then to a permanent desert pond, then down along a perennial streambed, and finally along a path shaded by arid land plants imported by Boyce Thompson from all over the globe.

Outdoor education classes are offered to all grades, including college credit courses. The arboretum holds spring and fall plant sales, drawing folks from all over the state. Contact the Boyce Thompson Arboretum, P.O. Box AB, Superior, AZ 85273, (602) 689-2811.

PHOENIX MOUNTAINS PRESERVE REGION

This collection of city parks is a major focal point for Phoenix day hikers. It consists of the Squaw Peak Park Area, Lookout Mountain Area, North Mountain Park Area, Echo Canyon Area, and South Mountain Park Area.

Easily accessible from I-17, these mountains and rolling desert parks are oases of play and relaxation, offering the day hiker unlimited opportunities to roam and explore the geology and plant and animal life of the Sonora Desert. From sharp-peaked summits and ridgelines to hidden valleys and drainages, this urban calm in the middle of the urban hustle is a welcome respite for the desert dwellers of Phoenix.

Trails are so numerous in the preserve that different day hikes could be taken on successive weekends for a year and not be repeated. There are elevation gains of a thousand feet on some of the preserve peaks. Desert valleys can be found within the area where there is no sign, sound, or evidence of the metropolis. One can literally get lost in the Phoenix Mountains Preserve.

We won't get lost, but we'll explore some exciting trails in the preserve that take us to vistas of both the Southern Deserts and Central Mountains provinces. We'll hike up the faces of fault-block mountains, along their edges, and in the basins between them. We'll find our way through jumbled volcanic remnants, across dry desert washes, and into exotic riparian habitats. We'll hike right along a mountain edge that separates the Central Mountains Province from the Southern Deserts Province.

Area facilities include picnic ramadas, restrooms, drinking water, and fire pits.

Campgrounds There are no public campgrounds within the Phoenix Mountains Preserve Region, only picnic areas. Use Tonto National Forest or Maricopa County Park campgrounds (listings included in subsequent trail descriptions).

Squaw Peak Park Area

The Squaw Peak Park Area is composed of the tops of fault-block mountains worn down by time so that what remains is the tops of the ancient peaks with the eroded debris lying between them. Most of the rocks are composed of metamorphosed (changed by heat and pressure) materials. The bottom layers of Squaw Peak are very old grayish-colored gneiss and schist. These old rocks were heated and compressed below the surface, causing their crystals to align themselves in layers, forming this foliated, striped rock, streaked with infused white quartz. The middle layers of the peak are composed of meta-rhyolite (metamorphosed volcanic ash) from ancient volcanic eruptions. The top of the peak is made up of quartzite (metamorphosed sand). Milky white quartz outcroppings can be seen throughout the park. Vegetation is the typical mixture of Lower and Upper Sonoran desertshrub with plenty of saguaros, ocotillos, barrel cactus, palo verde, and mesquite.

While hiking in this park, there is a good chance of seeing—or hearing—coyotes, lizards, cactus wrens, thrashers, doves, owls, ringtail cats, and gopher snakes. You'll also scare up bunches of black-throated sparrows and quail.

Day Hike Area Takeoff Point—Navajo Ramada Turn east off I-17 on Glendale Avenue. Drive to 16th Street where Glendale turns into Lincoln Drive. Go east on Lincoln and exit north on Squaw Peak Drive (between 16th and 24th Streets). This road leads up into Squaw Peak Park, where the ramadas blend into the mountainside. After entering the park, turn left into the first parking lot, just south of the Navajo Ramada.

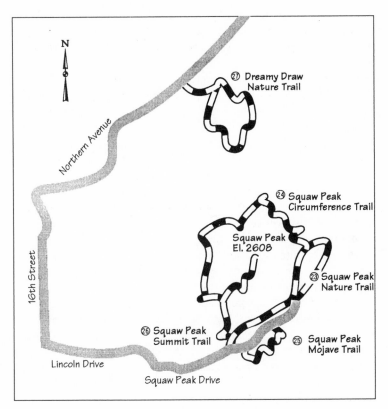

Squaw Peak Park Area

23. Nature Trail

Time: 1 hour. *Distance:* 1.5 miles roundtrip. *Elevation Gain:* 250 feet. *Rating:* Easy.

Trailhead: From the Navajo Ramada, follow the park road up to Apache Ramada. The trailhead is at the square, brown trail post near the bulletin board.

High Points: Interpretive signs, identifying typical Lower and Upper Sonoran plant zone vegetation. A good introductory trail to the Squaw Peak Area.

Hiking the Trail: Follow posts for Trail #304, which parallels Trail #302, the Squaw Peak Circumference Trail, for about .5 mile, angling up northeast to a saddle. The first interpretive sign is for the palo verde tree. Go on to the ocotillo sign. This gangly plant may flower four or five times a year. If you sit and watch the flower stalks long enough, you may see a carpenter bee bore a hole in the side of the bloom to suck out the nectar. A little way past the ocotillo sign there is a large piece of pink quartz, striated with black lines. Quartz is beach sand that existed on the edge of ancient seas that was buried and metamorphosed to the milky-colored hard rock you see.

The Arizona fishhook cactus sign is next. These little beauties are protected against collectors by law—as are all Arizona cacti. You're walking on alluvium deposits that have been changed by heat and pressure into schist (gray) with quartz crystals (white) throughout. Orange and brown/black colors on the rocks are a patina of manganese and clay. Notice a boulder—about 55 paces past the sign—that contains groups of other white crystals between the schist and quartz. These are kyenite crystals, which make up the very hard rock used in the manufacture of spark plugs. During World War II, 38 tons of kyenite were mined from Squaw Peak Park.

The trail starts up a steep gully and goes on to the barrel cactus sign. Feel the sharp, curved spines of this plant—once used by desert Indians for sewing needles. This fascinating succulent contains chemicals similar to antifreeze, which help the cactus survive below 32° F temperatures. A little past the barrel cactus sign, you'll see a large outcrop of white quartz on the edge of an old mine prospect. The miners were probably looking for gold or mercury. No gold has ever been found, but some mercury has been taken out. Look inside the prospect and you'll see a dark greenish-gray rock. This was once a volcanic basalt and was metamorphosed about 1.7 billion years ago into "greenstone" or a metabasalt.

Keep to the left at the staghorn cholla sign. The staghorn grows edible buds in the spring. Indians baked the buds and rolled the spines off before eating. Hike to the brittlebush sign. If you are there from March through June, you'll see bright yellow blossoms of this scrub plant all over the south sides of mountains and in the flatlands. The saguaro cactus is next. Look for holes bored into the flesh of this giant apartment house for local owls, woodpeckers, and flickers. The Perl Charles Trail (1A) soon comes in from the left. This is the halfway point of the hike.

The teddy bear cholla sign comes into view next. A little farther and partway up the hill to the left is a large black rock outcrop. The black is a coating of manganese oxides and iron called "desert varnish." Early Native Americans drew petroglyphs on similar rocks by scratching through the varnish and exposing the lighter rock below. Proceed to the bursage sign. This plant grows in profusion in wet years, with thousands of blooms on the west-facing slope of Squaw Peak. The hedgehog cactus is next. These cucumber look-alikes grow in clumps and have an edible fruit. The slender Christmas cactus comes next. In winter, you can see the small bright-red fruits that remind you of Christmas balls or lights on a tree. The prickly pear cactus is next, with its ripe red fruit available in early summer, which you will see lying around where desert animals have feasted. The Mormon tea sign is next. The dried stalks make a strong tea. The creosote bush is the last plant sign. Smell the pungent leaves.

This delightful loop hike should whet your appetite for more knowledge of the desert landscape. Keep the plants and rocks you discovered on this hike in mind as you explore the other park trails.

24. Circumference Trail

Time: 5 hours. *Distance:* 4 miles roundtrip. *Elevation Gain:* 1,000 feet. *Rating:* Challenging.

Trailhead: The trailhead is located at the northeast end of the Navajo Ramada parking area. Look for the brown signpost for Trail #302.

High Points: Views of the entire Phoenix area, extending northeast to the Central Mountains Province. North and south slope desert vegetation changes. A complete circumference of Phoenix's most popular mountain.

Hiking the Trail: This is one of the best half-day desert hikes in Arizona, consisting of a 4-mile circle around, and up, Squaw Peak Mountain.

Round bunches of grass line the path in profusion when there's a wet winter, as do the short, wheatlike red brohm and schimus grass. Triangular-leaved bursage comes out every year, covering the east side of the slopes. About .25 mile along the trail, look left to a short, vertical wall of bright gray schist with foliations (bands). This was probably buried and compressed for a billion years before being exposed to surface erosion. Another .25 mile along, you'll find a stone seat. As you pass the last ramada on the right, the path dead ends into, and joins, Squaw Peak Nature Trail #304. Turn left here. The path-way becomes more rocky, narrow, and slightly steep in places as the combined Trails #302 and #304 angle up to the first pass. Before reaching the pass—about 100 yards up the trail—notice a deep desert wash on the right—evidence of the power of desert flash floods. This 10-foot vertical slash is usually empty, but heavy rains can slice through the alluvium like a knife. Climb up to the pass and look northeast to the skyline. The McDowell Mountains ridgeline will show up in the distance. Stay left as you leave the pass. You'll find the junction of the Perl Charles Trail (#1A) coming in from the left. Turn left here as Trail #302 joins #1A, heading northwest to another higher saddle. Subtle changes in plant life occur on the cooler and wetter north-facing slopes, giving rise to a mossy-looking plant growing along the trail. This is resurrection plant. It blooms bright emerald green during wet months and retreats to a dead-looking brown during drought. As soon as another rain comes, it "resurrects" to the lively green. Desert lavender starts to show up here with its sweet aroma. A saguaro cactus by the trail contains constricted rings around its stem. This is evidence of a slow growth season, when freez-ing temperatures or long-term drought was apparent. You will soon reach the main northwest saddle with its prevailing southwest winds. Head down the deeply eroded path as it turns southwest with views of the West Phoenix skyline. Continue until the junction where the Perl Charles Trail branches off to the right (northwest). Follow Trail #302 as it turns south, with brittlebushes along the slope. Their bright, yellow blooms explode, painting the mountainside in early spring. Make an abrupt left (east) and head up to the next pass, which connects with Summit Trail #300. Follow Trail #300 to the summit from here (500 feet elevation gain and .5 mile) or head back down to Navajo Ramada. (See Summit Trail #300.)

25. Mojave Trail

Time: 1 hour. *Distance:* 1 mile roundtrip. *Elevation Gain:* 300 feet. *Rating:* Easy.

Trailhead: From the Navajo Ramada parking lot, drive up the road a short way to the Mojave Ramada on the right and turn up into the top parking lot. The trailhead is to the right of Ramada #5, desig-nated by a square, brown trail post.

High Points: A short trek to great views of south and east Phoenix. A great lunch and sunset point. View of the main Squaw Peak Summit trail.

Hiking the Trail: This short, delightful trail takes you to a great view of east Phoenix and out to the city of Mesa and the Superstition Mountains. The trail climbs up steeply for about 150 feet to a junction. Turn 90 degrees right and follow a level contour along the slope. The predominant rock color is gray. Patina weathering processes, along with heat and pressure, add dark hues to the surface of this hard schist. Brittlebushes line the trail. Their gray-green leaves support single-stem flower stalks that stand up and out from the leaves. Sap from the stems was used by early Americans as a blood coagulant. An early-blooming blue dick plant may stick its solitary, foot-long stem into the air with its characteristic six-petaled flower head. The root is an edible onion.

The path opens at a small saddle offering views southeast to Phoenix and Tempe. A trail angles down left to a residential area. Stay right and climb up the next section to the ridgeline. The path surface is a brittle mica-schist metamorphic rock that breaks off as you walk on it. As you climb up to the next saddle, the color in the surrounding rocks changes again. Rust-colored bedrock is infused with a whitish quartz material. This extends to the top of the ridgeline. A short, steep climb takes you to the ridgeline summit and the horse trail to the right. You can sit on a rock that offers views of Squaw Peak, Phoenix, the Sierra Estrella range to the southwest, and South Mountain Park directly south. This is a great sunset viewpoint. Step back across the trail to a small pile of stones facing southeast. Camelback Mountain beckons about a mile away across Tatum Boulevard. Return to Ramada #4.

26. Summit Trail

Time: 2 hours. *Distance:* 2.5 miles roundtrip. *Elevation Gain:* 1,000 feet. *Rating:* Moderate.

Trailhead: The trailhead is located at the southwest end of the Navajo Ramada parking area, right behind the ramada.

High Points: 360-degree views of the Valley of the Sun. Excellent architecture of constructed rock trail. Views north to the rest of the Phoenix Mountains Preserve.

Hiking the Trail: This is a favorite trail of Phoenicians. Somewhat of a "social" trail, it gets very crowded in the evenings and on weekends and is covered with fireworks watchers on the 4th of July. At Christmas time, it is lined with luminarias (paper bags weighted with sand and lit inside with candles) for the annual Christmas luminaria hike. This trail was originally a horse trail, and some of the horse railings are still in place.

Due to heavy use, the first section of this favorite route has been "improved" with concrete binding materials and natural stone. This anti-erosion construction technique has been perfected by the Phoenix City Parks engineering department by blending in the material so well you hardly notice it. Climb up to the first stone bench.

Just below the .25-mile marker, the Alternate Summit Trail comes in from the left. Stone retaining walls have been built higher up to keep runoff channeled away from the path. The .6-mile marker is at the second stone bench close to the junction of Circumference Trail #302—located at a small pass. From this pass, you can see how the Squaw Peak Circumference Trail zigzags down to the lower, western slopes. A few switchbacks after the stone bench, the path goes up to a pass that takes it over to the west side of the mountain. Steep switchbacks on the west side take you to another pass and on to the summit scramble. From this summit you can see all of the Phoenix megalopolis, the surrounding desert mountain chains, and, to the northeast, the edges of the Central Mountains Province. The only higher point in the city is Camelback Mountain—about 30 feet higher and visible about a mile to the southeast. Descend by the same route or take the Summit Alternate Trail at the .25-mile marker. It takes you down a gully and around a couple of hills back to the parking area.

27. Dreamy Draw Nature Trail

Time: 1 hour. *Distance:* 1.5 miles roundtrip. *Elevation Gain:* 200 feet. *Rating:* Easy.

Trailhead: From the Navajo Ramada parking area, go back out of the park and turn right on Lincoln Drive and go to 16th Street. Turn right and drive to Northern Avenue. Follow Northern under the freeway to the Dreamy Draw Park sign. Turn into the park and drive through the tunnel. Just past the tunnel, notice the vertical, shiny gray wall of schist on your left. Go to the small parking area where drinking water, restrooms, picnic ramadas, and a ranger station are located. The trailhead is located on the north end of the parking lot by a wash.

High Points: Views north, east, and west to the surrounding desert mountains and the Central Mountains Province.

Hiking the Trail: Cross the wash and turn right at the Trail #220 signpost and "horse tunnel" sign. Walk along a wash with vertical bank cuts 20 feet high—an example of flash flooding. Planted barrel cactus with their curved spines, along with lots of brittlebush, line the route. When you exit the tunnel, notice the vertical, broken schist on each side of the wash. There are moss and lichen on the wetter, cooler north-facing side of the wash. There are a few beavertail cactus along the route, along with isolated pieces of quartz lying on the ground.

When you come to the junction of Trails 100 and 220, make a 90-degree turn to the right on 220. Pass an old "creosote bush" and "staghorn cholla" sign. Look up and see the twin summits of Squaw Peak—the higher one on the right. Hike along an undulating ridge-line path that changes colors from gray to red to buff, according to the different mineral content of the rocks that make the gravel. Keep heading south until dropping into a wash with lots of ironwood, oco-tillo, and triangular-leaved bursage, where you turn left. Stay left and head back out of the wash. Keep looking for the Trail #220 signposts. The trail turns gradually north and up the steep-gullied side of a knoll. Climb up to a small ridgeline that leads to the highest spot on the trail, a small knoll. This is the halfway point. Look northeast to the McDowell Mountains range and notice the granite knobs along the ridgeline. A little left of the range, you'll see a sharp rock peak—Pinnacle Peak. Look west to the hazy skyline of the White Tank Mountains. The route now heads down and to the north and passes a saguaro cactus where the trail splits around it. The needles, the waxy skin, and the edges have been damaged, perhaps from frost or drought. Make a sharp left and head back to the horse tunnel and to the trailhead.

Lookout Mountain Area

Lookout Mountain, another fault-block remnant, is the northern-most part of the Phoenix Mountains Preserve. It is crisscrossed with many old roads, trails, and paths.

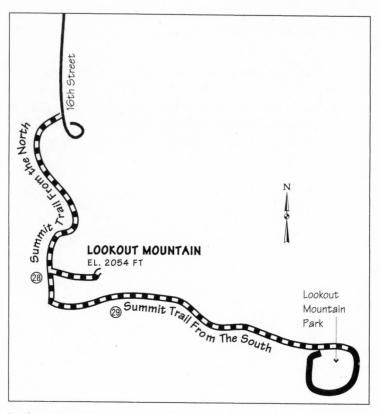

Lookout Mountain Area

Day Hike Area Takeoff Point Bell Road and 16th Street: Turn off I-17 on Bell Road. Turn east on Bell Road and drive to 16th Street.

28. Summit Trail—From the North

Time: 1 hour. *Distance:* 1 mile roundtrip. *Elevation Gain:* 550 feet. *Rating:* Moderate.

Trailhead: Turn south on 16th Street, past Greenway Parkway until the road stops at the gate to the Phoenix Mountains Preserve, where there is a small parking area. This is the trailhead.

High Points: Views north to Paradise Valley, Cave Creek area, and Pinnacle Peak area. Views to the edge of the Central Mountains Province.

Hiking the Trail: The major route to the summit is just past an information sign to the right. It is an old roadway that heads south to a brown, square trail post in the ground about 100 yards up the trail. It is marked #308 and #150. Take 150 to the south and toward Lookout Mountain. A large water tank looms to the left. Various trails and paths lead all over the place.

Follow the main zigzagging path to the obvious saddle between the west and east summits. The saddle opens up views of the rest of the preserve, as well as most of north Phoenix. Lookout Mountain Park is visible to the southeast. The maze of southside trails is also visible—and enticing. From this saddle you can climb both the east and west summits, the east being the highest. Climb both to get views of both east and west Phoenix. Look northeast to Pinnacle Peak and the McDowell Mountains range and to Black Mountain by Cave Creek. On the far horizon is the prominent Four Peaks massif, the very edge of the Central Mountains Province. In winter months, you may see hot air balloons climbing into the morning sky. Slightly northwest on the horizon, you can see the Bradshaw Mountains—also at the edge of the Central Mountains Province. Look south to Squaw Peak Park and the rest of the Phoenix Mountains Preserve. See South Mountain Park on the southern skyline with the Sierra Estrellas in back of it.

By going back to the saddle, you have various options for returning to the parking area: (1) follow your original route, or (2) go right to a large, wide saddle and the path that leads to it; from that saddle, follow another wide roadbed down to the right of the water tank and back to your vehicle.

29. Summit Trail—From the South

Time: 1 hour. *Distance:* 1 mile roundtrip. *Elevation Gain:* 550 feet. *Rating:* Challenging.

Trailhead: This route starts from Lookout Mountain Park, located on the south side of the mountain. The park is a new addition to the city park system and offers a pleasant respite from the busy intersections surrounding it. Drive east on Bell Road, past 16th Street to Cave Creek Road. Turn south on Cave Creek Road to the huge First Assembly Church on the left. Look for Sharon Street at the light. Turn right on Sharon and go down to 20th Street. Turn right on 20th Street and follow it all the way to Lookout Mountain Park. The trailhead is located at the north end of the parking area.

High Points: Short ascent to great views of the valley, same as Summit Trail #150.

Hiking the Trail: The trail angles northwest toward the Lookout Mountain saddle, crossing the Circumference Trail. Continue up to the saddle and on to the east and west summits of Lookout Mountain. Return by the same route.

North Mountain Park Area

North Mountain Park, another erosional remnant, is the westernmost area in the preserve. It has historical significance as an early camping area for pupils and families from the Phoenix Indian School, a facility for teaching Arizona tribal youngsters English, math, history, and U.S. government. Facilities include ramadas, picnic tables, restrooms, and drinking water.

Day Hike Area Takeoff Point Ranger Office in North Mountain Park: Turn off I-17 east onto Thunderbird Road. Follow Thunderbird to 7th Street. Turn south on 7th Street to the park entrance at Peoria Avenue.

30. North Mountain Nature Trail

Time: .5 hour. *Distance:* .25 mile. *Elevation Gain:* Level. *Rating:* Easy.

Go to the northwest corner of the Havasupai parking lot. A self-guided loop runs adjacent to the picnic areas and provides a good introduction to the park. Plant identification signs are planned for the future. Look for bird life and nests among the shrubs and cactus plants. Short, five-minute trails branch off almost every picnic ramada in this park.

31. National Trail

Time: 1.5 hours. *Distance:* 1.5-mile loop. *Elevation Gain:* 600 feet. *Rating:* Moderate.

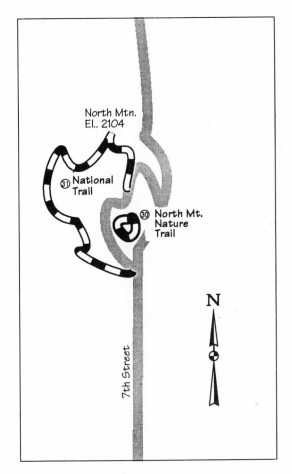

North Mountain Park Area

Trailhead: The trailhead is at the north end of the Maricopa picnic area, by a drinking fountain.

High Points: Short hike to great views of north and west Phoenix.

Hiking the Trail: The trail starts up a short, steep pitch until it reaches a set of stone steps leading up to a roadway. Turn left and follow the road up to the tower gate, past the road cuts and the thinly layered bands of metamorphosed schist running vertically along the cuts. Look for a place on a corner where the layers become horizontal

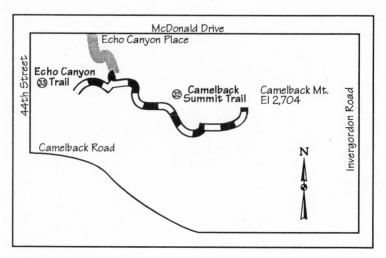

Echo Canyon Area

in orientation. This is where tectonic pressures folded the rock. The rock colors change from greens to rusts to grays, depending on the rock's mineralization and chemistry. Views of Paradise Valley and north Phoenix open up as the paved road ascends to the radio towers. Lookout Mountain is the next desert peak slightly to the northeast.

At the end of a small block wall is a trail that angles off and up to just below the radio towers. It should be marked #44A. Take this up to the towers and follow it along the ridgeline south. It offers great views of the entire Phoenix skyline and out to Cave Creek to the north. The trail gets fairly steep as it angles back down to the park road. Follow the road back up to the Maricopa picnic area.

Echo Canyon Area

This small park is located a couple of miles southeast of Squaw Peak Park. It contains most of Camelback Mountain and the surrounding rock formations.

The park has one parking lot, two ramadas, and a drinking fountain at the trailhead. In addition to hiking trails, the park is a favorite place for rock climbers to practice their skills on huge brecciated boulders.

Camelback Mountain—centerpiece of the park—was a landmark

for early Native Americans as well as traveling pioneers due to its easily identifiable "camel kneeling down" profile. It has been reported that desert bighorn sheep once roamed the mountain.

A long legal and fiscal battle was waged over saving the mountain from development. With Senator Barry Goldwater's support, the top part was finally saved and access gained so that today Echo Canyon Park is maintained for hikers, climbers, and picnickers.

The Camel's Head area of the park (ramadas, climbing boulders, and short trails) is composed of erosional remnants of ancient brecciated sandstones laid down between 70 million and 100 million years ago. These rocks have been eroded and sculpted by wind and water to provide caves, alcoves, and climbing areas.

The Camel's Hump area is different. It is a much older Precambrian plutonic granite that was eventually uplifted and exposed to the surface to be eroded by wind and water. It is about 1.5 billion years old—equivalent to the inner gorge schists of the Grand Canyon.

The Head and Hump join at the "neck," which is actually coincidental, because they are millions of years apart geologically.

A typical Sonoran desertshrub plant community covers most of the mountain, with some additional species that prefer the cooler temperatures of the shaded areas on the north side.

Day Hike Area Takeoff Point Echo Canyon Parking Lot: Turn off I-17 on Glendale Avenue. Turn east on Glendale Avenue and follow it until it turns into Lincoln Drive at 16th Street. Continue on Lincoln past Squaw Peak Park to Tatum Boulevard. Turn south on Tatum for a half-mile to McDonald Drive. Stay in the right-hand lane at the light and turn left (east). Another quick right takes you onto Echo Canyon Place, which leads up to the parking area.

32. Camelback Summit Trail

Time: 3 hours. *Distance:* 2.5 miles roundtrip. *Elevation Gain:* 1,300 feet. *Rating:* Challenging.

Trailhead: From the Echo Canyon parking lot, go to the ramada and drinking fountain on its east end. The trailhead starts at the ramada.

High Points: Exhilarating, varied trail sections. Varied plant life. Dramatic volcanic architecture. This is the second most popular trail in Phoenix due to its central location and aesthetic appeal. Dramatic rock formations line the path. Views of both central and north Phoenix present themselves along the way. Color contrasts between the reddish sandstones and darker granites provide a dramatic backdrop to the greens and browns of the vegetation. This trail offers a strenuous workout for those seeking cardiovascular exercise, due to its many boulder hops and stretches.

Hiking the Trail: Follow the obvious route from the ramada down and back up to a large boulder used for rock-climbing practice. This rock is one of many eroded sandstone remnants of ancient sea beaches that contain multisized pebbles and rocks intruded into the matrix (breccia). This ancient sandstone is easily eroded, and you can see the many holes, caves, and caverns carved out of the Camel's Head. Creosote bush, brittlebush, and a few palo verde trees line the path as it goes up the broken rocky route to the first saddle overlooking Paradise Valley to the north.

The trail skirts the huge sandstone face, along the base of what seems like a planted garden of wildflowers and shrubs. This well-shaded, cool hiding place is a microhabitat of lush desert plant life— globe mallow, resurrection plant, grasses, mosses, chuparosa, desert lavender, palo verde, and ironwood. The wall is undercut due to the soft alluvium underlying harder sandstone. A handrail provides assistance up a steep, slippery section of exposed granite. This continues to another handrail and up another slippery boulder route to a pass that overlooks central and south Phoenix.

Follow the trail along the "neck" between the Head and Hump to a gully. Continue right to another pass that opens views to South Mountain Park with the radio towers on top. The ominous Sierra Estrella range looms to the right and rear of South Mountain Park. You are now hiking on 1.5-billion-year-old decomposed granite surrounded by bedrock.

Continue along the ridgeline as it angles back and forth across the north and south sides of the mountain. A steep, wide gully leads to the summit slopes. This section requires hopping large boulders and can be quite strenuous. The gully tops out on the last sloping section to the summit. The entire Valley of the Sun appears on a 360-degree skyline at the top. Look north and northeast to Four Peaks and the Bradshaw range at the edge of the Central Mountains Province. Look east to the farmland that runs along Pima Road. This is the edge of the Salt River Indian Reservation. Return by the same route to the Echo Canyon parking area.

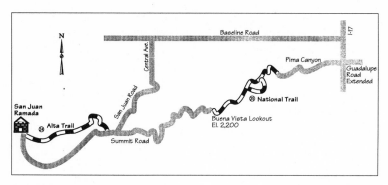

South Mountain Park Area

33. Echo Canyon Trail

Time: 1 hour. *Distance:* .5 mile roundtrip. *Elevation Gain:* 50 feet. *Rating:* Easy.

Trailhead: From the Echo Canyon parking lot, go east to the ramada and drinking fountain, where the trailhead is located.

High Points: Introduction to the Camelback Mountain area. Various rock formations to explore.

Hiking the Trail: Start on the main summit trail and look for the first trail to the right. Follow this down and up a series of gullies. It flanks a private-property fenceline, circles a couple of small hills, and branches out into Echo Canyon. The canyon itself offers a series of trails for exploring the base of the sandstone walls and caves. Take your choice for a leisurely stroll through desert vegetation and boulders. You can spend a half-hour or half a day exploring this area. One branch loops back to the old stone ramada and then back to the main trail.

South Mountain Park Area

South Mountain Park is the largest municipal park in the country with over 16,000 acres of recreation area. With over 40 miles of hiking trails in the huge park, the day hiker can spend many weekends exploring this vast and legendary desert area. South Mountain was an Indian hunting ground. It contains numerous shrines, petroglyphs, and corn-grinding holes.

The western part of the range is composed of older Precambrian granitic gneiss (coarse-grained and banded light and dark minerals) and schists (layered and cleaved along lines of weakness). The eastern end contains younger granites.

Over 300 species of desert plants grow in the park, including a great variety of cacti that includes saguaro, barrel, hedgehog, pincushion, teddy bear, Christmas, staghorn, and prickly pear, along with palo verde and ironwood trees.

Other than insects and birds, most of the fauna is nocturnal, as it is in all the deserts. Sun spiders, centipedes, scorpions, beetles, ants, bees, wasps, and tarantulas are prevalent. Desert rodent, reptile, and mammal species inhabit the mountains. The Maricopa Audubon Society lists 54 bird species. As South Mountain Park has become more popular, some of the wildlife has migrated across the basin to the Sierra Estrella range.

South Mountain Park facilities include picnic areas, a kitchen, grills, catering facilities, restrooms, and a storage area.

Day Hike Area Takeoff Point Junction of Central Avenue and Baseline Road: Take I-17 south and turn east on I-10 to Tucson. Look for the Central Avenue turnoff. Turn south on Central Avenue and drive to Baseline Road.

34. Alta Trail

Time: 5 hours. *Distance:* 4.5 miles one-way. *Elevation Gain:* 700 feet. *Rating:* Challenging.

Trailhead: Continue south on Central Avenue to the South Mountain Park entrance. Follow San Juan Road west, past the Summit Road junction. A short way past the junction, start looking for the Alta Trail sign on the right. A few feet beyond the sign, turn into a small parking area. Walk back to the trailhead.

High Points: Exhilarating ascent from base of uplift to ridgeline with great views of Phoenix and the surrounding desert mountains. Close-by views of the White Tank Mountains and the Sierra Estrella Mountains. Subtle vegetation changes with altitude.

Hiking the Trail: This 4.5-mile trail offers a cross-section of most of the plants in the park. It follows a ridgeline that provides views of most of central and west Phoenix and the Sierra Estrella range to the southwest. Several rock benches, built by the Civilian Conservation Corps in the 1930s, are found along the path. This trail is best completed with a shuttle from the trailhead to the San Juan Ramada on the west end of the route. The trail heads north along a gently sloping bajada. There is a profusion of staghorn and teddy bear cholla to either side. Palo verde and ironwood mix with creosote and bursage. The first saguaro cactus along the side of the trail on the right has a stunted growth ring about head-high. It was probably caused by either freezing weather or a drought.

Just beyond the saguaro are some barrel cactus, many of which have fallen over and exposed their shallow roots. Most cacti have shallow root systems that allow them to take advantage of scant rainfall as soon as it hits the ground. But when heavy rains loosen the soil and heavy winds catch the wide stems, cacti can be blown over.

Right by the barrel cactus is an ironwood tree with dark bark on the bottom that turns to gray on the way up. Leaves are gray-green and extend down to the main branches.

Exposed pieces of gray banded gneiss with orange and brown patina splotches are scattered along the route. A large pile of rocks greets you at the first sharp left turn. The trail steepens here and zigzags up to a bench built into the hill. A series of switchbacks steepens the trail. As you near the ridgeline, look right at the exposed wall of brown and white banded rock. The white minerals were pushed into the bedrock when great heat and pressure melted the material.

Switchback up to the ridgeline and follow this to a high point with a small rock pile. The Superstition Mountains are visible on the east skyline. The White Tank Mountains are not that far away to the northwest.

A stone bench can be found along the ridge. The route crosses back and forth on the north and south sides of the mountain, exposing the orange/gray lichen and moss on the north side where the soil is wetter and cooler. Much of it never sees the sun, while the south side is always bathed in it.

The route descends to the north past the highest point on the mountain (Maricopa Peak). It climbs up again and continues along the ridge on both sides until it starts descending on the north side. It follows a steep, heavily vegetated wash down to the San Juan ramada. Orange/pink globe mallows and the bright red berries of the tomatillo line the wash. As you reach the lower slopes, the vegetation changes to creosote bush and desert grasses. The path continues on to the San Juan ramada.

35. National Trail

Time: 4 hours. *Distance:* 7 miles roundtrip. *Elevation Loss:* 1,000 feet. *Rating:* Moderate.

Trailhead: Follow Central Avenue south through the park entrance and continue along San Juan Road west to the junction of Summit Road and the Buena Vista Lookout sign. Turn left on Summit Road and drive up to the Buena Vista Lookout. The trailhead starts here.

High Points: Panoramic ridgeline views both north and south to Phoenix and the entire Valley of the Sun. Views east to the Superstition Wilderness. Dramatic exposed granite formations along ridgelines and interior valleys. Small, vegetated desert-mountain valleys between ridgelines, containing wildflowers and water in the spring. Early 1930s rock ramada architecture.

Hiking the Trail: This trail can be done in a couple of ways. You can hike the entire route from Buena Vista Point to Pima Canyon — a downhill hike of 7 miles, losing 1,000 feet of elevation. Or, it can be taken the opposite way with 1,000 feet of elevation gain. Both require a vehicle shuttle, unless you want to hike both ways.

Another option is to hike as far as Hidden Valley — about the midway point — from either direction, and return to the respective parking area. I'll describe the one-way, downhill route from Buena Vista Lookout to the Pima Canyon parking area.

The path starts out on the north side of the mountain with views extending across the Salt River Valley, the Phoenix metropolis, and all the way to the Bradshaw Mountains and Four Peaks — the edge of the Central Mountains Province. You'll pass brittlebush, Mormon tea, palo verde, creosote bush, bursage, wild buckwheat, desert sage, catclaw, saguaro, hedgehog, agave, and staghorn. Look for the 4-inch-square brown trail marker signs that say National Trail with a white arrow pointing to the direction.

The path ascends to the top of the ridgeline, then descends into a valley between the ridges where water collects in runoff channels and in bedrock tanks during the spring. Southwest breezes flow along this ridgeline, coming from across the open Lower Sonora Desert to the west. A mile from the trailhead, you'll find a junction with a sign that shows Hidden Valley to the right. You can continue straight on the National Trail or take the alternate loop through Hidden Valley back to the National Trail. Hidden Valley is worth the detour. Take the trail right at the junction and you'll immediately drop down into Fat Man's Pass, a short, narrow passage that requires a squeeze to pass through. The trail continues along a streambed, over and through rock slabs, and down into the wash again. Look for red-tail hawks, dove, cactus wrens, and quail in this area. You'll see giant bursage in the wash. Keep your eyes peeled for petroglyphs along the wash. Follow the drainage trail until you come to the "tunnel," an enclosed overhang of granite slabs. This leads back to the National Trail marker. Turn right and continue as the path leads back up to the ridgeline and the Phoenix valley. Four Peaks will grace the eastern skyline in the haze.

You'll top a ridge and spot the dirt road that leads from the Pima Canyon parking area to a small rock ramada. The path will gradually descend to the ramada and the old dirt road that is now closed off to vehicles. A gradual descent takes you to the ramada. You can follow the dirt road to the Pima Canyon parking area (about a mile) or follow the wash to the left that goes to the same parking area. The wash contains petroglyphs and heavier plant growth, as well as many lizards and birds. There is a pit toilet and drinking fountain at the Pima Canyon parking area. There is also a small hill just to the south of the parking lot that has a path leading to an inscription in stone made by Fray Marcos de Niza, an early Spanish explorer. This is an open, shadeless trail with no water in the washes except in the early spring or after rainfall.

MARICOPA COUNTY REGIONAL PARKS

Far-sighted planning in the past, along with wise management in the present, accounts for this "ring" of exceptional county parks surrounding Phoenix and the Salt River Valley. Large land tracts of desert/mountain terrain were acquired with bond money, with the idea of preserving park land for a "regional" concept of outdoor recreation resources for the burgeoning Phoenix metropolis. These parks surround the urban population but still have the "remote" quality and "wilderness" feel about them.

With over 100,000 acres of land, this system is recognized as the largest county park system in the country. Development is centered around hiking, horseback riding, picnicking, camping, nature study, photography, and sightseeing.

These parks used to be Arizona's best-kept secret due to their seeming remoteness. Not anymore. Due to recent picnic area and RV overnight accommodations improvements, they have become popular winter destinations for outdoor folks from all over the country.

Each park has a resident host who takes fees, manages camping spaces, and maintains the park. Campground hosts are usually retirees, with a trailer, who volunteer to oversee a campground or popular hiking trailhead in cooperation with a land-management agency. Contact them upon entering the park. For more information, call or write Maricopa County Parks and Recreation Department, 3355 W. Durango Street, Phoenix, AZ 85009, (602) 272-8871.

Estrella Mountain Park Area

This park sits at the northern base of the Sierra Estrella Mountains and includes the northern tip of this 22-mile-long fault-block range. The park contains 19,200 acres with elevations ranging from 900 feet to its high point of 3,650 feet in the southeast corner. All the hikes within the park are on the low desert or the undulating foothills at the base of the peaks. There are few trails into the Estrella range itself. This range is one of the most rugged desert uplifts in the state.

Early Pima Indians lived at the base of the range. Early Spanish explorers like de Niza, Coronado, and Kino passed by gravesites and grinding holes. The range was used as a landmark by trappers along the Salt River and by California gold seekers.

This area is a huge fault-block formation composed of gneiss and granites of Precambrian (500 million to 1 billion years old) origin. This range is so steep that rain runoff zooms down the washes and leaves little water on the mountain itself. There are some drainages that contain exposed granite bedrock tanks with water in them, but they are only reliable after rainstorms.

Day Hike Area Takeoff Point Estrella Mountain Park Entrance: Take I-17 south to I-10. Take the Los Angeles (west) exit and follow I-10 to the Litchfield Road turnoff. Turn south for about 3.5 miles to State

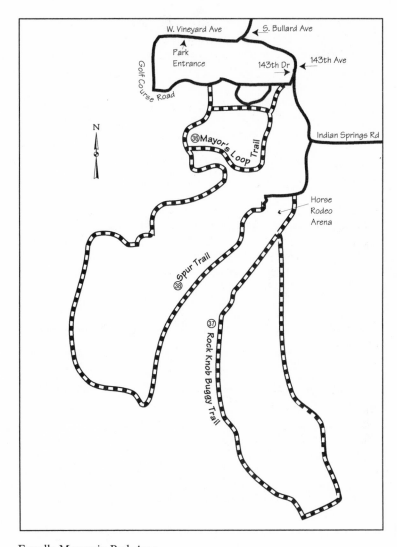

Estrella Mountain Park Area

Route 85. Turn west on 85 and drive to Bullard. Turn south on Bullard to West Vineyard Avenue. Go west on Vineyard Avenue to the park entrance.

Campgrounds The park contains a group campground, individual camp sites, and RV hookups. Check at the park entrance for current facilities. Contact the Maricopa County Parks office for current hours at (602) 272-8871.

36. Mayor's Loop Trail

Time: 1 hour. *Distance:* 1.75 miles roundtrip. *Elevation Gain:* 200 feet. *Rating:* Easy.

Trailhead: From the park entrance, turn left on Casey Abbott Drive North and follow it around to Casey Abbott Drive South. Turn right and drive to the amphitheater entrance and exit roads. One trailhead starts just before the exit road. The other trailhead starts east of the exit road at the edge of a vehicle turn-in.

High Points: An introduction to the Lower Sonoran desertshrub plant zone. Views of the Sierra Estrella range to the south.

Hiking the Trail: This trail loops around the small knobs south of the amphitheater. There are many paths and side trails to this loop. The main loop is pretty obvious and is marked with red engineer tape, tied to creosote bushes. Parts of the trail are quite steep but worth the climb for the quick views they offer of southwest Phoenix and the White Tank Mountains to the northwest. The typical desertshrub vegetation is more sparse than in the other county parks due to its lower elevation, close to the Salt River bed. Most of the plant life exists in the washes. Evidence of past mineral exploration is evident on this trail from the presence of small mine-shaft digs.

37. Rock Knob Buggy Trail

Time: 4 hours. *Distance:* 6 miles roundtrip. *Elevation Gain:* 250 feet. *Rating:* Moderate.

Trailhead: From park entrance, take Casey Abbott Drive east around to 143rd Avenue. Take 143rd Avenue to the horse arena. Just as the road turns to dirt, look left for the trailhead sign and a vehicle pullout.

High Points: Remote wilderness experience at the edge of the Gila Indian Reservation. Views south into the Sierra Estrella range and the Lower Sonoran desertshrub.

Hiking the Trail: The trail starts off as a 20-foot-wide road track. A prominent 600-foot knob juts up ahead to the left. The track meanders through desert scrub and slowly angles up to the gap between the rock knob on the left and another prominent ridgeline on the right. At about the 2-mile mark, you will reach a saddle and Rainbow Valley spreads out below—a long, flat bajada stretching to the far distant ranges. The route narrows and angles down left to meet the short section of the Pack Saddle Historical Trail.

Return by the same route or follow this path a couple of hundred yards until a junction marked with signs pointing to the left appears. This is the Rainbow Valley Trail, which you can follow back to the rodeo arena. This portion of the trail narrows and provides many ups and downs as it heads back north. It goes up and over Rock Knob Pass, then descends slowly toward the arena, which is now in view. The Rainbow Valley Trail connects again with the Rock Knob Buggy Trail about .25 mile before reaching the rodeo arena.

38. Spur Trail

Time: 2 hours. *Distance:* 3 miles roundtrip. *Elevation Gain:* 200 feet. *Rating:* Moderate.

Trailhead: Follow the paved road around the rodeo arena to where it ends in a parking lot. There is a trailhead sign on the right as you enter the parking area.

High Points: Views of the White Tank Mountains and desertshrub vegetation that extends south into the Lower Sonora Desert.

Hiking the Trail: The trail skirts a deep wash as it heads southwest along a well-defined route. Rock Knob forms an impressive pointed summit off to the left. About 1 mile out, a loop branch comes in from the west. It is just past two signposts marked with green arrows. Walk past this and continue straight for another .75 mile to the Rainbow Valley junction, marked with two more posts—one with a green arrow and one with a red. Turn right onto Rainbow Valley Trail. The path is marked with both red and green ribbons. It is the most scenic part of the hike as it climbs up to a saddle overlooking a desert valley and the White Tank Mountains to the northwest.

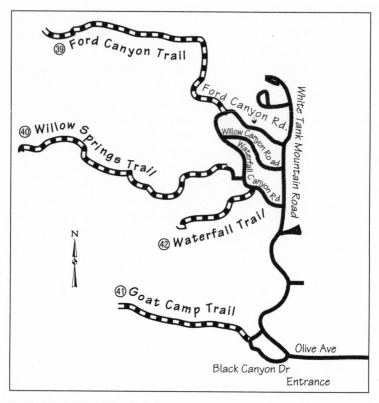

White Tank Mountains Park Area

The route curves north and down to a junction where the afore-mentioned loop trail comes in from the east. The trail continues with green ribbons showing the way. It connects with the Mayor's Loop Trail and doubles back to the rodeo arena.

White Tank Mountains Park Area

White Tank Mountains Regional Park, the largest park in the county system, encompasses over 26,000 acres of Sonoran desert/mountain terrain. The mountains that make up most of the park are fault block in origin. The range goes from 1,400 feet at its lowest to over 4,000 at its summit. The upper levels are deeply eroded and helped cut the deep canyons of the eastern face.

Early Hohokam Indians built at least seven villages along the White Tanks. Many petroglyphs are found near the village sites. The lower slopes of the mountains were seasonally grazed by small cattle herds. Presently, the outwash bajadas on the eastern flanks contain numerous citrus orchards and farming communities, with Luke Air Force Base in the middle.

Movement of the earth's crust and the fault blocks that resulted caused the uplifting of the White Tanks in typical Southern Deserts fashion. Rock structure is mainly Precambrian gneiss and granite intrusions. The granite "tanks" were formed when water torrents carrying rock debris scoured out the depressions.

Day Hike Area Takeoff Point Park Entrance: Take I-17 north to Dunlap Avenue. Drive west on Dunlap until it turns into Olive at 43rd Avenue, then follow Olive all the way to the park entrance.

Campgrounds The park contains a group campground, individual campsites, and RV hookups. Phone: (602) 272-8871.

39. Ford Canyon Trail

Time: 5 hours. *Distance:* 5.6 miles roundtrip. *Elevation Gain:* 900 feet. *Rating:* Challenging.

Trailhead: From the park entrance, follow White Tank Mountain Road to Ford Canyon Road. Turn left and continue until you find the Ford Canyon Trail sign. This is the trailhead.

High Points: Remote wilderness experience at the western edge of the Salt River Valley. Views of west Phoenix and the Sierra Estrella range. Water tanks and riparian vegetation with abundant bird life.

Hiking the Trail: This wide path is lined with river rocks—placed there long ago by prison inmates. It is very easy to follow. There are a couple of junctions where convening trails make a hodgepodge connection. The path generally follows the edge of Ford Canyon and gradually angles up into a side canyon that starts displaying white granite bedrock tanks—the range's namesakes. These tanks contain varying amounts of water accumulated from previous rainfalls. The gradual climb along Ford Canyon brings the western part of Phoenix into view. The higher you climb on the trail, the closer you get to the main streambed.

Take a walk over to the exposed granite and see if you can find any water in the tanks. Look for remnants of old rock dams and water catchment basins. Also look for stone fencing and small corrals, which are remnants of cattle-grazing days.

The trail at the top of the canyon crosses the main drainage. Our day hike ends here, but you can continue upstream if you desire. Return by the same route.

40. Willow Springs Trail

Time: 5 hours. *Distance:* 5 miles roundtrip. *Elevation Gain:* 900 feet. *Rating:* Moderate.

Trailhead: From the park entrance, drive to Willow Springs Road. Turn left and follow the road to the Willow Springs trailhead sign.

High Points: Views across the White Tank range. Views of west Phoenix and the Sierra Estrellas. Upper Sonoran vegetation habitat. Riparian habitat vegetation and bird life.

Hiking the Trail: Elevation gain starts quickly and the trail climbs to a junction of the Rock Knob and Waterfall trails. The path steepens and heads for a prominent saddle. Look down to the right from the saddle and you can spot Mesquite Spring down in the Mesquite Canyon wash with its exposed white granite bedrock and pools. Descend into the Mesquite Canyon wash and follow the wash upstream for about 50 yards until you find a cairn marking the trail exit to the right, out of the wash. This will take you over to Willow Canyon and to Willow Springs. This makes a good lunch spot. On the return, you can take the Waterfall Trail turnoff to the right and descend via that trail to the White Tanks waterfalls and back to the trailhead.

41. Goat Camp Trail

Time: 5 hours. *Distance:* 6 miles roundtrip. *Elevation Gain:* 1,600 feet. *Rating:* Challenging.

Trailhead: From the park entrance, turn left at the road sign for "Picnic Area and Goat Camp Trail." Drive past the sign for "South Loop Goat Camp Trail" and continue to the turnout for the Goat Camp trailhead.

High Points: Views of the White Tank range. Views of west Phoenix and the Sierra Estrellas. Riparian vegetation and bird life.

Hiking the Trail: River rocks line this path as it follows the Goat and Black Canyon drainages. The South Loop Trail comes in from the left in about .75 mile. The trail crosses Goat Canyon from north to south, then steepens.

Goat Canyon is typical of the White Tank drainages: granite bedrock with water pools scattered along the course (depending on rainfall patterns). Dramatic rock formations greet you as you climb steadily.

Just as the trail steepness eases off, there is a small waterfall with a large pool beneath it that waters a huge mesquite tree right by the trail. This is a good lunch spot, or you can go another quarter-mile to the rock dam and boulder fences of Goat Camp. This is as far as most day hikers go. Return by the same route.

42. Waterfall Trail

Time: 1 hour. *Distance:* 2 miles roundtrip. *Elevation Gain:* 200 feet. *Rating:* Easy.

Trailhead: Take the park road to Waterfall Canyon Road, turning left until you reach the trailhead sign.

High Points: The waterfall and surrounding vertical walls. Riparian vegetation and bird life.

Hiking the Trail: This short, popular trail meanders along a wash to some large boulders. A flat spot opens up just before the trail climbs up to the impressive waterfall that runs after local rain showers. It may be tempting to climb on the walls around this area, but it is not recommended since a number of climbing deaths have occurred here. Return by the same route.

McDowell Mountain Park Area

This park is a desert oasis in the midst of ever-increasing Scottsdale and Fountain Hills development. It is located in the Lower Verde Basin between the McDowell Mountains to the west and the Verde River and the Fort McDowell Indian Reservation to the east.

Nearby Fort McDowell, a former military outpost, was established in 1865 to prevent Apache attacks on local ranchers and miners. In 1890 it was transferred to the Bureau of Indian Affairs, where it pro-

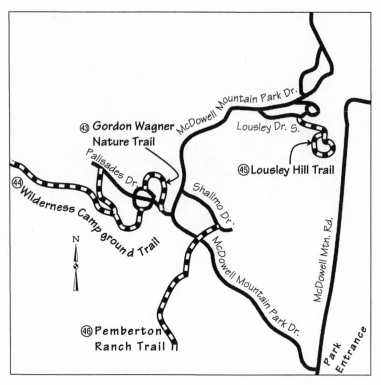

McDowell Mountain Park Area

vided local services of mail, a constable, and marriages. The area also served as cattle-grazing country.

The fault-block mountain range on the park's western boundary is composed of mostly granites, schists, gneiss, and quartzite. Picturesque rock formations of exposed granite invite the hiker to the mountain slopes.

The bajadas that slope eastward toward the Verde River are alluvial fans and arroyos, draining into the Verde. Elevations range from 1,600 feet in the southeast corner to over 3,000 feet along the west boundary. The lush desert vegetation invites hikers at all times of the year except June, July, and August.

Day Hike Area Takeoff Point McDowell Mountain Park Entrance: From I-17 drive north to Bell Road, turn east, and follow Bell to Pima

Road. Turn north on Pima to Pinnacle Peak Road, turn east and follow the signs to Rio Verde Drive. Follow Rio Verde Drive east to the end of the road where Rio Verde Estates begins. Turn south and go through the community of Rio Verde until you see the McDowell Mountain Park sign that directs you west for 4.5 miles to the park entrance.

Campgrounds The park has a group campground, individual campsites, and RV hookups. Phone: (602) 471-0173.

43. Gordon Wagner Nature Trail

Time: .5 hour. *Distance:* .5-mile loop. *Elevation Gain:* Level. *Rating:* Easy.

Trailhead: From the park entrance, follow McDowell Mountain Park Drive to Group Campground #6. Turn into the campground and look for the trailhead sign along the road.

High Points: An introduction to McDowell Mountains plant life. A short overview of the area.

Hiking the Trail: This short nature trail combines with the Cornell Club Trail to form a numbered and signed plant interpretive trail. The loop comes back into the Palisades Circle North campsite area. Pick up a copy of the Campground Interpretive Guide from the park host.

44. Wilderness Campground Trail

Time: 3.5 hours. *Distance:* 3 miles roundtrip. *Elevation Gain:* Level. *Rating:* Moderate.

Trailhead: From the park entrance, drive to Family Campground #7. Take the Palisades Way North Road to the northwest end. The trailhead sign is located here.

High Points: Remote wilderness experience. Lush Upper Sonoran desertshrub plant life. Abundant animal and bird life. Great views of McDowell Mountain granite skyline and the Verde River watershed.

Hiking the Trail: This great wilderness trail heads west-northwest along a huge drainage, through undulating terrain, to reach a designated wilderness campground. Look for lizards and other reptiles along this flat route, as well as for the Harris hawk with its brown body and white-striped tail; it nests in the McDowell area frequently. The primitive camping area is nestled between boulder piles at the site of an old, dilapidated cattle tank. If you want to continue on the trail past the campground, climb out of the campground to the west and pick up an old horse path that goes another mile and connects with the Pemberton Trail. From this higher elevation, the east faces and slopes of the McDowell Mountains stand out with their dramatic, boulder-edged skyline. This trail provides the hiker with the best half-day "wilderness experience" within the park.

45. Lousley Hill Trail

Time: 1 hour. *Distance:* 1 mile roundtrip. *Elevation Gain:* 500 feet. *Rating:* Moderate.

Trailhead: From the park entrance, follow McDowell Mountain Park Drive around to Lousley Drive South. Turn right on this road and follow it to the Ironwood picnic area. Look for the trailhead sign for Lousley Hill Trail on the right, by a turnout.

High Points: Hilltop views of the McDowell Mountains skyline to the west. Lush Upper Sonora Desert plant zone. Abundant bird life.

Hiking the Trail: Follow the rock-lined path along a streambed until it starts up Lousley Hill. Follow this to a sitting bench located where the trail steepens. As you ascend this trail, views of the Goldfield, Four Peaks, and Superstition Mountains rise up in the east. The steepest part of the trail goes up to another benched overlook. From there, an easy slope goes to the top of Lousley Hill, where a 360-degree panorama of desert skyline presents itself. If you look southeast, you may catch the Fountain Hills development 500-foot-high water spout, with its aerating rooster-tail spray. It's the highest man-made fountain in the world. Northwest lie the Pinnacle Peak and Cave Creek areas. A look west takes in the entire McDowell Mountain Park, right up to the edge of the range.

There is a lot of loose teddy bear cholla lying on the ground along this trail. The path can be followed back the same way or a loop can be made back to the original trail and back to your vehicle.

46. Pemberton Ranch Trail

Time: 3 hours. *Distance:* 3 miles roundtrip. *Elevation Gain:* Level. *Rating:* Moderate.

Trailhead: From the park entrance, drive along McDowell Mountain Park Drive to Shallmo Drive. Turn right on Shallmo Drive and go about a mile to the Group Horse Staging Area. The Pemberton Ranch trailhead starts here.

High Points: Lush Lower or Upper Sonoran desertshrub plant life. Remnants of an old cattle ranch.

Hiking the Trail: This pleasant, level walk goes through the lush Upper Sonoran bajada of the McDowell Mountains, skirting saguaro, bursage, crucifixion thorn, pincushion, Christmas cholla, barrel cactus, wild buckwheat, buckhorn cholla, Mormon tea, ocotillo, palo verde, jojoba, hedgehog cactus, teddy bear cholla, creosote bush, mesquite, and desert hackberry. It is like walking through a planned garden, intermixed with outcroppings of granite surfaces. The McDowell Mountains range outlines the western skyline, with its granite boulders, spires, and outcroppings.

The route angles south-southwest across the bajada for about .75 mile until it drops into a huge drainage that angles down from the northwest. Jackrabbits, cottontails, coyotes, gray foxes, and the usual assortment of desert birds frequent the area. As the path approaches the embankment of the southern edge of the wash, look on the left for evidence of old concrete cattle tanks, an old and dilapidated metal cattle tank, and steel posts. The remnants of a windmill and a wellhead are found next to a dug-out cattle tank, the remnants of Pemberton Ranch. Return by the same smooth, sandy path.

Usery Mountain Park Area

This park is relatively small in comparison to the other regional county parks but has some great hiking trails. It contains over 3,000 acres of lush Upper and Lower Sonoran desert terrain, surrounded by the Superstition Mountains to the east and the Goldfield Mountains to the northwest.

In reality, the trails in this park fall within the jurisdiction of both Maricopa County and Tonto National Forest. The lowland trails are

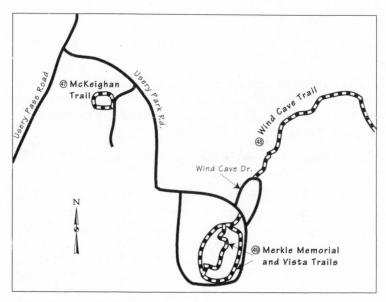

Usery Mountain Park Area

in the county, and the mountain trails are in the national forest. Elevations range from 1,700 to 2,750 feet.

This area, located in the pass between Pass Mountain and Usery Mountain, was once a hangout for King Usery, a desperado and horse thief who lived in the area during the nineteenth century. Some grazing and homesteading occurred in the past. The area has little mineralization.

The park is located on a sloping granite pediment, with fault blocks making up the mountain section. Volcanic "tuff" lava caps Pass Mountain and has been hollowed out in places by erosion to form "caves." (Tuff is formed when volcanic eruptions spray various consistencies of material out over the ground. It contains a lot of air and other gases, and when it solidifies, it forms a light, porous material subject to quick erosion, thus, the caves.)

Day Hike Area Takeoff Point Park Entrance: Drive south on I-17 and turn east onto the Superstition Freeway. Take this out through Tempe and Mesa to Power Road. Turn north on Power Road until it turns into Bush Highway. Follow Bush Highway to the Usery Mountain Recreation Area park entrance.

Campgrounds The park contains a group campground, individual campsites, and RV hookups. Phone: (602) 272-8871.

47. McKeighan Trail

Time: .5 hour. *Distance:* .5 mile roundtrip. *Elevation Gain:* Level. *Rating:* Easy.

Trailhead: From the park entrance, follow Usery Park Road for a short distance until you meet Buckhorn Camp Drive on the right. Turn into Buckhorn and drive to the campground host trailer. The McKeighan trailhead sign is on the right.

High Points: Local plant life signs and general overview of the area.

Hiking the Trail: This is a self-guided nature trail with plant identification signs that give hikers a good introduction to Upper Sonora Desert plant life.

48. Wind Cave Trail

Time: 2 hours. *Distance:* 2.75 miles roundtrip. *Elevation Gain:* 800 feet. *Rating:* Moderate.

Trailhead: Take Usery Park Road to Wind Cave Drive West. Turn left to a parking area. The trailhead sign can be found behind the washroom.

High Points: Views looking west to the Salt River Valley. Volcanic outcroppings amid Upper Sonoran desertshrub vegetation.

Hiking the Trail: The path gradually ascends to a barely discernible sign for a rest area to the left about .5 mile from the trailhead. This is a small rest loop for horses. The main trail steepens and winds around as views of Mesa, Tempe, and Phoenix come into view. The angle eases off as the route traverses below the lava tuff cliffs that lead to the hollowed-out area called Wind Cave. From the cave, one can pick out the McDowell Mountains to the northwest, the White Tanks on the far west horizon, Squaw Peak and Camelback Mountain due west, and South Mountain to the southwest. The Merkle Memorial and Merkle Vista trails are visible just past the left edge of Wind Cave. Return by the same route.

49. Merkle Memorial and Vista Trails

Time: 1 hour. *Distance:* 1.5 miles roundtrip. *Elevation Gain:* 200 feet. *Rating:* Easy.

Trailhead: From the park entrance, take Usery Park Road just past the turnoff to Wind Cave Drive West. A sign on your right directs you to Headquarters Hill trailhead. Both trails start from the Merkle Memorial parking area on the south side of the paved loop road. One trail goes around Headquarters Hill and the other goes up and over the hill, connecting at two places.

High Points: Plant identification signs along route. Vistas from Merkle hilltop.

Hiking the Trail: The loop trail (Merkle Memorial) is a nature hike in that it has plant identification signs along the route. It is a flat path that takes in views of the Superstition Mountains to the east. It's a good trail for getting the feel of the Upper Sonoran desertshrub plant community. A leisurely stroll makes a complete circle around the hill, allowing for a gradual and short climb on the Merkle Vista Trail for those wanting a higher view of the surrounding terrain. The hilltop trail (Merkle Vista) gives the hiker a commanding view of the Superstitions and surrounding desert basins. There are a couple of good lunch spots on top and along the ridgeline. Return by either route.

SUPERSTITION MOUNTAINS REGION

This fabled mass of volcanic remnants is one of the most popular hiking areas in Arizona. Its jagged, vertical walls, twisting canyons, spikes, spires, and pinnacles make it the home of many stories, some true, many just romantic tales. The famed Lost Dutchman Gold Mine is the focus of many books, searches, and endless discussion. It has yet to be found, but a lot of gold has changed hands in the form of dollars traded for secret maps, books, papers, and verbal descriptions of just where the gold is located.

About 50 miles east of Phoenix, this intriguing backcountry lies on the border between the Southern Deserts and Central Mountains provinces, forming a transition from Lower-Upper Sonora Desert to chaparral and pinyon-juniper plant communities. Its jumbled topography makes quick believers of those who would venture cross-country afoot without direction. Just about every hiker this author knows, including himself, has been temporarily confused about where they might be in the "Supes" at one time or another.

Various hunting and gathering Indian groups frequented the area around 800 A.D. Later, Hohokam agricultural villagers filled the surrounding landscape. From about 1500 A.D. to the middle of the 1800s the area was frequented by the Yavapai Indians with occasional forays by Apaches.

The first Europeans were Spanish explorers in the 1500s, looking for gold. They had little luck, and it wasn't until the 1800s that mining became a factor in the Superstition area. Although there is no recorded gold mine within the Superstition Wilderness itself, there is at least one in the range just to the west of it—the Goldfield. The first recorded mining effort was in the 1890s, and many small prospects produced gold up into the 1900s. There was no great strike of record, but the Lost Dutchman mine has been the one claimed by fable to contain wild riches. It was supposedly found by Jacob Waltz with the aid of a relative of the original discoverer, Miguel Peralta of Mexico. The "Dutchman" as he was called—a German immigrant—reportedly brought gold out of the Superstitions to nearby Globe and Miami where he had it assayed. Waltz died in Phoenix in 1891 without leaving any information about the mine. Modern prospectors and mining buffs have been looking for the mine ever since. A few ranches were established within the mountains. They supplied beef to the early military forts surrounding the mining towns.

The Superstitions officially became a Wilderness Area in 1964, which now contains 159,780 acres of remote, awe-inspiring terrain that ranges from 2,000 to 6,265 feet in elevation. The nationally known Weaver's Needle monolith rises in the middle of the Supes and is used for navigation and orientation throughout the area.

The Superstition Mountains and surrounding formations were formed by violent volcanic eruptions from 29 to 15 million years ago. A series of events folded the terrain into fantastic forms of lava remnants that have been eroding and faulting for the last 15 million years. The range is composed of heavily weathered tuff, ash, and lava deposited on top of Precambrian granite. This makes for thin, finely textured, easily eroded soils. Many rock formation "monsters" have been created in the Supes and a night hike can expand the imagination into the twilight zone.

The Supes contain plants from the Sonoran desertshrub community, desert grassland, chaparral, oak-pine woodland, and even some junipers, as well as riparian vegetation that grows along the many intermittent streambeds.

Since this mountain range is on the border of the Southern Deserts and Central Mountains provinces, there is a wide mixture of animal life from both these zones.

Perhaps more wildlife can be heard in the Supes than seen, due to the great variety of birds. The cactus wren seems to make more noise than the other animals put together. It flits from creosote bush to saguaro cactus, scolding intruders with its raucous, scratchy squawk. Thrashers, cardinals, Gila woodpeckers, and quail intermix with owls, hawks, and buzzards.

First Water Area

Day Hike Area Takeoff Point First Water Parking Area: From I-17, get onto the Superstition Freeway (State Route 60) heading east to Apache Junction. Turn off the freeway on Power Road and head north to Apache Boulevard. Turn right on Apache Boulevard and go east to Apache Junction. From Apache Junction, turn northeast on State Route 88. Drive past Lost Dutchman State Park and look for the First Water trailhead sign. Turn right on this dirt road and drive for about 2.5 miles to the trailhead parking lot.

Campgrounds National Forest campgrounds located at Canyon Lake include Acacia, Palo Verde, Laguna, Boulder, and Tortilla. Open camping is also allowed along the First Water trailhead road, the Peralta Canyon road, and other areas of the Tonto National Forest. Camping is also available in Lost Dutchman State Park.

50. Second Water Trail

Time: 6 hours. *Distance:* 6 miles roundtrip. *Elevation Gain:* 400 feet. *Rating:* Moderate.

Trailhead: The trailhead starts at the Superstition Wilderness boundary at the east end of the parking lot on the old ranch road that goes to the remnants of the long-abandoned First Water ranch.

High Points: Views of Superstition Mountains and Weaver's Needle. Desert riparian vegetation and bird life. Garden Valley flat area

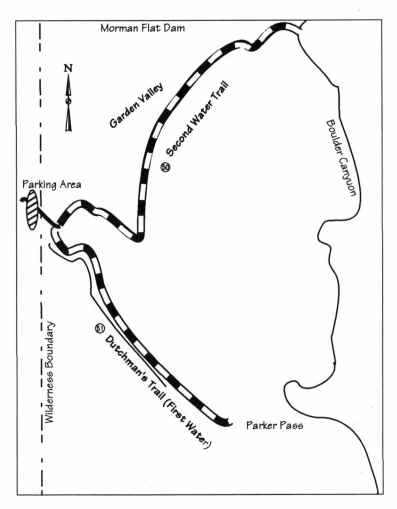

First Water Area

that offers possible wildlife viewing. Dramatic volcanic formations along trail.

Hiking the Trail: Cactus landscaping lines the first part of this trail with prickly pear and staghorn cholla predominant. The bright green (almost chartreuse) turpentine bush lines the trail everywhere. You come to a major junction of the Dutchman's Trail #104, going right, and the Second Water Trail #236, going left. Go left. You'll pass an old wellhead and cattle corrals—evidence of this area's historic ranching activity. The first drainage is First Water Creek. It has water in the spring but can be dry in summer. Hackberry Spring Trail takes off to the left at this drainage. On the way to the next drainage, you pass through a forest of chain-fruit cholla with their dangling, edible fruit clusters drooping toward the ground.

As the path heads down to the large drainage, the plant life transitions into jojoba bush and hop bush and wild cucumber vine, twisting itself among the palo verde trees and hackberry bushes. Walk along on volcanically deposited ash, tuff, and agglomerate, surrounded by yellowish-orange volcanic rocks. This soft, porous material erodes quickly, forming holes, overhangs, and grotesque formations throughout the range. A black and reddish patina forms on many of the rock surfaces.

The path crosses the Hackberry Spring runoff drainage, then turns directly north and angles up to a level area called Garden Valley. Look for coyotes, cottontails, and jackrabbits dashing through the cholla. It's also a good place to spot thrashers, wrens, and sparrows as they dash between nests in the predominantly chain-fruit cholla and prickly pear cactus forest.

Superstition Mountain is the main mountain in the Superstition range. Its vertical stone columns are part of the skyline to the right. Four Peaks comes into view to the northeast. The black basalt cap of Black Mesa looms to the near southeast. This black basalt layer is the latest of the volcanic outpourings that covered the terrain. It is evident in many areas of the Supes and can be seen again in the immediate northeast cliffs. The tip of Weaver's Needle comes up to the south. The huge yellow volcanic walls of Battleship Mountain and Geronimo Head loom in the foreground, across Boulder Canyon.

Continue on down the rough path to Second Water Canyon with grayish-black bedrock water pools scattered along the wash on the right. This is a spring-fed wash and offers cooling desert waters most of the year. Giant bursage plants, with their long, arrowhead-shaped leaves, line the drainages. The wide bed of Boulder Canyon comes into view. Trail #236 and Boulder Canyon Trail #103 meet in a flat area. To the right of the junction is an ephemeral trail, Trail #103, which requires a lot of boulder hopping and is washed out much of the way. To the left, the trail goes on to the Canyon Lake trailhead near Laguna and Boulder campgrounds. Take a few steps left from the junction and you'll see the white bedrock of the last part of Second Water Canyon. This is a great lunch spot. Return by the same route.

51. Dutchman's Trail (First Water)

Time: 4 hours. *Distance:* 4 miles roundtrip. *Elevation Gain:* 350 feet. *Rating:* Moderate.

Trailhead: The trailhead starts at the east end of the First Water parking lot, which is the boundary of the Superstition Wilderness.

High Points: Desert riparian vegetation and bird life. Dramatic volcanic landscape streamside. Great vistas of Weaver's Needle and Superstition Mountains.

Hiking the Trail: Hike along the old road to the junction of the Dutchman's Trail #104 and Second Water Trail #236. Go right on #104, heading for Parker Pass, about 2 miles southeast along the trail. This is a nice half-day roundtrip hike along slightly ascending terrain that skirts First Water Creek for a mile. It culminates in great views of Weaver's Needle. The path crosses First Water Creek about .25 mile from the junction and follows it along for another .75 mile. The creek may run all summer, depending on the previous winter rainfall. A forest of hop bush, burro bush, and scrub oak lines the creek—along with chain-fruit cholla with bird's nests built between the stems. Large boulders and walls of volcanic agglomerate intermixed with decomposed granite line the creek path.

Just after the trail leaves the creekbed, heading uphill, the tip of Weaver's Needle comes into view and continues to show itself all the way to Parker Pass. Black Mesa, with its level top of black basalt and lower horizontal layer of yellowish volcanic tuff, looms on the skyline to the left. Parker Pass is the last saddle before the trail descends to Aylors Caballo Camp. Most of Weaver's Needle and its base are seen from here. Notice that the Needle has two parts—one large spire, closest to you, the second smaller one split by a deep ravine. This ravine can be climbed and the large needle ascended. It is possible to spend the night on the summit. Return to the trailhead by the same route.

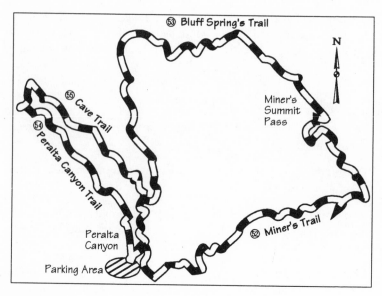

Peralta Canyon Area

Peralta Canyon Area

The Peralta family were early Spanish explorers and miners in the Superstition Mountains area. They developed a few mines around the mountains and have figured in the stories and legends of the Lost Dutchman Gold Mine.

Peralta Canyon is on the south side of the wilderness area and provides the most popular trail in the Superstitions — Peralta Canyon Trail. The Peralta Canyon parking area is the hub of a number of trailheads into the Supes, radiating out into the range. It offers many choices for short or long day hikes and is a favorite spot for spotting spring wildflowers.

Day Hike Area Takeoff Point Peralta Canyon Parking Area: From I-17, get onto the Superstition Freeway (State Route 60) heading east to Apache Junction. Turn off the freeway on Power Road and head north to Apache Boulevard. Turn right on Apache Boulevard and go east to Apache Junction. From Apache Junction, take US Route 60-89 southeast for 8 miles to the Peralta Canyon turnoff. This road goes north 6 miles to the Peralta Canyon trailhead parking area.

Campgrounds See First Water Area.

52. Miner's Trail

Time: 4 hours. *Distance:* 6 miles roundtrip. *Elevation Gain:* 900 feet.
Rating: Moderate.

Trailhead: All Peralta Canyon trailheads start at the north end of
the parking area. There is a pit toilet in the parking area but no water.

High Points: Hiking the very southern edge of the range with views
to the south across the Southern Deserts Province. Dramatic volcanic landscape adjacent to the trail. Close-up of Miner's Needle formation. Views north into the range from Miner's Saddle.

Hiking the Trail: Just past the trailhead you will find the junction
of Dutchman's (Miner's) Trail #104 and Bluff Spring Trail #235. Go
right on Dutchman's (Miner's) Trail. The brittlebush-lined route
climbs up and south around a high point to a saddle that overlooks
Coffee Flat Valley and a view of Miner's Needle 2 miles east. The
trail slowly angles down to the flat area where giant bursage, globe
mallow, and jojoba line the path. When you reach the first drainage—
Barks Canyon—walk upstream and see the small waterfall. Chain-
fruit cholla line the path as you continue. The fruit is edible in summer. Chain-fruit cholla gives way to a prickly pear forest. Prickly pear
fruit also ripen and become edible in summer.

The route heads northeast toward the southern edge of the Supes
and meets a second drainage. To the right, a profusion of saguaro
cactus fills Coffee Flat Valley. Apartment-dwelling birds use the holes
in the saguaro, made by the Gila woodpecker. The inside of the saguaro is cooled by shade and its internal water-transport system,
making it a perfect summer shelter for winged animals. After the Gila
woodpecker makes the apartment, it may live in it for a season. Then
other birds, such as owls, doves, thrashers, and sparrows, rent it out.

The path continues east along the base of jumbled volcanic rock
formations. Cross another drainage close to the junction of Coffee
Flat Trail #108. This is Miner's Canyon. Upstream you might find
a shady spot to sit.

Walk a little farther around the switchbacks that head up to Miner's Summit and look up at the Miner's Needle monolith. You might
see rock climbers working through the eye of the needle on their way
up the rock face to the summit. As you start up the switchbacks heading northwest to Miner's Summit, notice the granite boulders lining
the path. You are walking in Precambrian granite bedrock, charac-

terized by the whitish-gray rock with black mica, gray feldspar, and clear quartz crystals. This clearly contrasts with the higher-elevation volcanic material, composed of the yellow-brown-buff volcanic dacite tuffs and agglomerates. Brown-black-rust-colored patina is apparent on the rock surfaces.

Granite gives way to grayish-brown agglomerates as you ascend the trail. You are now traveling through a forest of ocotillo. Continue northwest and up until you cross the main Miner's Canyon drainage. Resurrection plant is located near the cooler, wetter drainage. Continue up to Miner's Summit Pass, where Trail #104 is joined from the east by Whiskey Spring Trail #238. This is a good lunch spot with views that extend both north and south.

Return by the same route.

53. Bluff Spring Trail

Time: 6 hours. *Distance:* 7 miles roundtrip. *Elevation Gain:* 900 feet. *Rating:* Challenging.

Trailhead: This is a continuation of the Miner's Trail, so the trailhead can be found at the north end of the Peralta Canyon parking area.

High Points: North-slope vegetation along a drainage. Crystal Spring. Streambed water most of the year. Possible water pools. Fantasyland of eroded spires, columns, and monsters.

Hiking the Trail: Take Miner's Trail to the Miner's Summit pass. Continue on Trail #104 from Miner's Summit to the junction of Trail #235 and back to the Peralta Canyon trailhead.

The path to Crystal Spring is a gradual descent through a north-facing vegetated slope. Strong-smelling buckbrush, mountain mahogany, scrub oak, and sugar sumac start appearing. The south-facing slopes have saguaro cactus, but those facing north don't. A few juniper trees are scattered on either side of the trail. After the junipers, you enter a prickly pear forest—again, mostly on the south-facing slopes. A few sotol plants with their agavelike forms shoot up next to the trail. Their leaves are long and thin and edged with spines. The stalk is a straight, thin tower of vegetation. The prickly pear forest gives way to a chain-fruit cholla forest.

Crystal Spring is identified by the cottonwood trees growing in the area. Go upslope a bit from the junction of Trails #235 and #104 to find the spring. Follow Bluff Spring Canyon Trail #235 west, boulder hopping and sloshing for about a mile before turning south. Look for rock cairns as you follow the streambed. Weaver's Needle is visible again as you turn south and run into the junction of Trail #235 and Trail #234 (Terrapin Pass Trail), located in a bedrock streambed. This waterway runs most of the year, and if you follow it down a short way it forms deeper pools. Go off the trail and down the canyon a bit to find the pools. It's a good place to take a cool dip, but remember that there are no lifeguards and you swim in these areas at your own risk. The water is warmed as it runs along the flat bedrock, absorbing the heat from the stone.

The trail heads downhill towards Bark's Canyon. The next mile is "fantasyland" mile, with all sorts of eroded rock monsters, needles, windows, and balanced boulders formed from the volcanics. Huge sugar sumac trees appear, with their dark green, shiny, arrowhead-shaped oval leaves and reddish branch tips. Scrub oak and barberry oak become abundant. Barberry is the holly-leaved brushy plant with extremely sharp points on the leaves. The wood is yellowish and is used for carving.

The route angles up and away from Bark's Canyon to a pass that offers views of the Coffee Flat Valley and the southern end of the wilderness. It makes a sharp right to the west and goes about 100 yards before turning south again. At this turn, look for the junction with Cave Trail #233, which comes in from the right. This is a return route from the Peralta Canyon Trail, which we'll take at another time. Notice the return of south-slope vegetation—like jojoba, brittlebush, globe mallow, and hop bush. You soon arrive at the overlook for views down into Don's Camp southwest of the trailhead. This also overlooks Peralta Canyon and the trail that ascends to Fremont Pass. Return to the parking area via the rocky descending path.

54. Peralta Canyon Trail

Time: 4 hours. *Distance:* 4 miles roundtrip. *Elevation Gain:* 1,400 feet. *Rating:* Moderate.

Trailhead: From the trailhead at the north end of the Peralta Canyon parking area, turn left at the sign.

High Points: Rich riparian vegetation and bird life. Dramatic volcanic rock color and formation changes. Grotesque volcanic architecture. Breathtaking views of Weaver's Needle and the northern Superstition range from Fremont Saddle.

Hiking the Trail: This is the most popular trail in the Supes because of its climactic view of Weaver's Needle from Fremont Saddle. The route follows the Peralta Canyon streambed and crosses it at various places. Water runs in spring and early summer if rainfall allows. The water goes underground and resurfaces at various spots. This trail, with its return by way of the Cave Trail, is a great introduction to the Superstitions. There is constant topographic, vegetative, and scenic variety along the entire roundtrip loop. The route starts out heading north and angles northwest all the way to Fremont Saddle. The path is lined with agglomerate boulders with various sizes and shapes of stones infused in the cementlike rock formations. A white coating covers many of the boulders. On the vertical volcanic columns above, a dark brown and black patina hides much of the original rock surface. Higher up the skyline to the right are the yellow and tan volcanic ash layers that lie atop vertical basalt columns.

Early on, two small abandoned mine sites greet the hiker. About 100 yards up the trail, you pass a vertical stone wall to the left. Growing on this wall are two rare plants, *Gila paritili* and maple leaf mirandia, the latter found only in the Superstition and Usery mountains. The ascent is gradual and crisscrosses the streambed. Various shaded spots offer cool respite at the crossings. Large scrub oaks and sugar sumacs provide the shade, while the canyon wrens provide the music. Deer vetch shows its small, bright yellow-orange flower.

As you ascend farther up the trail, Geronimo Cave comes into view on the right along a line of yellow volcanic tuff. You will pass that cave on the return path. The trail ascends away from the streambed and up a series of switchbacks directed through layers of multicolored volcanic tuff, ash, and agglomerate. Various shades of purple, buff, orange, pink, brown, and cream permeate the landscape. Much of the trail is now on bedrock. One last water course crosses the trail as a bedrock stream channel. This is a good spot for sitting and looking out over Peralta Canyon and part of Coffee Flat Valley. This small water flow can last throughout spring and some of summer. The vertical "people" rocks on the western canyon edge come into prominent view. Look up for ravens, hawks, and vultures soaring across the canyon. A "one-eyed monster" lurks by the trail.

More pastel-colored bedrock trail surface leads you past the monster and on to Fremont Saddle, where the overpowering Weaver's Needle looms to the north. This is a good lunch and snooze spot. Trail #102 continues down to East Boulder Canyon and over to the

First Water trailhead. Return to the Peralta Canyon trailhead by the same route or take the Cave Trail loop back to the Peralta Canyon trailhead.

55. Cave Trail

Time: 2 hours. *Distance:* 2 miles one-way. *Elevation Gain:* 1,400 feet downhill. *Rating:* Moderate.

Trailhead: See Peralta Canyon Trail. Fremont Saddle is the trailhead.

High Points: Exhilarating ridgeline hiking with mixed rock scrambling. Sweeping overlooks into Peralta Canyon and the southern range. Variety of route finding and trail configurations.

Hiking the Trail: Hike Peralta Canyon Trail to Fremont Saddle and return by this little-known alternate route, rather than by the same Peralta Canyon route. Cave Trail is one of the best-kept day-hiking secrets in the entire Superstition Wilderness, with unique views of the Superstition range. The route angles northeast for about 100 yards from the end of the Peralta Canyon Trail at Fremont Saddle, then takes a sharp turn to the north. Follow that for a short distance and watch for another sharp turn back to the southeast and down a short way to where the trail skirts the edge of Peralta Canyon, heading for Geronimo Cave, that large, dark area you saw in the yellow-banded rock as you came up the trail.

Follow the sometimes-hard-to-see path, looking for rock cairns along the route. The path is mixed dirt and bare rock surface. Keep looking ahead for more cairns. They will lead you along the sloping rock surface of the buff-, brown-, and orange-colored tuff that makes up the Geronimo Cave layer. Follow these until you pass below a couple of overhangs. Keep going until you see the huge cave above and to the left. There is a short path up to the cave. Climb up into it and sit a spell.

The next section of the trail is tricky, but challenging and fun. A series of steep gullies and sloping rock faces leads to a small flat area. You can choose from a couple of options: take the gullies down, which involves some bushwhacking, or take the rock faces down, which requires some careful foot and hand placements. You can slide on your butt down these faces.

Stay right and follow the path and cairns to another short face that leads to a small vegetated valley. The path splits to the right and left in the valley. Stay left, following the path around the valley and up to a series of large boulders. The route continues along the ridgeline and eventually crosses over to the northeast side of the ridge, where great views open up to Weaver's Needle to the northwest and Miner's Needle to the east. The path becomes more obvious at this point, angling around and through boulder piles. The surface is mixed foot-path and bedrock. Keep looking for cairns. You'll eventually come out to a series of small saddles that look down to Peralta Canyon and the trailhead parking area. Follow this last part downslope to the junction of Bluff Spring Trail #235 and back to the trailhead.

Lost Dutchman State Park Area

Lost Dutchman State Park is named after the Lost Dutchman Mine, supposed site of gold ore that has yet to be found. The legendary site was supposed to have been worked by early miner Jacob Waltz, with findings carried to the nearby town of Globe to be assayed. Other miners followed Waltz into the Superstitions but usually met un-timely deaths at the hands of Apache Indians, other unknown adven-turers, or perhaps Waltz himself.

The park is located close to the Superstition Wilderness Area, making it an ideal area for hikers. Sheer-walled escarpments rise above the 300-acre park. Palo verde, ocotillo, cholla, saguaro, and many ground flowers dot this volcanic desert landscape.

The park contains a nature trail, 35 undeveloped campsites, rest-rooms, and picnic facilities.

Day Hike Area Takeoff Point Apache Junction: From Apache Junction, take State Route 88 northeast about 5 miles to the Lost Dutchman State Park sign. Pull in and park in the visitor parking area to the right of the entrance station.

Campgrounds Individual and group campgrounds available in the park. Phone: (602) 982-4485.

56. Native Plant Trail

Time: .5 hour. *Distance:* .25-mile loop. *Elevation Gain:* Level. *Rating:* Easy.

Trailhead: The trailhead starts at the edge of the parking area.

High Points: Identification signs and bird-watching bench.

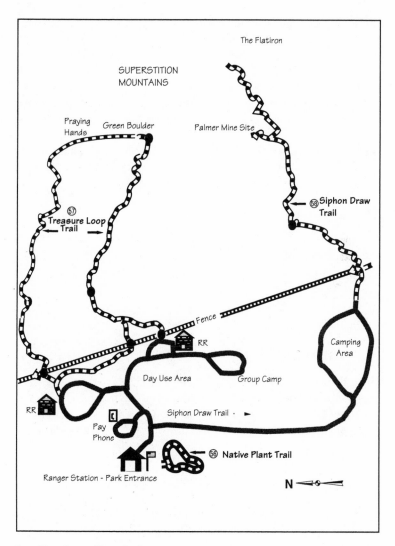

The Flatiron

SUPERSTITION
MOUNTAINS

Praying
Hands   Green Boulder   Palmer Mine Site

⑤⑧ Siphon Draw
Trail

⑤⑦
Treasure Loop
← Trail →

Fence

RR

Camping
Area

Day Use Area   Group Camp

Siphon Draw Trail · ►

Pay
Phone

⑤⑥ Native Plant Trail

Ranger Station - Park Entrance

N ◄●►

Lost Dutchman State Park Area

Hiking the Trail: Hiking this nature trail provides a good introduction to the plant life of the Superstition Mountains. There's a series of plant identification signs, along with observation benches.
The identified plants include bursage, foothill palo verde, chain-fruit
cholla with bird's nests, Christmas cholla, teddy bear cholla, jojoba

bush, staghorn cholla, mesquite tree, prickly pear cactus, saguaro cactus, brittlebush, fishhook and barrel cactus, ocotillo, Mormon tea, creosote bush, desert broom, buckhorn cholla, and white ratany. If you can get these plants in your mind and remember them, you will see them again frequently in the surrounding terrain. There is an observation spot for watching birds flit in and out of a constructed feeder. Look for dove, house finch, northern flicker, ash-throated flycatcher, black-tailed gnatcatcher, red-tailed hawk, Anna's hummingbird, Harris hawk, great horned owl, mockingbird, phainopepla, Gambel's quail, roadrunner, curved-bill thrasher, starling, towhee, verdin, Gila woodpecker, cactus wren, and turkey vulture.

57. Treasure Loop Trail

Time: 2 hours. *Distance:* 2.5 miles roundtrip. *Elevation Gain:* 500 feet. *Rating:* Moderate.

Trailhead: From the Lost Dutchman State Park entrance station, keep left and go to the Cholla Day Use Area. Park here and look for the trail sign just to the right of the restroom facility. Follow the path north past a couple of picnic ramadas to the Superstition Wilderness boundary fenceline (gate) with a trail sign that reads Treasure Loop Trail #56. This is the trailhead.

High Points: Panoramas of the Valley of the Sun to the south, west, and north. Vistas northeast to the McDowell Mountains, Four Peaks, and the beginning of the Central Mountains Province. Dramatic views of the volcanically jumbled Superstition Mountains headwall.

Hiking the Trail: Follow the flat, well-maintained trail as it gently slopes up toward the Superstition Mountains headwall. You'll be looking up at this headwall for the first half of the loop. It is made of volcanic ash and lava with intrusions of welded tuff, breccia, dacite, basalt, and some conglomerate. The headwall is an eroded remnant of an upthrust of thick lava within a caldera that has subsequently been eroded away to its present form.

You'll pass lots of bursage, tomatillo, and jojoba bushes, along with palo verde trees and pleasantly spaced saguaros. The path drops down across a couple of small drainages and meets up with Jacob's Crosscut Trail #58 on the right. (This crosses over to the return path of the Treasure Loop Trail and can be taken for a shorter day hike.)

Continue straight ahead on the Treasure Loop Trail as the uphill angle steepens a bit. Just past the junction, there is a saguaro cactus on the left with many holes in the stem in which birds live. A way up the trail, you'll pass through a forest of chain-fruit cholla with lupine, golden poppy, mallow, daisies, and blue dicks growing alongside. A bench provides a place to sit. Continue up the trail to the apex of the hike—at another bench.

At this apex, the skyline—from west to east—includes the White Tank Mountains, Camelback Mountain, Squaw Peak, the Goldfield, the Mazatzal Mountains, and Four Peaks. A small trail goes up to the headwall from here but is not recommended. Thin rock fins jut up around the base of the headwall. These are favorite rock climbing areas. The path passes through an area of hop bushes—willowlike plants with thin clustered leaves and three- to four-petaled flowers. Then it passes over a bedrock drainage that is covered with green algae and called the Green Boulders.

Another aluminum bench is found close to the junction of Prospector's View Trail #57 and the continuation of Treasure Loop Trail #56. Take #56 south from this point, angling down over some rounded wooden trail supports. The huge boulders on the right are made up of breccia and ash and are easily eroded. They provide a rock climber's practice area, commonly called a "bouldering" area. You will find another bench on the down-sloping trail. Then you'll cross Jacob's Crosscut Trail #58 again. Another chain-fruit cholla forest precedes a junction of small paths. Stay right and head back to the Cholla Day Use Area.

58. Siphone Draw Trail

Time: 2 hours. *Distance:* 3 miles roundtrip. *Elevation Gain:* 600 feet. *Rating:* Moderate.

Trailhead: From the park entrance station, go to the main camping area. The trailhead starts on the east end of the parking area.

High Points: Panorama of the Valley of the Sun to the west and south. Dramatic volcanic architecture of the Superstition Mountains headwall. Old, abandoned mine site. Springtime wildflower displays.

Hiking the Trail: The path starts relatively level and encounters the Tonto National Forest gate in about .25 mile. In another .25 mile, Prospector's View Trail #57 is met. Just past that, Jacob's Crosscut Trail #58 crosses the path. (For another day hike, take the Crosscut back over to Treasure Loop Trail #56 and descend to the day-use area and back to the main camping area.)

Follow the trail as it climbs up to the turnoff to the old Palmer's Mine. Turn left off the trail for a view of the mine site and return to the main trail. The designated trail stops at the foot of the draw that leads up to the Flatiron. This is the end of the described trail. It is possible to continue up to the Flatiron, but not recommended for casual hiking. It is steep and slippery and difficult going. Return to the camping area by the same route.

PART TWO

CENTRAL MOUNTAINS PROVINCE

CHAPTER 6

Forming the Central Mountains Province

Geology

The Central Mountains Province lies between the Northern Plateau Province to the north and the Southern Deserts Province to the south. The northern edge is sharply defined by the prominent Mogollon Rim escarpment running slightly southeast by northwest across the center of the state. The Mogollon Rim rises vertically from 1,000 to 2,000 feet along its meandering path above the towns of Payson, Pine, and Strawberry on the west and McNary on the east. It is the southern edge of the Northern Plateau Province exposing the eroded layers of Northern Plateau sediment. In some undetermined time in the future, it will have eroded back to the Arizona-Utah border. The southern boundary of the Province is where these Central Mountains flatten out into the lower peaks, slopes, bajadas, and valleys of the Southern Deserts.

In earlier geologic time, the Central Mountains Province was covered with many of the same layered sediments that constitute today's Northern Plateau Province. About 38 to 33 million years ago, colliding continents pushed volcanic intrusions of light-colored ancient granite, darker basalt, and various metamorphic complexes up, into, and over some of these overlying layers of gray, red, and white limestones and sandstones, cracking them and hastening the erosive forces of wind and water. The softer sedimentary layers gradually eroded away, leaving 1- to 2-billion-year-old metamorphic intrusions in the form of today's Central Mountains Province ranges. These ranges are, in general, higher and more closely spaced than the ranges of the desert, but they run in the same general northwest/southeast direction. Among these ranges are the Bradshaws, Mazatzals, Sierra Anchas, Superstitions, Pinals, Whites, Hualapais, Junipers, and Weavers.

The silted-in valleys between these ranges are generally shallower and narrower than those of the desert ranges. An exception to this is a series of broad valleys that run in a northwest/southeast line through the center of the state. They include Chino Valley, Verde Valley, Tonto Basin, and the Gila River Valley.

The northern part of the Central Mountains Province (at the base of the Mogollon Rim) is made up of the lower sedimentary layers of this 2,000-foot escarpment. It's a land of broken limestones, sandstones, conglomerates, and shales, which creates an area of rugged canyons and waterways that drain off the plateau.

Another factor in the Central Mountains landscape is the ever-present volcanism that covers so much of Arizona's surface. Great shield volcanos, such as Mt. Baldy in the White Mountains exemplify this process where many square miles of basalt lava poured out, covering the surrounding land and creating a low shield-shaped mound. The shield volcano is not as dramatic as the cone of an explosive volcano, but it is more prevalent. In many instances, this lava was harder than the underlying layers, and after millions of years of erosion took their toll on the softer sediments, the harder basalt "caps" remained and formed flat-topped "mesas."

Speaking of erosion, it must be remembered that this province contains the majority of the streams, springs, creeks, and water holes in the state. With the exception of the Colorado River, the headwaters of most of Arizona's river and stream systems start in these mountains. These drainages provide water for the thirsty crops and human population of the Phoenix metropolitan area—and provide groundwater for Tucson's growing population.

Climate

Northern Plateau Province weather comes in from the continental mass to the north and reaches down across the Mogollon Rim, dumping wind and rain on the Central Mountains. In contrast, in summer months, the desert marine climate comes up from the south and dumps moisture in the Central Mountains Province. The unpredictable high-altitude jet stream moves back and forth over this area, greatly influencing the amount of precipitation the region receives.

The Central Mountains, with their high peaks and increased rainfall, create the wettest province and the summer vacationland for dry desert dwellers to the south.

Summer weather varies tremendously in this province, due to the vertical nature of the terrain. Mountain peaks and wide valleys help create local weather changes out of the bigger patterns that flow over them. It can get hot during midday in the Central Mountains valleys—sometimes 100 degrees Fahrenheit—but it cools off to the pleasant 60s and 70s at night and in the morning. Afternoon showers are usually short and sweet and increase in intensity through July and August.

Fall is fairly dry, depending on how soon the Pacific Northwest storms start their journey across the continent. The deserts are still hot and dry during these months, but there is a distinct crispness to the air in the Central Mountains Province.

Winter weather is heavily influenced by Pacific storms. Covering large areas with a fairly uniform cloud base, these storms drop rain, snow, hail, and sleet in the Central Mountains—again, with the help of the jet stream. Due to vertical relief, it can be snowing on the upper levels of some peaks while raining on the lower slopes. The freezing level of the precipitation can change hundreds of feet in one day. Towns such as Prescott, in the middle of the Province, can experience snow, rain, then snow again within minutes. Temperatures in Prescott sometimes dip below freezing at night but seldom stay that cold during the daytime. There are some areas in the eastern White Mountains where especially frigid temperatures make Hawley Lake the nation's coldest spot on certain nights.

The state's largest ski area—Sunrise Ski Area—exists within those same White Mountains. It normally receives the greatest and longest-lasting snow cover in the state.

The lower parts of the Central Mountains—the aforementioned wide valleys—fall midway between the deserts and mountains in climate. They are warmer than the mountain communities and usually not as wet. It can be raining or snowing in Prescott at 5,500 feet while sunny in the Verde Valley, just an hour away.

Spring is the magic season for all landscapes, and the Central Mountains Province is no exception. Winter storms have left the ground soaked and wildflower seeds ready to explode. Animals are giving birth to young that will feed on the new growth. The weather is warming and the snow is melting, creating the waterways that will run into summer. Hikers are getting out their maps and planning.

Plant Life

The great range of weather and mountain-valley elevation changes in this province creates a tremendous variety of plant life. In fact, representatives of almost all Arizona plant communities live in this province—from desertshrub to spruce-fir-aspen.

The grassland community includes varieties such as fescue, lovegrass, and gramas. These grasslands are a southwestward extension of the Great Plains. Most of the grassland occurs at elevations between 5,000 and 7,000 feet. Some reach down to 3,500 feet. In many areas, the grassland commingles with higher-elevation desert plants such as sotol, beargrass, and mesquite.

The oak-pine-woodland community includes trees such as the emory oak, Arizona oak, Mexican blue oak, silverleaf oak, Arizona cypress, and netleaf oak. Intermingled with the oaks are Chihuahua pine, Apache pine, and Mexican pinyon. These oaks and pines are warm-weather woodland plants that comprise the northern extension of woodlands originating in Mexico. They inhabit elevations from about 4,000 to 7,000 feet.

Chaparral plants are characteristically tough-leaved evergreen shrubs that grow in dense stands and cover large areas of landscape. They exist between 3,500 and 7,000 feet. Scrub oak is the dominant species. This mixes with hollygrape, manzanita, hackberry, sotol, squawbush, agave, sugar sumac, buckthorn, mountain mahogany, and cliffrose. Trees found in this community include the desert willow, Utah juniper, one-seed juniper, alligator juniper, pinyon, and Arizona cypress.

A little higher up in the Central Mountains Province plant-community profile is the pinyon-juniper woodland. Dominated by the juniper half of the equation, these trees exist at elevations between 5,500 and 7,500 feet. They also grow in grassland and chaparral but many times stand alone in pure juniper profiles. It is easy to identify this community, due to the dominance of these two tree species. Arizona cypress sometimes grows within the community.

The higher elevations within the Central Mountains Province support the ponderosa pine and spruce-fir-aspen communities with stands of Douglas fir, white fir, subalpine fir, Gambel oak, Arizona white oak, and maples. There is a large variety of understory plants in some places. In other areas, the ponderosa pine is so dominant that little else exists around it. These communities exist from 6,500 up to 10,000 feet and create a shady, cool, forest environment that so many Phoenix residents seek in the summer.

Animal Life

As you would guess, animal life in the Central Mountains Province is just as varied as the plant life due to the same geographic variations. More cover, water, and food are available in this province than in the Southern Deserts Province. This allows for an increased number of browsing and grazing animals—especially mule deer, white-tailed deer, antelope, and elk. The lower-elevation mule deer will move up into the Central Mountains during the summer, and the white-tails will move down into this warmer climate during cold winters. Predatory mountain lions and bobcats may follow.

The abundance of cone- and nut-bearing trees provides food and shelter for smaller animals such as squirrels and chipmunks. Other wild animals include wild turkeys, skunks, porcupines, and badgers. Birdlife includes Arizona jays, bluebirds, juncos, sparrows, ravens, hawks, quail, warblers, and nuthatches.

The permanent riparian habitats of this area contain the greatest variety of fishes in the state and include large-mouth bass, crappie, bluegill, catfish, striped bass, and pike. Higher-elevation species include rainbow, German brown, and Eastern brook trout. These year-round oases provide habitats for many water-loving birds and amphibians.

Reptiles include the western diamondback rattler, gopher snake, and mountain king snake.

COMMON CENTRAL MOUNTAINS PROVINCE PLANTS

Chaparral

Shrub Live Oak One of the most common Central Mountains plants, this shrublike tree has an edible acorn that was utilized by early Americans. Leaves are gray-green and hollylike. This plant can grow in dense thickets and be difficult to hike through.

Manzanita A shrub that can grow to tree height. Its characteristic smooth red bark catches the hiker's eye. Fruits and flowers are edible. This plant grows in a very dense manner and can be almost impossible to hike through.

Squawbush A deciduous shrub whose leaves turn red in fall. In summer produces an edible berry with a strong citrus taste.

Harris hawk

Hackberry Often grows with shrub live oak. Similar in size to shrub live oak. Grayish-green leaves with rough, sticky surface. Edible berries in the fall.

Sotol Yuccalike leaves but thinner. Produces a tall, thin flower stalk with small cream-colored flowers. Leaf fibers were used by early Americans for basketry.

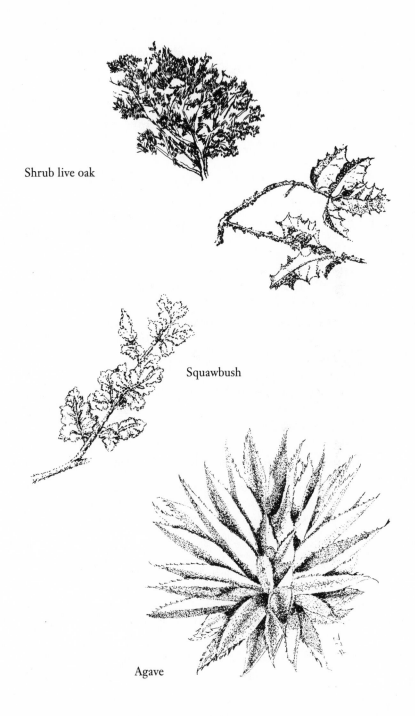

Shrub live oak

Squawbush

Agave

Hollygrape Very sharp-leaved shrub that produces small blue berries. Leaves are thin. Difficult to hike through.

Agave Sometimes called century plant. Looks like a yucca but has spines along leaf margins. Very showy flower stalk with large, cream-colored flowers. Spines used for sewing and fiber used for basketry. Blooming stalk used for food.

Oak-Pine/Pinyon-Juniper Woodland Communities

Utah Juniper Very common with small, scalelike leaves that overlap like shingles. Berries are edible after they fall to the ground and sweeten up. Trunk branches close to ground. Grow 25 to 30 feet tall.

Alligator Juniper Larger and thicker than Utah juniper. Bark resembles alligator skin, broken up into square plates. Berries also edible.

Arizona Cypress Sometimes mistaken for a juniper, this tall, conical tree has a smooth, reddish bark that detaches in strips.

Pinyon Pine This shrub or smallish tree has stout leaves that grow in pairs. Pinyon nuts are edible.

Cliffrose Tree/shrub that produces sweet-smelling summer flowers. Seed pods produce characteristic white plumes in fall. This is deer and livestock browse.

Ponderosa Pine/Spruce-Fir-Aspen Communities

Ponderosa Pine Very prominent, large, tall tree that can grow over 100 feet high. Has long needles attached to twig in bundles of three. Bark smells like vanilla or butterscotch. Bark is dark and rough on young trees, changing to smoother and orange on older trunks.

Douglas Fir Large tree with needles growing all along twig. Smooth needles. Grows with ponderosa pine but not as prevalent.

Arizona Pine Resembles small ponderosa. Produces long needles in bundles of three or four. Also found in southeastern Arizona "sky-island" mountains.

White Fir Often confused with Colorado blue spruce. Needles are short, flat, attached singly, and grow along twig. Cone is smooth.

Utah juniper

Cliffrose

Pinyon pine

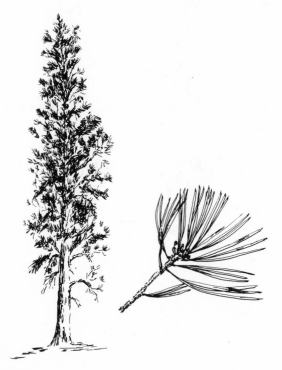

Ponderosa pine

Gambel Oak Very prominent lobed leaves that drop off in fall. The bark is rough and gray. Fruit is an acorn.

Arizona White Oak An evergreen tree with leaves taking many forms. Acorn bearing. Found throughout the Central Mountains Province.

Various Maples Characteristic maple-shaped leaves that turn yellow and purple in fall.

Sugar Sumac Characteristic large, shiny-green leaves produced by oval-shaped shrub.

Wild Cherry Small tree with small, bitter fruit.

Riparian Habitat Plants

Riparian habitat covers all three provinces, since streambeds run through them, but the majority of running water is found in the Central Mountains Province.

Poison Ivy Shrub or vine with three-lobed leaves. Shiny green surfaces turn red in fall. Produces small, white berry. Causes severe skin irritation in allergic individuals. Found along stream beds.

Cottonwood This huge, water-loving tree grows in the Southern Deserts Province and the lower areas of the Central Mountains Province. Its bright green, quaking-aspenlike leaves provide shady respite for desert animals. The soft wood is used for carving, and the flesh inside the bark contains the same chemicals as aspirin. Early Native Americans and early settlers chewed the bark pulp for pain relief.

Willow Companion tree to the cottonwood, with long, slender leaves. Grows in clusters and forests next to streambeds. Used for basketry, wickiup construction, bows and arrows.

Tamarisk Known as salt cedar, this introduced tree is now considered a pest, having taken over much of the willow and cottonwood habitat. Forms thickets along streambeds. Has sweet-smelling purple flowers in summer.

Sycamore This characteristic tree displays a smooth, gray, brown, green, and white bark. Large five-lobed leaves. Trunk can grow in any direction and sometimes forms weird shapes along streambeds.

Box Elder Tree that has leaves resembling poison ivy.

Arizona Walnut Produces long compound leaves with toothed edges. Small, smooth nuts, 1 inch or less in diameter.

Mountain Alder Small riparian tree with conelike fruit.

COMMON CENTRAL MOUNTAINS PROVINCE ANIMALS

Badger Feeds mostly on rodents by digging them out of burrows with strong front paws. Nocturnal during summer but visible during the rest of the year. Seldom preyed upon because of its strong defensive posture and aggressive counterattacks. Lives in open grasslands.

Black Bear Eats a wide variety of plants and animals. Shy and seldom seen, inhabits forests, chaparral, oak-pine woodlands, and canyons. Black and brown mixed colors.

Bobcat Feeds on rodents, birds, and other small animals. Inhabits rocky areas and canyons. Yellowish-brown to gray.

Elk Grazer and browser. Lives in timbered forest and chaparral. Head and shoulders are dark brown with dark legs. Body is brown to cream with white rump patch.

Gray Fox Most common of Arizona foxes. Eats rodents, lizards, birds, fruits, and nuts. Distinguishing mark is dark stripe extending length of tail. Reddish-brown stripe down back. Body gray with dark face. Lives in brushy, rocky terrain.

Mule Deer Browser that lives in forest, chaparral, and desert grassland. Summer coat varies from yellowish to reddish. Winter coat is dark gray. Short, stubby tail tipped in black.

Mountain Lion Largest carnivore in Arizona preys on deer, javelina, desert sheep, and elk. Resides in mountain ranges, rough canyons, and rocky outcrops. Tan or gray in color with white underparts.

Javelina Piglike peccary that eats a wide variety of fruits, nuts, and plants. Lives in oak-woodland, chaparral, desert grasslands, and desertshrub. Grizzled black and gray hair.

Porcupine Feeds mostly on woody plants. Lives in most areas of Arizona.

Elk

Javelina

Pronghorn Antelope Fastest runner in Arizona. Grazer that lives in grasslands and mountain canyons. Golden tan with white rump patch and throat bands.

Snakes The western diamondback resides here along with the gopher snake, blue racer, garter snake, mountain king snake, and hognosed snake. Snakes are rare to see and pose little threat to hikers—unless the hiker bothers the snake.

FISHES OF THE CENTRAL MOUNTAINS PROVINCE

This province has the majority of running water in the state, therefore the majority of fish species. Common fishes of the many lakes, streams, tanks, and rivers include bass, bluegill, crappie, catfish, pike, and trout.

Lake fishing is done at the many reservoirs, and stream fishing is practiced in the drainages that flow off the edges of the Northern Plateau—as well as along the White Mountains and Gila Mountains drainages of eastern Arizona.

CHAPTER 7

Prescott Day Hikes

Prescott

Mingus Mountain Area

Granite Mountain Area

Groom Creek Area

Thumb Butte Area

Lynx Lake Area

PRESCOTT

Prescott became the territorial capital of Arizona in 1864, shortly after gold was discovered in the Bradshaw Mountains north of town. The community soon became the business and cultural hub of north-central Arizona due to burgeoning ranching and mining activities.

Prescott has become one of the nation's most desired areas for retirement, due in part to its clean air, mile-high altitude, and mild climate. It's a two-hour drive from Phoenix and serves as a summer weekend getaway for thousands of desert dwellers. When it's 100 degrees Fahrenheit in Phoenix in July, it's between 75 and 80 degrees Fahrenheit in Prescott—usually with afternoon clouds and thundershowers.

Close to being surrounded by over 1 million acres of national forest, this mountain community offers close access to many great hiking trails. You can hike along mountain trails on Thumb Butte, Granite Mountain, Mingus Mountain, and Spruce Mountain, climbing to views of the Mogollon Rim and Sedona Red Rocks (southern edge of the Colorado Plateau), San Francisco Peaks, and the Grand Canyon North Rim.

Horseback riding is another favorite pursuit along many of the mountain and grassland trails. Granite Mountain, west of Prescott, is one of Arizona's favorite rock-climbing areas. In the Lynx Lake area, you can see remains of Native American settlements.

When to Go

The best hiking weather is spring, summer, and fall. Winter is normally too cold and wet for enjoyable tramping, but sunny and mild days do occur. The main winter desert-hiking areas are only a couple of hours south in the Southern Deserts Province.

Places to Visit

Visits to the *Sharlot Hall Museum* and the *Smoki Museum* give the hiker a taste of the cultural history of the local area. The *Prescott Public Library* and the *Prescott College Library* offer special sections on Arizona natural history. For more information, contact Sharlot Hall Museum, 415 W. Gurley, Prescott, AZ 86301, (602) 445-3122, and Smoki Museum, 100 N. Arizona, P.O. Box 123, Prescott, AZ 86301, (602) 445-1230.

The *Prescott Animal Park* is a small zoo with close-up views of coyotes, mountain lions, pronghorn antelopes, white-tailed deer, and coati-mundis, along with a clouded leopard, black jaguar, and Bengal tiger. Phone: (602) 778-4242.

Nearby *Jerome* is a historic mining area with its own museum. Jerome State Historic Park is located in the mining town of the same name built and preserved on the side of Mingus Mountain. The park displays early mining relics and offers some of the best scenic views in Arizona.

Directions to all Prescott Day Hike Area Takeoff Points start from the Prescott Chamber of Commerce, located at 117 West Goodwin Street, Prescott, Arizona 86302-1147, (602) 445-2000.

Mingus Mountain Area

Mingus Mountain is the local name for a fault-block range of mountains running northwest by southeast along the western boundary of

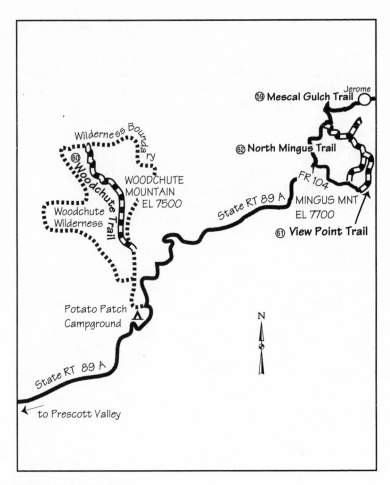

Mingus Mountain Area

the Prescott National Forest–East Half. The official name for the range is the Black Hills, derived, no doubt, from the layers of black basalt lava that cap it.

At one time, Mingus contained millions of dollars worth of copper, silver, and gold but now lies dormant as a mining area. Its main tourist attraction is the community of Jerome, once a ghost town perched on a 45-degree slope.

Mingus displays 1.7-billion-year-old metamorphic rhyolite bedrock at its base. This underlies limestone and sandstone layers and is capped by many episodes of volcanic basalt.

Mingus starts in desert grassland and changes into oak-pine woodland, chaparral, and pinyon-juniper woodland with the summit plateaus and colder drainages displaying ponderosa pine community. The highest summit of the range is 7,743 feet with an east-facing escarpment of 4,700 feet overlooking the Verde Valley below.

A second growth of ponderosa pine covers the top of the Mingus chain, the original forest having been cut down years ago for shoring timbers at the Jerome mine. Stumps of the old forest are visible among the newer growth of pines.

Day Hike Area Takeoff Point Potato Patch and Mingus Mountain campground turnoffs: From Prescott Chamber of Commerce, turn north (left) on Cortez and go to the stoplight on Gurley. Turn east (right) on Gurley and follow it to the intersection of State Route 89N. Keep left as you reach the intersection, go under the overpass, and follow 89N to 89A (5 miles). Turn east (right) on 89A. Follow 89A through the grasslands of Prescott Valley to the base of Mingus Mountain and the Prescott National Forest boundary, looking on either side of the highway for pronghorn antelope and coyotes.

Drive up to the highest road elevation in the mountains, a pass at 7,022 feet, and look for the Potato Patch campground entrance on the left, with the Mingus Mountain Campground sign to the right.

Campgrounds Potato Patch, Mingus Mountain, open National Forest camping.

59. Mescal Gulch Trail

Time: 4 hours. *Distance:* 4 miles roundtrip. *Elevation Gain:* Level. *Rating:* Moderate.

Trailhead: From Potato Patch campground, continue on the highway, looking for mile marker 339. Slow down, looking for the next marker—338 on the right-hand side. There is a small pullout on the left just past the marker. Cross the highway on foot to the 338 marker and head down the dirt road to a metal gate. The Mescal Gulch trailhead starts here.

High Points: Mescal Spring. Stone structure remains. Old mine sites. Mescal Creek. Spectacular vistas of the Verde Valley and the edge of the Northern Plateau Province.

Hiking the Trail: The trail follows the roadbed, which follows the Mescal Gulch streambed. This is lined with large ponderosa pine, alligator juniper, and Arizona walnut. Surrounding plant life consists of Fremont barberry (yellow carving wood), cliffrose, penstemon, horehound, manzanita, and mullein. Follow the road for about .75 mile to what remains of an old limestone building structure. Mescal Spring—a large, square, spring-fed tank—sits just past the structure. The spring originates just above the tank, flowing out of an abandoned mine prospect, the entrance covered with moss and watercress. In winter and spring, water will be flowing down the mountainside all around this site. It flows out of porous limestone at weak points on the surface. Water also flows along the interface between the porous limestone and underlying impenetrable rhyolite bedrock, surfacing along the seams. A separate road branches to the right at the spring. Stay left, following our road away from the spring.

The path passes an old corral made from juniper wood posts. Just past the corral, take a right-hand detour for an overlook down into Mescal Creek as it cuts steeply through the bedrock, forming pools and waterfalls below. Go back to the road and follow it past a fenced vertical mine shaft to the right. Evidence of copper ore abounds in this area and pieces of green, ore-infused rock lie about.

As the road curves north, views of Verde Valley 3,000 feet below open up, along with views of the higher, level Mogollon Rim. Soon, the towns of Camp Verde, Cottonwood, Sedona, and Clarkdale come into view on the valley floor. The skyline is outlined by the San Francisco Peaks (highest summits), Kendrick Peak, and Bill Williams Mountain. Follow the road another couple of hundred yards to a fenceline with a gate. In winter and springtime, water gushes down the mountainside from the left in another display of limestone porosity. This water coats the surrounding limestone with a travertine deposit—a chemical precipitate. Return by the same route.

60. Woodchute Trail

Time: 5 hours. *Distance:* 5.5 miles roundtrip. *Elevation Gain:* 600 feet. *Rating:* Moderate.

Trailhead: From Potato Patch campground, follow FR 106 for .3 mile to the powerline and powerline cattle tank. A Forest Service gate is ahead. Go through the gate and follow the jeep road to the Woodchute #102 trailhead at a narrow fence gate to the right. This is the Woodchute trailhead.

High Points: Great vistas north to the Northern Plateau Province and Red Rock country. Vistas east to the Verde Valley and the Mogollon Rim. Changing vegetation zones from chaparral community through pinyon-juniper to ponderosa pine.

Hiking the Trail: The route was originally a bulldozer track used to create cattle watering tanks on Woodchute Mountain. Woodchute Mountain got its name when loggers built a chute for sending timber down the north side of the mountain to loading platforms for the narrow-gauge railroad that served Jerome. The Woodchute Trail is formed on top of the basalt lava cap that covers the Mingus Mountain chain. Lava rock cobbles, evident in the few streambed crossings, show various shades of brown, red, cream, and black. They also vary in weight, showing the different lava consistencies, depending on the amount of gas bubbles that perforate the rocks during eruption. Vegetation is dominated by ponderosa pine, juniper, scrub oak, and various grasses. There are some Gambel oaks, mountain mahogany, agaves, penstemon, and prickly pear cactus scattered around, but since this is a full-growth ponderosa forest, these big trees shut out most other trees on the plateau, creating an open forest to walk through. The trail slowly angles up and onto the east side of the mountain where views of the Verde Valley and State Route 89A appear. A little way farther, views open up to the west where Chino Valley, Prescott Valley, Granite Mountain, and Granite Dells appear. The route then generally follows the ridgeline with views in both directions. A couple of spots offer views of the San Francisco Peaks, Mt. Elden, and Bill Williams Mountain.

Notice the unusually large-trunked juniper and Gambel oak trees along this relatively flat first part of the Woodchute Trail. You'll approach a major drainage angling down to your right. This has water in it during spring and summer, depending on rainfall. Cross the stream, then start angling up away from it on the steepest part of the trail to the plateau in the area of the Woodchute Wilderness. Look back as you start up and you'll see Woodchute Tank. The fairly level plateau is even more open, again dominated by the large ponderosa pine. But even the pines thin out and open space continues to increase as the trail goes north. Old stumps from the early tree cuttings are visible. The miners practically leveled the area, and the present growth is all new forest.

Continue along the meandering plateau trail until you start to see piles of stones along the path. You'll run into a fenceline as the plateau slopes off to the north. The trail turns to the left of the fence and an old sign says Sheep Camp. This is the turnaround point on the trail. If followed, it would continue down to an old road at the base of the northern end of the plateau. From this turnaround point, you can see the edge of the Northern Plateau Province—conspicuous by the layered red and white sandstone formations to the north. This is a good lunch spot, but there is a better one a short way back and to the east. Look for the high elevation spot of 7,648 on the topo map, just at the northeast end of the plateau. Walk off-trail to this high area. The views north and east are breathtaking. The entire Verde Valley opens up—Camp Verde, Cottonwood and Clarkdale, Sedona, and an edge of Jerome close in to the right. Old mining roads angle down the east slope of Mingus and invite exploration.

The Verde Valley is ringed with whitish layers of sediment along the edges. These are ancient lake sediments, laid down millions of years ago. They contain salt beds as well as prehistoric mammoth, camel, horse, and human bones.

61. Vista Point Trail

Time: 3 hours. *Distance:* 3 miles roundtrip. *Elevation Gain:* 700 feet. *Rating:* Moderate.

Trailhead: From the Mingus Mountain campground turnoff, take FR 104 right for about 2.5 miles to the Mingus Mountain campground. The trailhead, #106, is located at the east end of the campground, just to the left of the campground host.

High Points: Fantastic views of the Verde Valley, 3,500 feet below, and the edge of the Northern Plateau Province to the north and east. A botanist's paradise of southern-exposure vegetation, consisting of mixed ponderosa pine, pinyon-juniper, and chaparral—with an abundance of spring and summer wildflowers.

Hiking the Trail: This trail starts with a view and it only gets better as the hike progresses. It drops right off the southeast-facing edge of Mingus Mountain with the Verde Valley and Northern Plateau Province rim as a backdrop. Looking east the Northern Plateau rim can be almost all the way to Payson. Look close right to the escarpment profile of Mingus and the radio towers. Stretching out below are Camp Verde, Cottonwood, and the Verde River floodplain.

The white layers, exposed by the roadcuts, that lie on the valley bottom are remnants of prehistoric freshwater lakes that filled the valley when local volcanism blocked the river and dammed up the valley.

Let your eye follow the plateau rim from right to left and see the red and white sandstone layers defining the Sedona area.

The path surface is a rocky volcanic mixture, due to the basalt layer that caps Mingus Mountain.

The vegetative mix on this side of Mingus is in some places backward from the normal vertical zones. While the top of Mingus is heavy with ponderosa pine, it stops right at the rim and the chaparral takes over just below the rim, followed by some pinyon-juniper with ponderosa pine again lower down. You first enter a Gambel oak mini-forest that canopies the trail. Next will be a mini-forest of Apache plume and penstemon. Then a mini-forest of scrub oak, mixed with New Mexico locust. Flowers and vines and low-growing shrubs dominate this thick underbrush amid the oaks, pines, and junipers—wild rose, lemonade berry, manzanita, locust, mountain mahogany, grasses, hackberry, yuccas, agaves, prickly pears—Brer Rabbit's briar patch.

The route angles down steeply at first but then levels out to traverse the southeast face. Then you see the pinyon-juniper belt with the ponderosas below it. It's a fairyland of plant life that continually amazes the hiker heading down the trail. A small rise leads you to a view north to the San Francisco Peaks, Mt. Elden, Kendrick Peak, and Bill Williams Mountain. The junction of Trails #106 and #105A occurs about 1.5 miles from the trailhead. Return the same way, or turn left on #105A and follow it to the junction of #105, taking #105 back up to the top of Mingus and back down another half mile to the original trailhead (see North Mingus Trail).

62. North Mingus Trail

Time: 3 hours. *Distance:* 3 miles roundtrip. *Elevation Gain:* 750 feet. *Rating:* Moderate.

Trailhead: From the Mingus Mountain campground turnoff, turn right on FR 104 and drive about 2.5 miles to the campground. From the campground host trailer, follow the road left as it climbs up and goes past radio towers and stops at the hang-glider site. This is where the bird-men and -women fly off the Mingus escarpment and float down to the Cottonwood airport below. The trailhead starts here. Look left for the North Mingus Trail #105 sign.

High Points: Views across the Verde Valley, Jerome, and Sycamore Wilderness Area to the north, and to the Woodchute Wilderness Area to the northwest. Tremendous variety of north-slope vegetation mixes.

Hiking the Trail: The trail starts just at the edge of the hang-glider ramps that overlook the Mingus Mountain escarpment. Take a look off the ramp across the Verde Valley to the edge of the Northern Plateau Province and the rim that extends across the state. Follow the path and volcanic stone cairns as the route traverses the edge of Mingus through ponderosa pine, Gambel oak, and juniper trees. There is little underbrush due to the heavy overhead canopy.

The trail drops down off the northwest-facing slope of Mingus, exposing views to the Woodchute Wilderness area, Jerome, Clarkdale, and the Northern Plateau Province rim to the north. The San Francisco Peaks, Kendrick Peak, and Bill Williams Mountain set the skyline backdrop to the scene. A mini-forest of Gambel oak greets you as you start descending.

Soon you pass through Douglas fir, ponderosa pine, white fir, and aspen on this northern exposure. Chaparral underbrush is mixed with the trees, along with numerous wildflowers such as lupine, wild rose, penstemon, paintbrush, and deer vetch. The trail angles down for about 1.25 miles to a junction on a promontory with a large pile of rocks. Trail #105 continues left for another 3 miles to Mescal tank if you want a longer hike. This will require a car shuttle. Trail #105A turns right and goes across the east face of Mingus, connecting up with Trail #106 for a loop. Take a walk out on the promontory for one of the best views of the Verde Valley anywhere.

Return by the same route or follow Trail #106 to its trailhead in the Mingus Mountain campground and walk back to your vehicle.

Granite Mountain Area

About 5 miles west of Prescott, the Granite Mountain Wilderness Area includes a spectacular granite outcropping that dominates the

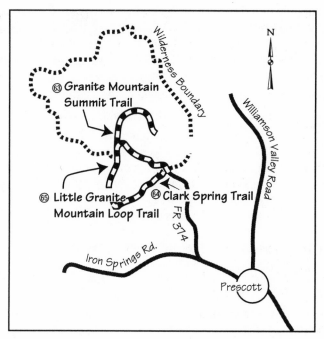

Granite Mountain Area

skyline. Granite Mountain is the main hiking attraction in this expanded forest-recreation area.

This entire region was once plutonic granite that rose close to the surface along the edges of converging earth plates. Millions of years of erosion weathered the softer surface around the pluton and exposed the granite we see today, creating a jumbled topography of huge rounded and shattered boulders and smooth, slick rock faces.

Chaparral, oak-pine woodland, pinyon-juniper woodland, and ponderosa pine communities dominate the area. A variety of bird life and small mammals, including deer, bobcat, and mountain lion, also inhabit this wild place.

With the elevation variation creating its own weather, it's best to prepare for storms any time of the year by carrying a rain parka, wool hat, and warm underwear.

Day Hike Area Takeoff Point Parking Area at the End of Forest Road #347: Go west on Gurley to Grove. Turn right on Grove, which turns into Miller Valley Road and proceeds into the intersection of Iron Springs Road and Willow Creek Road. Turn left onto Iron Springs Road and follow it for about 5 miles to the Granite Basin Lake turnoff. Turn right and follow the newly constructed road (FR 374) for about 4 miles to the campground/picnic area entrance. Stay left another mile past the campground to the parking area.

Campgrounds Three developed facilities service the Granite Mountain hiking area: (1) Granite Basin Campground, (2) Granite Basin Group Reservation Campground, and (3) Granite Basin Picnic Area. All three sites are located on FR 374 about 4 miles from the turnoff from Iron Springs Road. The campsites are currently under expansion and may be completed as of the publication of this book. Remember, open camping is also permitted in Prescott National Forest.

63. Granite Mountain Summit Trail

Time: 7 hours. *Distance:* 7 miles roundtrip. *Elevation Gain:* 3,000 feet. *Rating:* Challenging.

Trailhead: A gate entrance at the west end of the parking area is the trailhead.

High Points: Shade, mountain vegetation along a riparian habitat. Views of the Prescott area from Granite Mountain lookout site. Possible views of rock climbers on granite walls.

Hiking the Trail: The trail goes for about 1 mile to Blair Pass. Blair Pass is the junction of Trails #261, #37, and #41. On the way, you pass pinyons, junipers, ponderosa pines, and a lot of scrub oak, spread out along the usually dry streambed that follows the trail. Scattered wilderness campsites are found along the route. This is a pleasant, short day hike in itself. You may see or hear rock climbers on the massive granite wall to your right.

To continue on to the top of Granite Mountain, turn right on Trail #261. This is the strenuous part of the trail as it switchbacks up the Granite Mountain massif for about 1.3 miles to the main saddle. The all-uphill climb switchbacks across many small (usually dry) stream courses. You are walking on crushed granite gravel from the surrounding boulders. In fact, you are surrounded by erosional remnants of this granite pluton as you ascend to the summit. As you climb up the trail, the western part of Yavapai County comes into view—

rolling hills, mountains, and grassland. Little Granite Mountain is to the south below you. As you ease over the rounded saddle below the summit boulders, you'll notice a trail branching to the right. Take this branch. About .5 mile along this path, you'll encounter granite boulders about 1.7 billion years old. Campsites are found alongside the path.

Follow this until you reach a vista that offers spectacular views of Prescott and the mountains to the south. Looking back (north) from this vista, a narrow trail through the brush leads to a jumble of granite rocks. This pile of rocks can be climbed, and offers a 360-degree summit view to the Northern Plateau Province sedimentary layers to the north and to the older metamorphic mountain chains to the south. This view is one of the finest in all central Arizona. Often, flocks of jet-black ravens cavort over these crags, dipping, diving, and swirling along their slow, lazy sky path. Swallows do the same, only with blinding speed.

Another short route from back at the main saddle goes north (left) to a view of the San Francisco Peaks, Bill Williams Mountain, and the Sycamore Wilderness. Either one of these overlooks is a good late-lunch and snooze spot. There is no water along this route, except during spring runoff. It is hot in summer, and you should carry at least two quarts of water, after tanking up before heading out. Return by the same route.

64. Clark Spring Trail

Time: 2 hours. *Distance:* 3 miles roundtrip. *Elevation Gain:* 450 feet. *Rating:* Moderate.

Trailhead: Trailhead #40 begins about 4.5 miles in on FR 374, about .25 mile back from the parking area for the Granite Mountain Trail #261 trailhead. Park there and walk back to the Clark Spring Trail #40 sign by the side of the road. This is the trailhead.

High Points: Riparian vegetation along a flowing streambed with a spring site. Views of Granite Mountain Wilderness Area. Views north to the San Francisco Peaks. Views south and west across Skull Valley to the southwestern edge of the Southern Deserts Province.

Hiking the Trail: The path starts out quite steep and angles up in a southwesterly direction. The trailbed is composed of somewhat slippery decomposed granite. About .25 mile in, an old stone structure with barred windows stands on the left. It holds a modern water pump. A large, out-of-place apple tree stands next to it. The trail continues up to views of Lizard Head rock to the right and the granite-bouldered ridges surrounding Granite Mountain. The path is bordered by manzanita, mountain mahogany, juniper, scrub oak, agave cactus, prickly pear cactus, and various spring wildflowers. As you climb gradually, views include the south-facing slabs of Granite Mountain—a spectacular white face of smooth, rock-climbing stone. After about a mile of steady climb, you will cross a streambed and baby cottonwood trees will be visible. A string of seeps parallels the trail on the right. In about a mile, the concrete holding tank of Clark Spring appears on the right.

Hike another steep .5 mile through stands of Emory oak, Arizona walnut, cedar, and ponderosa pine to the junction of the Little Granite Mountain Loop Trail #37—evident from the gate and trail signs that direct the hiker either right to Blair Pass and a loop back along Trail #261 to the parking area—or—go left for 1.5 miles to the Trail #37 trailhead on Iron Springs Road. Turn right and head up Trail #37 for about .25 mile to the ridgeline, where great views of western Yavapai County open up. This is a good lunch spot. Return by the same route.

65. Little Granite Mountain Loop Trail

Time: 5 hours. *Distance:* 6.5 miles one-way. *Elevation Gain:* 700 feet. *Rating:* Challenging.

Trailhead: This is a continuation of the Clark Spring Trail. Trailhead #40 begins about 4.5 miles in on FR 374, about .25 mile back from the parking area for the Granite Mountain Trail #261 trailhead. Park there and walk back to the Clark Spring Trail #40 sign by the side of the road. This is the trailhead.

High Points: Views of western Yavapai County. Great spring wildflower displays.

Hiking the Trail: Take Clark Spring Trail #40 to the junction of Little Granite Mountain Trail #37, as described in the Clark Spring Trail hike. At this junction, #37 goes right and left. Our trailhead turns to the right and heads up to the shaded ridgeline that runs south. This is a great lunch spot as it opens up vistas west and south to Skull Valley and the rolling ranch land leading to it.

The first part of the route from the ridgeline angles down steeply in places and gradually eases off, crossing several drainages coming down from Little Granite Mountain on the right. You pass through a gate, crossing over a vein of broken quartz fragments. The remains of a brush fire are obvious, with the blackened scars of chaparral vegetation sticking out amid the new growth. There is little shade on this west-facing part of the trail, but the prevailing southwest breezes cool you off. The huge white face of Granite Mountain gradually comes into view to the north as the trail curves north by northeast. You pass through a long-stemmed grassy area with bizarre black and white remains of burned-out juniper trees permeating the area. Huge granite boulders enhance the scene even more, making it seem like a surrealistic painting. More chaparral, pinyon-juniper, and ponderosa pine appear as the trail continues to curve to the north. Gradually, north-slope vegetation takes over and shady areas start to appear. You reach Blair Pass at the junction of Trails #261, #37, and #41. Follow #261 back to the trailhead.

Groom Creek Area

This mountain community is made up of many summer-cabin users along with year-round residents. It is definitely "in the pines" with ponderosa pine prevalent. It also contains Goldwater and Hassayampa lakes, two small reservoirs that offer short day hikes around their shores.

Being 1,000 feet higher than Prescott, the air is cooler and wetter during local storms. It receives more rainfall and snow than Prescott, and many times when the trails in Groom Creek are covered with snow, other day-hike areas in the lower surrounding hills of Prescott are open. Conversely, when it gets a bit hot in May and June around the territorial capital, Groom Creek elevation becomes more appealing for the local foot-tramper.

Campgrounds Upper and Lower Wolf Creek and open National Forest camping.

Day Hike Area Takeoff Point Horse-Camp Parking Area: Turn south off Gurley onto Mt. Vernon. Mt. Vernon turns into Senator Highway. Follow Senator Highway up the paved road as it climbs into tall stands of ponderosa. The road turns into rolling up-and-down terrain until it reaches a small store, signaling the middle of the Groom

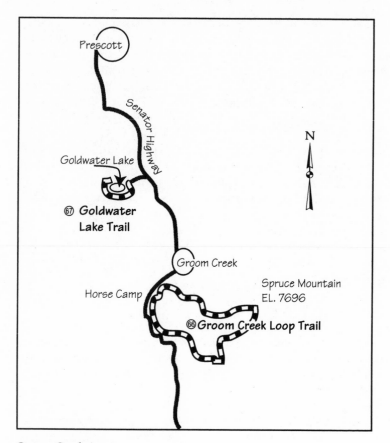

Groom Creek Area

Creek community. Drive past the store for another mile to the horse camp, a prominent facility for horseback riders on the west side of the road. Immediately across from the horse camp is a parking area for hikers. Groom Creek Trail #307 and Groom Creek Loop Trail #307 start and end here.

66. Groom Creek Loop Trail

Time: 5 hours. *Distance:* 7.5 miles roundtrip. *Elevation Gain:* 1,500 feet. *Rating:* Challenging.

Trailhead: Look for the Groom Creek Loop #307 signs just past the restrooms at the parking area on the east side of the highway. This is the trailhead. Even though the trail is called a "loop," it is an out-and-back by the same route.

High Points: Cool, shady, forest/mountain hiking. Unparalleled views north, east, and west across Prescott, Prescott Valley, Mingus Mountain, and the Bradshaw Mountains.

Hiking the Trail: Turn left at the trailhead sign and follow the logs put in the ground to delineate the route. The path crosses a dirt road and continues straight, slowly angling away from the Senator Highway and starting up Spruce Mountain. This is a hike through a predominantly ponderosa pine forest with lots of shade and occasional views west to the lower grasslands. You pass large boulders on the left, used by local rock climbers as practice areas. The trail steepens, turning east as it climbs up to a small pile of boulders on the right. This provides a good sunset view on the way back. The going is shady and cool.

About .5 mile later at a junction, a large #307 sign directs you left. Continue up and along this forest path. It will start down for about .25 mile until it reaches a second trail sign. This is the halfway mark. The route gets steeper from here for the climb to the summit lookout tower. There is one more level section that follows a drainage. Look for a small spring site to the right and the remains of a log cabin. Log railings start appearing on the trail.

More steepness leads to the summit picnic area and the short trail up to the lookout tower at 7,693 feet. A short walk past the tower brings you to a group of boulders that provide spectacular views of Prescott, Prescott Valley, Granite Dells, Mingus Mountain, Thumb Butte, Granite Mountain, the San Francisco Peaks, and the sandstone rims of Sedona. This is another of the great views of central Arizona. Return by the same route.

67. Goldwater Lake Trail

Time: 1 hour. *Distance:* 2 miles roundtrip. *Elevation Gain:* Level. *Rating:* Easy.

Trailhead: Look for the Goldwater Lake sign on the left about 2.5 miles up Senator Highway on the way to the horse-camp parking

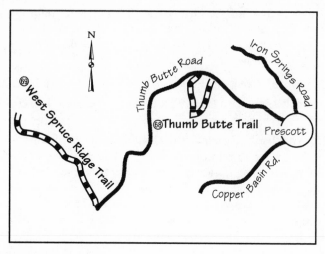

Thumb Butte Area

area. Turn right onto the short paved road that leads to the lake parking area. The trailhead is down to the left of the ramada and picnic benches, just at the edge of the lake.

High Points: Refreshing hike along a scenic lake. Riparian bird life.

Hiking the Trail: Lakes are few and far between in Arizona. Goldwater Lake is a backup to the regular Prescott water supply. It is also a recreation lake with a large covered ramada and picnic tables. Water and restrooms are also available. The path skirts the lake edge, taking you through the mixed riparian and forest plant zones—ponderosa pine, scrub oak, Gambel oak, and manzanita blends with willow, cottonwood, walnut, alder, and cattail. Bird life is abundant, with the addition of shore-hugging redwing blackbirds and lake birds such as coots, wood ducks, and blue herons. There is a picnic bench halfway around the lake. The trail ends at the Goldwater Lake dam. Return by the same route.

Thumb Butte Area

Thumb Butte has been Prescott's landmark forever. It is a basalt remnant from ancient lava flows and is a favorite area for hikers, runners, and horseback riders. It rises a thousand feet above the town of Prescott with a vertical columnar lava face that seems to overlook the town.

One first sees it on the western skyline coming into Prescott on State Route 69. Its main trail offers a bit of solitude for hikers and runners just a few minutes away from downtown Prescott.

Day Hike Area Takeoff Point Thumb Butte Recreation Area: Travel west on Gurley for 2.5 miles to Thumb Butte Road. Continue northwest on Thumb Butte Road for 1.5 miles to the recreation site at the base of the butte.

Campgrounds Open camping is available in the Prescott National Forest nearby. There are three picnic areas at the base of Thumb Butte— two are group reservation areas and one is open for picnicking.

68. Thumb Butte Trail

Time: 1.5 hours. *Distance:* 3 miles roundtrip. *Elevation Gain:* 600 feet. *Rating:* Moderate.

Trailhead: The trailhead is just across the street from the recreation and picnic area. A large sign identifies the start of the path. It shows the route of the trail and lists the viewpoint highlights.

High Points: A nature trail with plant identification posts along the route. Views of the Bradshaw Mountains, Prescott, Prescott Valley, and Granite Mountain Wilderness Area.

Hiking the Trail: The trail starts out fairly steep in the shade of ponderosa pine. There is little underbrush on this north side of Thumb Butte due to the competition for sun from the ponderosa. The path angles up along the west side of the butte where scattered chaparral starts to appear—Emory oak, Gambel oak, mountain mahogany, manzanita, silk tassel, scrub oak, buck brush, Apache plume, prickly pear, and yucca. As the trail turns to the hotter, drier southwest side, the ponderosa gradually disappear and are replaced by pinyon-juniper and thicker chaparral. This is a perfect example of the north/south vegetation change determined by the cooler, wetter north side in comparison with the hotter, drier south side.

Gradually, you will break out into the open on the northwest corner of the butte. The path angle lessens and the junction of the vista points appears. Views of Groom Creek can be had to the right. Granite Mountain can be seen from the vista to the left. Climb up to the

Groom Creek vista. Views include the Groom Creek area and the Bradshaw Mountains, Prescott, Mingus Mountain in the northeast distance, the edge of the Northern Plateau Province, and the San Francisco Peaks. Climb back down to the junction and go over to the Granite Mountain vista, which looks west to north out over Granite Mountain, Little Granite Mountain, and the Sierra Prieta range. A short trail heads up to the base of the butte itself. Rock-scrambling chimneys go to the summit blocks, but this activity is not recommended unless you have some free-climbing skills. The loop trail back to the picnic area is a bit longer due to many switchbacks, but offers unparalleled views of the Granite Mountain area on the way back down.

69. West Spruce Ridge Trail

Time: 3 hours. *Distance:* 3 miles roundtrip. *Elevation Gain:* 500 feet. *Rating:* Moderate.

Trailhead: From the Thumb Butte Recreation Area, stay on the main dirt road that turns into Thumb Butte Loop Road until you reach a junction with a sign that says "Lookout 4 Miles." Turn left here. Look for the Trail #264 trailhead sign about 3.5 miles from the junction. Pull out to the right of the sign.

High Points: Spectacular views across Kirkland, Skull Valley, and the Weaver Mountains to the south and west, and the Granite Mountain area to the north. Mixed ponderosa pine, pinyon-juniper woodland, and chaparral vegetation. Cool elevations with prevailing southwest breezes.

Hiking the Trail: The trail starts off fairly level and meets a fence along the west-facing ridgeline. Follow the fence to a break in the ridgeline vegetation to the left. Climb through the fence for a dramatic view of Skull Valley and Copper Basin directly below. Mining exploration has revealed the presence of copper in the area. About .5 mile along the path, at a log railing to the right, a side path takes you past the railing to an open area overlooking Granite Mountain, Prescott, and Chino Valley. The trail goes down a side slope and makes a 90-degree turn to the right. You walk through mini-forests of Gambel oak and huge juniper trees. You also walk in the shade of ponderosa pine, oak, mountain mahogany, Emory oak, and New Mexico locust. Views of the San Francisco Peaks and the Northern Plateau

Province will appear to the right between the ponderosa. Look for an open area to the left of the trail at the top of a small hill. There is a stone bake oven on top of the hill.

Continue along the trail that goes down to Copper Basin. A little farther along, the ponderosas phase out to the chaparral vegetation of scrub oak, silk tassel, manzanita, and mountain mahogany. Look up and left to a ridgeline that displays a mixture of both north- and south-facing vegetation. There is a dramatic line between the two slopes, with the higher ponderosas and Douglas firs on the north and the pinyon-juniper and chaparral on the south. This route continues for another 5 miles down to Iron Springs Wash and requires a vehicle shuttle. You can turn around on this trail anywhere you like and return to the parking area.

Lynx Lake Area

Lynx Lake is the most popular recreation lake in the Prescott vicinity, providing opportunities for day hiking, boating, fishing, canoeing, bird watching, or just loafing around the lake.

The lake is manmade—a Civilian Conservation Corps project created as both a recreational resource and a backup to the town water supply—and collects water from the Lynx Creek drainage and the surrounding Bradshaw Mountains. Once a rich gold-mining area, the creek still provides local panners with flakes and dust from the precious metal.

Day Hike Area Takeoff Point Corner of State Route 69 and Walker Road: Drive east on Gurley past the Chino Valley intersection and out past the Frontier Village Shopping Mall. Look for Walker Road, which turns right alongside the "Ranch" residential development. This is the corner referred to above.

Campgrounds Lynx Lake, Hilltop, and surrounding National Forest open camping areas.

70. Lake Shore Trail

Time: 2 hours. *Distance:* 1.5-mile loop. *Elevation Gain:* Level. *Rating:* Easy.

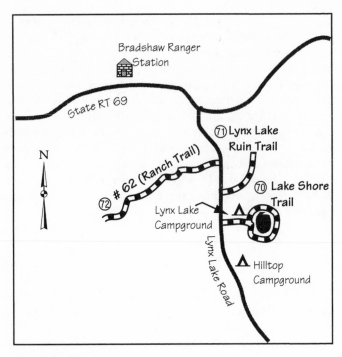

Lynx Lake Area

Trailhead: Follow Walker Road about a mile to the Lynx Lake store parking area. From the store parking area, look for the paved walkway leading down to the lake shore. This is the trailhead.

High Points: Both shore-bird and water-bird life abound at the lake's edge, living in the equally abundant mixture of lakeside and forest vegetation.

Hiking the Trail: Walk down the paved walkway and turn right onto the obvious trail that surrounds the lake and loops back to the store. The path follows the shore, heading through large ponderosa pines and scrub oaks. Short side trails lead to fishing spots all along the route. The vegetation is quite open under the ponderosa as the trail loops around the south end of the lake to the Lynx Lake parking area. This is the main picnic and bank-fishing place, where the majority of visitors head. Benches line the bank for relaxing and kibitzing.

The path leaves the parking area and angles down to the mouth of Lynx Creek itself, where the creek drains into the lake. In spring and summer, the stream flows intermittently. Gold panners search along this stretch most of the year, trying to sluice out what remains of a once-rich gold region. You'll feel like you're hiking along a jungle stream. It's surrounded by willow, wild grape, tall grasses, vines, New Mexico locust, yellow columbine, cattails, mullein, and lots of birds— doves, blackbirds, robins, brown creepers, jays, and water fowl such as grackles, coots, ducks, and herons. A small dam blocks the mouth of the stream as it pours into the lake.

The trail skirts the dam and continues along the shore. Oak, ash, cedar, thistle, ponderosa, juniper, and lots of cattail line the route, along with huge yellow clover bushes. The route passes more small bank-fishing spots and heads for the main storage dam at the north end of the lake. This dam is earth covered and allows a slow summer drainage to flow down lower Lynx Creek. (A branch off the Lake Shore Trail angles down next to the dam and follows the creekbed down to homesites below.) Return by crossing the dam and heading back up to the store area.

71. Lynx Lake Ruin Trail

Time: 1 hour. *Distance:* 1.5 miles roundtrip (loop). *Elevation Gain:* Level. *Rating:* Easy.

Trailhead: From the corner of Walker Road and State Route 69, follow Walker Road for about .75 mile to the Lynx Creek Ruins sign. Turn left onto the road that takes you to the ruins parking area. This is the trailhead.

High Points: A pleasant, short hike to a 700-year-old Yavapai Indian ruin site highlights this trail. Rest benches situated with spectacular views add to the pleasure.

Hiking the Trail: The trail is considered part of an interpretive site administered by the Arizona State Historic Preservation Office. Signs describing the early Native American civilization are posted along the route. The path winds through ponderosa pine, scrub oak, juniper, manzanita, lemonade berry, yucca, and local grasses. There are six benches along the route, offering views of Granite Mountain, Thumb Butte, the San Francisco Peaks, and the Bradshaw Mountains. The trail goes to a ruin site, believed to have been inhabited by 25 to 30 people about 700 years ago. A thriving community existed in the area. They built stone and mud pueblos on the adjoining hill-tops that overlook Lynx Creek. They cultivated beans, corn, and squash on small terraces created with small earthen dams along the creek tributaries. The structures have deteriorated down to ground level, but distinct room walls are apparent. Return by the same route.

72. #62 Ranch Trail

Time: 5 hours. *Distance:* 5 miles roundtrip. *Elevation Gain:* 500 feet. *Rating:* Moderate.

Trailhead: From State Route 69 and the Walker Road turnoff, go along Walker Road for about .5 mile to the Trail #62 sign. Turn right into the parking area. Chances are you'll be greeted by the Forest Service trail host who remains on the premises during the summer. The trail is open to horses, trail bikes, and hikers. It is relatively new in the Forest Service system, and as of this book's publication date there is no published map of the route. The full trail goes about 4 miles to join up with Trail #299 in Groom Creek. The day hike described below goes to the halfway point, about 2 miles one-way, and back. The trailhead is located at a hinged gate on the west end of the parking area.

High Points: This hike takes you up to dramatic 360-degree views of the surrounding Prescott area mountains as well as the highest Northern Plateau Province mountains. These views are reached in a short, pleasant mile of hiking.

Hiking the Trail: The first part of the path is an old jeep trail that heads for the "Ranch" development. Follow the jeep trail for about .25 mile and look for a rock pile that signifies a sharp left onto Trail #62. About 1 mile up the path, you reach another gate. Pass through this and head up the narrow trail. Altitude increases steadily and then the trail drops into a wash. Turn right in the wash as the trail continues up a ridge. The angle steepens to another ridgeline where vistas of the San Francisco Peaks, Kendrick Peak, Granite Mountain, Prescott Valley, Granite Dells, Thumb Butte, and Mingus Mountain open up. A pleasant, level ridgeline trail carries you through juniper, scrub oak, manzanita, lemonade berry, mountain mahogany, ponderosa pine, pinyon, and a few yucca plants. The route now descends to a large drainage where it meets the junction with Trail #126, a somewhat nondescript connection from a drainage to the right. This is about a mile in and a good shady lunch break area and turnaround point for the return hike to the parking area.

Community Nature Center of Prescott Trail Area

The Community Nature Center of Prescott was developed on 20 acres in the early 1970s with the idea of providing environmental education experiences for schoolchildren. A nature trail was developed that passes through representations of chaparral, desert grassland, pinyon-juniper, ponderosa pine, and riparian plant communities. This protected area houses a great variety of Central Mountains Province animals, including ground squirrels, chipmunks, skunks, occasional javelinas, coyotes, cottontail rabbits, foxes, and bobcats. Bird species such as scrub jays, common bushtits, rufous-sided towhees, doves, and ravens frequent the area, which includes a permanent water pond. The trail has interpretive signs and a nature trail guide booklet.

Day Hike Area Takeoff Point Corner of Iron Springs Road and Williamson Valley Road: Go west on Gurley from the Chamber of Commerce to the stop light at Grove. Turn right on Grove, which turns into Miller Valley Road. Follow this to the big intersection of Iron Springs and Miller Valley Road. Turn left at the light and follow Iron Springs Road to the intersection of Williamson Valley Road. Turn right on Williamson Valley Road and look for the Community Nature Center sign just past the Fire Station, Abia Judd School, and Granite Mountain Middle School. Turn right into the parking area.

Campgrounds Open camping in Prescott National Forest or any of the listed campgrounds.

73. Community Nature Center Trail

Time: 1 hour. *Distance:* 1 mile roundtrip. *Elevation Gain:* 100 feet. *Rating:* Easy.

Trailhead: From the parking area, enter the gate and look for the log cabin headquarters for the area host. Ask the host for a Nature Trail Guide, which describes the interpretive signs along the route. The trailhead starts at the cabin site.

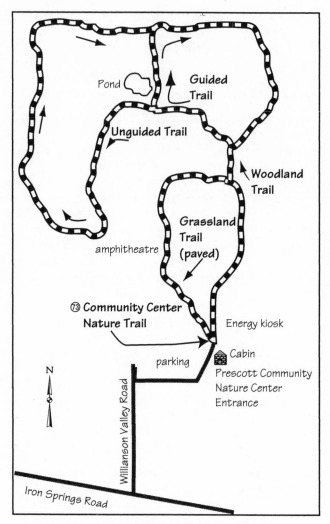

Community Center Nature Trail

High Points: Good introduction to Prescott area vegetation and wildlife. Interpretive signs along route.

Hiking the Trail: The trail starts in a grassland with various chaparral, pinyon-juniper, and ponderosa pine intrusions along its edges. It goes left and circles to a junction with the Woodland Guided Trail.

Take this trail left and follow it clockwise through the denser woodland habitat. You'll pass the pond at the junction of the unguided
trail. Stay right and follow the path back up through chaparral and
ponderosa pine to complete the loop back at the Woodland Trail
junction. Follow this back to the cabin and parking area.

CHAPTER 8

Verde Valley Day Hikes

Verde Valley

Wet Beaver Creek and

West Clear Creek Areas

Sedona Area

VERDE VALLEY

The Verde Valley encompasses mixed landscapes comprised of desert grassland, oak-pine woodland, chaparral, and pinyon-juniper communities at elevations ranging from 2,000 to 7,500 feet. It contains the communities of Camp Verde, Cottonwood, Clarkdale, Sedona, Cornville, and Jerome.

The valley itself is an ancient lakebed that drained its waters away millions of years ago, leaving limestone, chalk, and sandstone sedimentary layers that form the valley edges and floor. The fault-block Black Hills frame the valley on the west, while the Mogollon Rim frames it on the north and east. The Verde River runs through the valley, making the area agriculturally productive and providing riparian and aquatic habitats for abundant plant life and animal life.

The first written descriptions of the area were part of Antonio de Espejo's sixteenth-century expedition from the northern Hopi villages in his quest for the fabled cities of gold. The valley area was first settled by hardy ranchers who grew beef for the military in Prescott. Frequent raids by Yavapai and Apache Indians caused the establishment of Fort Verde in 1865, which became known as Camp Verde and remains a small town today.

Verde Valley offers year-round good weather. Summers are hot, but the streamside trails offer refreshing respite from the heat. Mild winter weather makes this valley a favorite place for Prescott and Flagstaff hikers on cold weekends. It is about one hour from each of those colder cities, and can provide a warm, sunny environment while Flagstaff and Prescott are under storm clouds.

Wet Beaver Creek and West Clear Creek offer trails that follow streambeds from the Verde Valley all the way up the drainages to the top of the Mogollon Rim and views out over the Northern Plateau Province.

Sedona is also year-round hiking territory, but winter storms can snow you out. Sedona is exceptional for its spectacular scenic backdrops, dramatic colored sandstone formations, and Oak Creek—a beautiful perennial stream formed from spring sites and carried down to the Verde River through the town of Sedona. This area is a fantasyland of day-hiking opportunities.

Places to Visit

A number of Indian and historic sites are scattered around the Verde Valley. *Tuzigoot* (602-634-5564), *Montezuma's Well* (602-567-4521), and *Montezuma's Castle* (602-567-3322) are national monuments displaying early Indian dwellings and culture.

Fort Verde State Historic Park is a preserved Army post in Camp Verde.

Dead Horse Ranch State Park is located along the Verde River and offers river-habitat information at the visitor center, which is located off 5th Street in Cottonwood. Phone: (602) 634-5283.

Directions to each Day Hike Area Takeoff Point begin at I-17 running north and south through the center of the state.

Wet Beaver Creek and West Clear Creek Areas

Both Wet Beaver Creek and West Clear Creek flow from near the top of the Mogollon Rim (southern edge of the Northern Plateau Province) down 3,200 feet to the Verde River. They slice through the edge of the plateau, exposing several geologic layers from the top of the rim down into the Central Mountains Province, including (1) a rim of basaltic lava; (2) Kaibab limestone deposited by marine organisms when the area was under water; (3) Toroweap sandstone from water-deposited sand; and (4) Coconino sandstone from windblown sand deposits. Many side springs and seeps drain into these

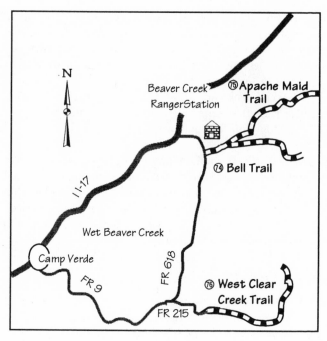

Wet Beaver Creek and West Clear Creek Areas

two beautiful streambeds. Remnants of many early American stone dwellings line the banks.

Hiking up these canyon trails from the bottom of the Verde Valley all the way to the top of the rim is similar to hiking from Mexico to Canada, considering the variation in plant life. From creosote bush through pinyon, juniper, and agave up to ponderosa pine and Douglas fir on the rim edges, these trails guide you right up from the Central Mountains Province to the Northern Plateau Province—in one hiking day. In addition to the vertical plant variation, streamside vegetation includes ash, cottonwood, alder, box elder, Arizona walnut, sycamore, wild grape, and poison ivy.

Because of the elevation gain (3,200 feet), climate can vary dramatically during winter and summer storms. It can be snowing on top of the Mogollon Rim while you are enjoying mild temperatures in the lower reaches of the Verde Valley.

Again, due to the great diversity of plant life, this area contains a wide variety of animal life, which includes white-tailed and mule deer, ringtail cats, coyotes, bobcats, javelina, beaver, black bear, and mountain lions. Elk occasionally wander down from the rim to the drainages.

Wet Beaver Creek Area Day Hike Takeoff Point Beaver Creek Ranger Station: From I-17, look for the State Route 179 turnoff. Go east at the turnoff onto FR 618 and drive to the ranger station, following the signs. The campground sign will also be posted.

Campgrounds Wet Beaver Creek and West Clear Creek campgrounds and open National Forest camping.

74. Bell Trail

Time: 4 hours. *Distance:* 5 miles roundtrip. *Elevation Gain:* 200 feet. *Rating:* Moderate.

Trailhead: From the ranger station, turn onto FR 618A for a quick .25 mile drive to the trailhead.

High Points: The entire trail is a high point due to its gorgeous variation of color, form, texture, and geography.

Hiking the Trail: The trail starts off as an old road, angling slightly upward for the first 2.5 miles until it reaches an old weir dam measuring station. As you start along the path, look left at the different sedimentary layers exposed along this escarpment. You are looking up at the very edge of the Northern Plateau Province. Notice the black basaltic lava on top, then the grayish Kaibab limestone below it, followed by the Toroweap sandstone and outcroppings of Coconino sandstone and red Supai sandstone. You'll notice flat ledges along the lower levels of the escarpment—possibly Indian ruin sites.

To the right is Wet Beaver Creek, engulfed in its own riparian vegetation, highlighted by huge sycamore trees. There is a small canal running alongside the creek that was used for irrigation by early Native Americans and European settlers who siphoned water from the main streambed higher up the drainage. About a mile along, a short roadbed leads down to a flat area by the creek. This is a good place to take a break to absorb the great variety of colors, sounds, and forms of this unique waterway. Continue along the roadbed, looking for the large stone on the left, directly beside the trail. This is Petroglyph Rock, probably carved into by early Yavapai people. Meander along the enchanting roadbed, looking right across the creek to the South-west Academy School, a private school for juveniles, located in one of the most beautiful settings in Arizona.

Continue to a junction with the Weir Trail. Turn right and pro-ceed along the narrow path that angles down to the remnants of an old water-gauging station. This is a delightful, curving path that takes you into the true wilderness of Wet Beaver Creek. The remains of the gauging station offer a flat lunch spot and the end of the half-day hike. A bit farther upstream, there are good swimming pools.

If you wish to go farther, continue up the trail past the gauging station as it crosses the creek and gradually angles up the escarpment to join the main Bell Trail. You can follow the Bell Trail all the way to the top of the Mogollon Rim, if you want to make a full day's hike out of it. Return to the trailhead by the same route.

75. Apache Maid Trail

Time: 5 hours. *Distance:* 6 miles. *Elevation Gain:* 2,000 feet. *Rating:* Challenging.

Trailhead: From the ranger station, turn onto FR 618A for a quick .25-mile drive to the trailhead.

High Points: Magnificent views of Wet Beaver Creek, Verde Valley, and the Red Rock Country around Sedona.

Hiking the Trail: Follow the Bell Trail about 2 miles to the Apache Maid Trail turnoff. The route takes you gradually up the escarpment that is the very edge of the Northern Plateau Province. You are climbing up through millions of years of sediment, laid down in an-cient seabeds. You are also climbing up through various vegetation zones, from desert grassland through chaparral, oak-pine woodland to the pinyon-juniper woodland, up to the ponderosa pine commu-nities on top of the rim. The surrounding views are unparalleled as you top out on the black basalt that caps the rim. This is a good lunch spot.

After lunch, take a short cross-country hike toward the San Fran-cisco Peaks, visible to the north. Continue over the basalt until the Sedona area becomes visible over the edge of the rim. You are looking at the volcanic field that caps the Northern Plateau Province around Flagstaff.

Return to the trailhead by the same route—or when you get back down to the Bell Trail, turn left and follow it to the junction with the Weir Trail. Take the Weir Trail to the old gauging station and return from there (see Bell Trail description).

West Clear Creek Area Day Hike Takeoff Point Camp Host at West Clear Creek Campground: From I-17, turn east onto State Route 260 and drive for about 6 miles to the turnoff sign to Bull Pen and West Clear Creek. Turn left onto the dirt road and drive until you see the next turnoff sign to Bull Pen and West Clear Creek. Turn right and go down the winding road that overlooks West Clear Creek. At creek level, a road angles off sharply to the right and to the campground host. Turn right and drive along to the camper that houses the host. Local conditions of the trail can be determined here.

Campgrounds West Clear Creek Campground and open National Forest camping.

76. West Clear Creek Trail

Time: 4 hours. *Distance:* 5 miles roundtrip. *Elevation Gain:* 1,000 feet. *Rating:* Moderate.

Trailhead: From the campground host trailer, go back on the dirt road, past the entrance road, and drive until you get to the gate at the end of the campground area. Park here. The trailhead starts here by either following the trail sign that heads north and up and around the previously privately owned strip of land or heading straight along the dirt road onto the flat area and to the stone dwelling with the prickly pear growing on the roof.

High Points: Like Wet Beaver Creek, the entire streambed is a high point, with many swimming and wading pools, along with a narrow chute for zooming headfirst over a short waterfall. Remember that there is no lifeguard and you swim in these areas at your own risk.

Hiking the Trail: The northerly option takes you up to a bench that traverses West Clear Creek for about a mile, then goes back down to the creekbed. This option gives you a great view up- and downstream and also great views of the 2,000-foot escarpment that defines the Mogollon Rim. When on this route, notice the sharp dividing line between the riparian habitat of the stream and the mixed surrounding vegetation of the lower slopes of the escarpment. This consists of desert grassland, chaparral, and pinyon-juniper communities that have intermixed due to the cold-air drainages that drop over the rim and the perennial water habitat that flows along the drainage. Look along the edge of the bench for evidence of ruins.

Both sides of the creek are guarded by the many layers of basaltic lava that cap the rim. Red-stained sandstone and limestone outcroppings add color and form to the slopes. There are very few places, anywhere, that have such an artist's blend of color. In one vertical gaze, you contrast the gray, black, and red of the streambed boulders, the black, green, and blue creek water, and the surrounding riparian vegetation colors from white-trunked sycamores to black-trunked alders. Many shades of green leaves fill out the riparian habitat that blends into the background of sliced sandstone and limestone creekbed walls. Above all this, the escarpment walls require at least seven different colors from the artist's brush. The entire scene is framed by the robin's-egg blue Arizona sky that carries puffy white clouds during summer monsoon afternoons.

The path leads down to a wide drainage that takes you to a sandy beach at the creek. The beach is at the edge of a great swimming hole. Wide, sandstone benches jut into the pool on the opposite bank. The original trail goes along the streambed and up on close-in benches, but a lot of it was washed away in the flood of spring 1992. Look for cairns and footprints that lead to the stream crossings. You can travel as far upstream as you want—or until you run into the steep-walled pools that require swimming. There are bunches of lunch spots and pools along the creek. After crossing the creek a couple of times, the trail stays about 50 to 60 feet above the streambed on the south side for about 3 miles. Various drainages lead back down to the water.

A long day's loop can be made by continuing along the trail until it heads up a canyon on the north side and climbs about 1,800 feet to connect to the parking area of FR 214A. Follow 214A to 214. Follow 214 about 1.3 miles to the Blodgett Basin Trail, which drops off the Mogollon Rim and follows a side canyon until it meets the West Clear Creek Trail and the original parking area.

A second option from the parking area follows the road past the gate and along the level path as it parallels West Clear Creek. The road will angle down to a favorite chute where the water funnels between huge boulders and provides a slide.

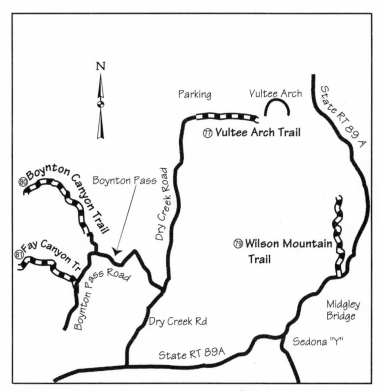

N

Parking   Vultee Arch   State RT 89 A

⑦ **Vultee Arch Trail**

⑧⓪ **Boynton** Canyon Trail   Boynton Pass

Dry Creek Road

⑧① **Fay** Canyon Tr

Boynton Pass Road

⑦⑨ **Wilson Mountain Trail**

Midgley Bridge

Dry Creek Rd

Sedona "Y"

State RT 89A

Sedona Area

Sedona Area

Few places in Arizona display such a variety of visual color and geographic diversity in such a small area as do Sedona and Oak Creek Canyon. "Red Rock Country" is world famous for its Coconino and Supai sandstone formations. Photographers and movie companies come to sample the "colored light" of this wonder of nature. It contains one of the few perennial water courses in the state, and along with its overlapping plant and animal communities has been dubbed an enchanted place by many local inhabitants.

Any way you look at the area, its cathedral-like rock formations take on spiritual proportions. One of the most beautiful waterways in the state, the canyon is named after the live canyon oak that fills

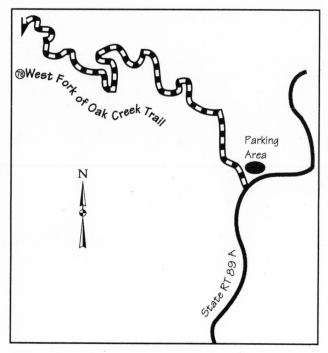

Sedona Area

the drainage alongside pinyon pine, Utah juniper, Arizona cypress, cottonwood, and Arizona sycamore. These trees intermingle with the vast array of streamside plants and groundcover that make up the canyon's riparian community.

The Oak Creek fault began about 7 million years ago, creating a streambed channel that eventually formed the present Oak Creek Canyon. The stream cuts down through the basalt, limestone, and sandstone layers of the Northern Plateau Province rim and drains into the Verde River. The layers of sedimentary rocks that line this fault are the same layers observed in the Grand Canyon. When these red, yellow, tan, and orange layers combine with the black basalt cap, the greens and browns of the surrounding vegetation and the blue water, they create an endless visual display of tone, shadow, and subtle color hues. The Sedona area provides the visual backdrop for painter, sculptor, and photographer—as well as day hiker.

Prehistoric peoples lived in and around the Sedona area, as evidenced by hundreds of ruin sites discovered within a 100-mile radius of the town. Spanish conquistadors passed through in 1583 looking for gold, found none, then left. A few settlers farmed near the creek after 1877. A cultured woman from Missouri and her husband moved to the creek area in 1901, becoming the fifth family to settle there. The lady's name was Sedona, and the local Postmaster General chose it for the town. Since Sedona Schnebley's death in 1950, Sedona, Arizona, has been "discovered" and developed to a point where preservationists are in constant battle with developers to maintain the character of this unique wonderland.

Over 200 bird species have been identified in Oak Creek Canyon, along with a mixture of both desert and forest mammals.

Sedona Area Day Hike Takeoff Point Sedona District Ranger's Office: From I-17, turn west onto State Route 179 and drive to the "Y" intersection of 179 and State Alternate 89 (89A). Turn left on 89A and go to Ranger Road. Turn left on Ranger Road and drive about .25 mile to the Sedona District Ranger's Office.

Campgrounds Chavez Crossing, Pine Flat, Cave Spring, Bootlegger, Banjo Bill, Manzanita. Open National Forest camping on the rim above Oak Creek Canyon.

77. Vultee Arch Trail

Time: 3 hours. *Distance:* 3 miles roundtrip. *Elevation Gain:* 200 feet. *Rating:* Easy.

Trailhead: From the Sedona District Ranger's Office, turn left on State Route 89A and continue to West Sedona and Dry Creek Road. Turn right on Dry Creek Road and drive about 2 miles to FR 152 and turn right. A sign designates Vultee Arch. Drive 4.3 miles to the end of the road and the trailhead.

High Points: Vultee Arch, a small, carved sandstone window with an accessible bridge. Huge Arizona cypress trees along the Sterling Canyon path. Mixed chaparral, pinyon-juniper, ponderosa pine forest, and riparian vegetation.

Hiking the Trail: This is a level 1.5-mile walk along Sterling Canyon and the creekbed that runs through it. It slowly ascends the canyon through mixed chaparral, oak-woodland, and pinyon-juniper vegetation zones, showing a few Arizona cypress, ponderosa pine, and Douglas fir species due to the cooler, wetter microclimate of the drainage. Microclimates permeate the Oak Creek Canyon area due to the riparian nature of the landscape. On this trail, which runs east and west, you can see moss growing on the north bank of the path but not on the south. Look up at the north bank to the larger ponderosa pines, Arizona cypress, juniper, and large oaks. Now look at the south bank and you'll see shorter junipers, chaparral shrubs, and scrub oaks.

Oak Creek is noted for its interbred varieties of oaks, and the same tree can have three different shapes of oak leaves. As the trail gains altitude, more oak varieties show themselves.

This trail is a good place to compare and differentiate between Arizona cypress and juniper. The cypress has branch bark that peels as it matures, showing a reddish/rust color underneath, while the juniper branches don't peel. The cypress normally has a lighter color of leaf also. This streamed trail displays some huge cypress. Notice the uprooted ponderosa pines, lying on their sides along the trail. It is thought they got top-heavy and toppled over when the floods of 1992 washed out the surrounding soil that supported them. Cacti species infiltrate the area also, with agaves, yuccas, and prickly pears predominating. After a little over a mile in, Vultee Arch becomes visible on the left—a small, low, level arch that blends into the background. A metal trail sign directs you to the left for better views of the arch. Follow the trail left to the sloping sandstone ledges that give great views of the arch. A fairly steep trail leads from the ledges to the arch.

A steep drainage flows under the arch and contains water during spring runoff. A short hike up the drainage behind the arch leads to views through the arch itself. Return to the sandstone ledges for lunch. Return to the parking area by the same route.

78. West Fork of Oak Creek Trail

Time: 4 hours. *Distance:* 6 miles roundtrip. *Elevation Gain:* Level. *Rating:* Moderate.

Trailhead: From the Sedona District Ranger's Office, turn right on 89A, drive through Sedona and about 8 miles north up Oak Creek

Canyon for a short distance past Don Hoel's Cabins. Look for the turnoff into the large parking area on the left. Look for the vertical trailhead sign for West Fork Trail #108.

High Points: Colossal sandstone walls, intricately carved streamside benches and overhangs. Continually changing riparian vegetation. Abundant bird life. A wonderland of changing color and light. Profusion of streamside wildflowers.

Hiking the Trail: This is one of Arizona's most popular trails. Be prepared to get your feet wet as the trail continually crosses the stream. In summer, this is refreshing and adds to the adventure. Every step of this hike is enjoyable as it winds through the watered canyon. Due to its "cold sink" environment, mixed plant communities exist side-by-side. Ponderosa pine, Douglas fir, and white fir co-exist with riparian plants such as sycamore, cottonwood, alder, and willow. Prickly pear cactus and yucca also make appearances.

Parts of this famous trail were washed away or covered with rockfall in the 1992 flood, but new routes will have been created by this time. The 6-mile distance mentioned above is arbitrary. This first 6 miles have been set aside by the Forest Service as a "Research Natural Area." Even a .25-mile hike in this canyon can be delightful. A full day is spectacular. Poison ivy is present along the streambed. The path zigzags back and forth across the stream, mostly in the shade of riparian trees and shrubs. Distance marker posts appear every .5 mile for the first 2 miles. Each turn and opening on this trail offers a new color palette of red and white sandstone mixed with the greens, yellows, blues, and purples of the local plant life and a backdrop of blue skies. Animal life includes both the desert and forest animals as both these zones come together in Oak Creek. Return by the same route.

79. Wilson Mountain Trail (to First Bench)

Time: 6 hours. *Distance:* 7 miles roundtrip. *Elevation Gain:* 1,700 feet. *Rating:* Challenging.

Trailhead: From the Sedona District Ranger's Office, turn right on 89A, drive through Sedona and about 2 miles north to Midgley Bridge. Turn into the parking area by the bridge. The trailhead is north from the parking area, just past a covered ramada.

High Points: Magnificent views east and south across Oak Creek Canyon to the red rock formations. Gardenlike path through mixed chaparral and pinyon-juniper plant zones.

Hiking the Trail: This trail reportedly originated during ranching days when horses were run up and down the mountain for grazing. Wilson Mountain is named for Richard Wilson, who was killed by a grizzly bear about 1885.

The path starts out with switchbacks up through mixed chaparral, pinyon-juniper, and grassland vegetation. This plant mosaic is so pleasant it seems that a master gardener planted it. Fantastic views across to Sedona, Steamboat Rock, Courthouse Butte, and Airport Mesa open up to the south. Teapot Rock and Thumb Butte are visible to the southwest. A short, level stretch eventually starts switchbacking again in a steep ascent up to the First Bench—a lava-covered plateau below the mountain summit, created when a huge fault block slid down from the main mountain. This level bench supported grazing at one time, and was even homesteaded for farming but failed because of the rocky soil. Some of the best views of the Sedona area are visible from this bench. This trail is open and hot in summer. Return by the same route.

80. Boynton Canyon Trail

Time: 4 hours. *Distance:* 5 miles roundtrip. *Elevation Gain:* 500 feet. *Rating:* Moderate.

Trailhead: From the ranger office, get back onto 89A and turn west. Go about 3 miles to Dry Creek Road on the right. Turn right and go north on Dry Creek 2.8 miles and turn left at the "T" onto Boynton Pass Road. Go 1.5 miles to Boynton Canyon Road. Turn right and go .25 mile to the parking area for the Boynton Canyon Trail. This is the trailhead.

High Points: Many early American cliff dwellings. Gradual ascent into very old vegetation.

Hiking the Trail: The path skirts the Enchantment Resort, starting in the open chaparral and pinyon-juniper communities. At the mouth of the canyon, huge red sandstone formations loom above. A look back down the canyon exposes great views of the Sedona area. This first stretch of trail is hot in the summer but soon ascends into the lush shade of the canyon. The route goes through a forest of manzanita before leading up to huge-trunked junipers and ponderosa pine. Some of the junipers are 2,000 years old.

There are many ruins in Boynton Canyon. They are remnants of the Sinagua ("without water") Indians who dwelt there between 1100 and 1250 A.D. Look for the ruins in alcoves about 100 to 300 feet above the canyon floor, with a southern or western exposure. The early Indians took advantage of seasons by locating their dwellings so as to face the sunlight in the winter and the shade in summer. There is a side path about 1.5 miles in that leads to a cliffside ruin. As you ascend into this canyon, you'll get more shade and see huge Douglas fir trees that might reach 130 feet in height. The route gradually steepens and ends at the head of the canyon. This is a good lunch spot before the return trip along the same route.

81. Fay Canyon Trail

Time: 3 hours. *Distance:* 3 miles roundtrip. *Elevation Gain:* 300 feet. *Rating:* Easy.

Trailhead: From the ranger station, go back out to 89A. Go west on 89A for 3 miles to Dry Creek Road. Follow Dry Creek Road for about 5 miles, following the signs for "Boynton Pass." The paved road turns into dirt just after the junction with the road to Boynton Canyon. The parking area is on the right side of the road. The trailhead is at the north end of the parking area.

High Points: Fay Canyon Arch and Indian ruins.

Hiking the Trail: The trail begins in an open, grassy area, dotted with yuccas. A turnoff to Fay Canyon Arch is about two-thirds of a mile in. It is marked with cairns along the way. It is about a .25-mile uphill hike to the sandstone Fay Arch and the ruins. The arch is difficult to spot since it is only about 10 feet from the surrounding wall. It is the longest arch in the Sedona area, measuring 94 feet long and 20 feet wide. It formed when a fracture near the edge of the canyon wall slid downward and intersected an alcove on the lower wall.

The main path goes up the canyon for another mile and into a shaded area of juniper and Emory oak. The path goes through the forest, then ascends to an open area with views of Capitol Butte and Courthouse Butte. For those more adventurous hikers who wish to continue farther, the trail gets interesting here as it narrows along a cliffside that offers views of various ruins. The trail fades out after another .5 mile at the end of the canyon. Return by the same route.

CHAPTER 9

Payson Day Hikes

Payson

Four Peaks Area

Mogollon Rim Area

PAYSON

This area was first inhabited by the Mogollon Indians. Mining brought settlers and ranchers. Timber became an economic activity. Today, tourism and summer vacationers from Phoenix make up a great deal of the local economy.

Payson lies close to the geographical center of the state at 5,000 feet elevation—just below the Mogollon Rim. It is the gateway to "Rim Country," where visitors stock up on food and provisions for fishing, hunting, camping, and hiking around the Payson area and up to the cooler plateau. It is only an hour to Payson from Phoenix (during the week). On weekends in the summer, it's best to start traveling early in the morning to avoid traffic on the single-lane highway.

Summer in Payson is Bluegrass Festival and rodeo time even though temperatures in town can get above 100 degrees Fahrenheit at midday. Another main attraction to the area is its visible and audible water. Many streams and creeks drain down from the Mogollon Rim above, along with seeps that pop up along the great escarpment. This is green and blue country, a definite contrast to the brown, dry desert to the south.

The trails in this chapter go up to the Rim (2,000 feet higher than town) and down to State Route 260. You'll have the opportunity to stand right on the edge of the Northern Plateau Province, looking one way to the top of Mt. Humphreys and the other way down into the Central Mountains. You can hike along perennial streams, stopping at springs and seeps to take a refreshing dip.

Places to Visit

The Museum of the Forest is located within the *Home of Northern Gila County Historical Society Payson Museum*. Recently dedicated (1990), the museum displays an original Forest Service ranger station along with an old fire tower. For more information, call or write to The Museum of the Forest, 1001 West Main, Payson, AZ 85541. Phone: (602) 474-3483.

Flowing Springs is a concrete ford connecting grassy flats and deciduous trees along a flowing streambed. The area extends for 2 miles, providing camping and wading places along the way. It is found by taking FR 272 about 4 miles up State Route 87 from Payson.

The *Tonto Natural Bridge* turnoff is about 8 miles north of Payson on State Route 87. Turn west on FR 583. A 3-mile drive leads to this newly formed state park, which guards the world's largest travertine arch—183 feet high, 150 wide, and 400 feet long. The arch was formed by water deposition of travertine solids that were subsequently eroded by stream action into an arch. For more information, write or call the Chamber of Commerce, P.O. Box 196, Pine, AZ 85544. Phone: (602) 476-3547.

The *Rim Lakes* and surrounding campgrounds are favorite summer vacation and weekend camping areas. These are manmade reservoirs providing fishing, boating, and camping facilities for heat-weary Phoenicians as well as locals.

Directions to all Payson Day Hike Area Takeoff Points start from the junction of State Routes 87 and 260 at the north end of Payson.

The best hiking weather occurs in spring, summer, and fall. Winters are usually too cold. The Rim itself, 2,000 feet higher than the town of Payson, can be snowed in during December, January, and February. But, Payson-based hikers can travel one hour south and hike in 60- to 70-degree weather in the middle of the Sonora Desert.

Four Peaks Area

The Four Peaks massif—a jagged 8,000-foot skyline—lies 30 miles east of Phoenix and provides a picturesque backdrop to the surrounding desert. Its huge bulk draws the explorer's eye to what looks like a far-distant range that would take days to approach—when, in reality,

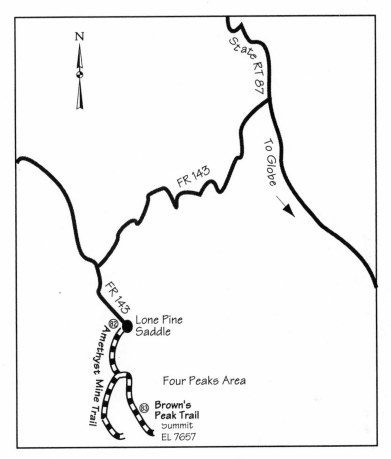

Four Peaks Area

you can drive to the base and climb one of the peaks in just one long hiking day.

There are three distinct topographic zones within the area: the craggy summits of the peaks; the complex series of ridges and drainages below the peaks; and the area of bluffs and short, steep gorges bordering the dammed-up lakes on the Salt River.

These dramatic differences reflect elevation changes and provide for widely mixed vegetation species growing side by side. They also provide for great variation in weather—especially during winter or summer storms. In a winter storm, ice and snow tear across the face of the peaks while the surrounding valleys are in the 60s and 70s.

Summer thunderstorms explode on the summits while the moisture evaporates before even hitting the ground on the desert floor below. The preceding factors make Four Peaks a unique desert "sky island"—one that shoots up from the desert floor and creates three life zones on its slopes. It is part of the southwest-facing edge of the Central Mountains Province.

Most of the surrounding area was leased for cattle grazing in years past. Much of the lower area still is. Many horse and cattle trails lead to springs and seeps on the mountain slopes. A small amethyst mine on the high southern flank was worked for years but is now closed.

The faces of the peaks themselves are composed of Precambrian shales and quartzite. The bulk of the mountain is made up of Precambrian granites and schists. The southern end of the range shows the volcanic tuffs and ash flows of the Cenozoic Age, which were deposited in the same time period as the Superstition Mountains just to the south.

Day Hike Area Takeoff Point Lone Pine Saddle Parking Area: Take I-17 to Northern Avenue. Turn east on Northern until it turns into Dreamy Draw and goes north to Shea Boulevard. Turn east at Shea and follow it all the way to its termination at State Route 87, the Beeline Highway. Turn north on the Beeline to State Route 188. Turn right on 188 and drive to El Oso Road (about .5 hour after the turn, just past Ash Creek). Turn right onto El Oso and immediately left on FR 143. This is a well-maintained, smooth dirt road that offers a pleasant, scenic trip up to Lone Pine Saddle.

Where the road turns left on 143, follow the ridgeline to the parking area at Lone Pine Saddle. Obvious camping spots appear along the ridgeline. An early start brings you to Lone Pine Saddle parking area from Phoenix in about 3 hours.

Campgrounds U.S. Forest Service campgrounds—Orange Peel, Bermuda Flat, Cholla, Cholla Bay, Bachelor's Cove, and National Forest open camping.

82. Amethyst Mine Trail

Time: 4 hours. *Distance:* 3 miles roundtrip. *Elevation Gain:* 1,000 feet. *Rating:* Moderate.

Trailhead: Steps at the southern end of the parking area lead up to a National Forest sign and a Four Peaks Wilderness sign. This is the trailhead.

High Points: Spectacular views of the Salt River Valley, the Southern Deserts Province, and the Central Mountains Province. The rugged escarpment and rocky peaks of Four Peaks Wilderness Area.

Hiking the Trail: The trail leads past the signs to a fenceline and a walk-through that marks the wilderness boundary. Slippery, decomposed granite provides the footing as the steeper part of the trail leads up to the broad saddle (Brown's Saddle) looking both east and west across central Arizona. Numerous campsites are available alongside the trail.

The air at 6,800 feet produces some huffing and puffing but helps get the desert dust out of your lungs. Sweeping views of the Tonto Basin and Roosevelt Lake catch your attention. The steepness of the escarpment is impressive and thoughts of cross-country travel through manzanita brush at a 50-degree angle bring horror to the mind.

When you reach the saddle, there is a good chance you'll feel the prevailing southwest wind. And when looking southwest, you'll see Phoenix, Mesa, and the Salt River Valley. You'll see the color changes from greens where you are standing to the browns, yellows, and grays of the desert floor. It looks a lot hotter and drier down there. It is.

A snack break at Brown's Saddle is in order. The trail splits here to go either up to Brown's Peak to the left or right to the Amethyst Mine. This split is not that obvious, so keep your eyes peeled. It's obvious if you've gone too far on the Brown's Peak Trail, for it will be heading for the peak itself. The Amethyst Mine Trail goes down and to the right. The hike to the mine goes up and down across the west face of Four Peaks and offers an unparalleled view of the Salt River Valley and the Southern Deserts Province.

The Superstition Wilderness volcanic labyrinth juts into view to the southeast, broken by the serpentine canyons of the Salt River dam compounds—compounds that serve water to a thirsty population of over 2 million desert dwellers in the Salt River Valley.

The mine site can be reached in about an hour and a half. The mine itself is on private land. It is unlawful to trespass around the mine site. Access to all four peaks is from this trail. Except for Brown's Peak, there is no established route to the other summits. Return to the parking area by the same route.

83. Brown's Peak Trail

Time: 4 hours. *Distance:* 2 miles roundtrip. *Elevation Gain:* 1,900 feet. *Rating:* Moderate.

Trailhead: See Amethyst Mine Trail.

High Points: Extended views in all directions from a 7,657-foot peak, including the San Francisco Peaks to the north and the very tips of the Santa Catalina Mountains outside of Tucson to the south on a very clear day.

Hiking the Trail: Follow the same route to Brown's Saddle as for the Amethyst Mine Trail. The route from Brown's Saddle angles left and up, heading for the scree chute that leads to the summit of Brown's Peak. The trail is broken and scrambles up over boulders and loose rock. It angles down into a gully just before heading up into the steep scree chute. This chute is loose, and rocks are easily dislodged on hikers below. It is all work until topping out on the summit flat of Brown's Peak. Then, one of the most spectacular views in central Arizona opens up.

You are standing on the edge of the Central Mountains and Southern Deserts provinces, 7,657 feet high with views as far north as the San Francisco Peaks and as far south as a hazy outline of Mt. Lemmon just north of Tucson. Many of the day-hiking areas covered in this book are visible from Brown's Peak, including Camelback Mountain, Squaw Peak, the McDowell Mountains, South Mountain, the Sierra Estrella Mountains, the White Tanks, and the Superstition Wilderness. The Sierra Ancha range spreads out to the east behind Roosevelt Lake. The Bradshaw Range lies to the north. The Mogollon Rim—where the Northern Plateau Province starts—lies along the northern horizon. The Mazatzals stretch out north along the same ridgeline as Four Peaks.

Lunch and a snooze is in order on Brown's Peak. Return by the same route.

Mogollon Rim Area

The "Rim" is the southern edge of the Northern Plateau Province, which itself is the southern edge of the Colorado Plateau. The Rim is an almost vertical escarpment that defines the end of the sedimentary-layered Northern Plateau Province that extends into Utah, Colorado, and New Mexico. The Rim extends from the Hurricane Cliffs in northwestern Arizona and proceeds in a generally east-southeast direction all across the state into New Mexico. The

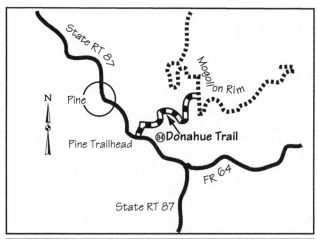

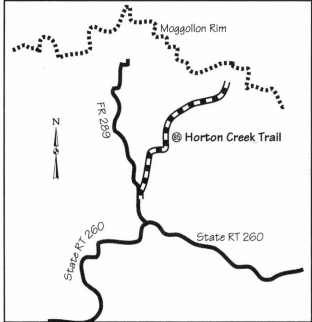

Mogollon Rim Area

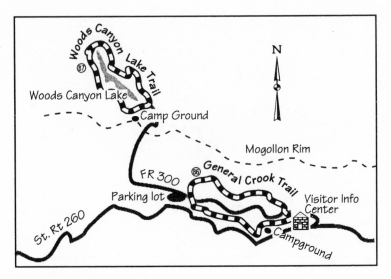

Mogollon Rim Area

most dramatic part of the Rim extends in an east-west direction about 20 miles north of Payson.

The escarpment varies between 1,000 and 3,000 feet along its course. Our day hikes focus on this area, along branches of the Highline Trail, which runs for 52 miles along the base of the Rim. The Highline Trail was used by early settlers on horseback as a commerce route. It is a year-round trail, closed occasionally by snow. Vegetation ranges from chaparral to pinyon-juniper to ponderosa pine communities. It crosses many streams and drainages that drop down from the Rim. It is connected by a number of forest roads that allow for all types of creative day hiking.

The Day Hike Area Takeoff Point for all hikes in this area is the junction of State Routes 87 and 260 at the north end of Payson.

Campgrounds There are over 20 open campgrounds along both the top and bottom of the Rim.

84. Donahue Trail

Time: 4 hours. *Distance:* 3.5 miles roundtrip. *Elevation Gain:* 2,200 feet. *Rating:* Challenging.

Trailhead: From the intersection of State Routes 87 and 260 East, drive north on 87 for about 19 miles to the well-marked Pine trailhead, just .5 mile south of Pine. Turn east at the sign and drive into the parking area. Look for the Highline Trail sign. This is the trailhead.

High Points: An ascent through a variety of vegetation life zones from the chaparral below the Rim up to the ponderosa pine forest on top of the Rim. Unparalleled views extend south through the Central Mountains Province, all the way to the edge of the Southern Deserts Province.

Hiking the Trail: This route was used by early settlers in the Pine area as an ascent route to the top of the Mogollon Rim. Follow the well-traveled Highline Trail along the level path for about 1.5 miles to the junction of the Donahue Trail. You will gain elevation fast as the 2,200-foot climb to the Rim begins. Typical chaparral vegetation with scattered prickly pear and hedgehog cactus greets you as you begin your climb. You'll travel from pinyon-juniper into oak woodland and then ponderosa pine forest as you ascend. You are climbing from the Central Mountains Province into the Northern Plateau Province on this one-day hike. Unlimited views to the south take your eyes across the entire Central Mountains Province to the edge of the Southern Deserts Province. The trail continues to FR 218. Return by the same route.

85. Horton Creek Trail

Time: 5 hours. *Distance:* 7 miles roundtrip. *Elevation Gain:* 1,000 feet. *Rating:* Moderate.

Trailhead: From the junction of State Routes 87 and 260 East, follow 260 just past Kohl's Ranch Resort and turn onto FR 289. Drive up 1 mile to the Upper Tonto Creek Campground. The trailhead is at the north boundary of the campground.

High Points: Streamside habitat in lush forest growth with Horton Springs as a destination.

Hiking the Trail: Horton Springs is an outlet for water filtered down from the Mogollon Rim, 2,000 feet above. It creates Horton Creek, one of many such drainages that will slowly erode the Rim back to the Utah state line over the next few million years.

This trail is a cool favorite among Phoenix residents in the summer as well as an autumn favorite when the Rim colors change. It has a two-in-one option. You can follow either an old roadbed to Horton Springs (a great lunch spot) or the less distinct path along the creekbed, which offers waterfalls and lush vegetation to sun-weary hikers. Follow the road up and notice the subtle vegetation changes as you slowly ascend to the springs. Notice the added riparian vegetation along the streambed. You are walking on top of parts of the eroded Northern Plateau Province that have fallen from the escarpment above. You are walking through millions of years of geologic time—the time it took to deposit the sedimentary layers of the area above you. The entire Rim in front of you has been eroding back to the north for millions of years and will continue to do so until it no longer exists. Return by the same route.

86. Rim Lakes Vista—General Crook Trail

Time: 3 hours. *Distance:* 6-mile loop. *Elevation Gain:* Level. *Rating:* Moderate.

Trailhead: From the intersection of State Routes 87 and 260, take 260 to the top of the rim and turn left on FR 300 and drive to the Rim campground. The trailhead is in the campground.

High Points: Unparalleled vistas from the edge of the Mogollon Rim out over the Central Mountains Province to the south.

Hiking the Trail: This is an undulating path that skirts the Mogollon Rim as you hike from one fantastic vista to the next. You are hiking in a ponderosa pine forest with open views. The dramatic geologic events that shaped the Rim become obvious as the steepness of this eroded escarpment strikes your senses. This is the same process that formed the Grand Canyon, only on a slower scale because there is no river to carve into the layers along the edge of the Northern Plateau—only rainfall and snow.

After 3 miles of hiking along the Rim, you'll run into the Military Sinkhole Vista parking lot and trailhead. Turn north onto Military Sinkhole Trail and follow it for about .5 mile to the junction of the General Crook Trail. Turn right and follow the General Crook Trail through the ponderosa forest to FR 300 and turn right along this road to head back to the Rim campground. Watch for deer, elk, and turkey along this Rim hike.

87. Woods Canyon Lake Trail

Time: 4 hours. *Distance:* 5.5 miles. *Elevation Gain:* Level. *Rating:* Easy.

Trailhead: From the intersection of State Routes 87 and 260, drive northeast on State Route 260 to the top of the Mogollon Rim. Turn left on FR 300 and drive to Woods Canyon Lake. Look for the trailhead at the lake amphitheater.

High Points: Rim lake environment with aquatic bird life. Short, .5-mile interpretive trail.

Hiking the Trail: Take the short, .5-mile interpretive trail at the west end of the Rocky Point picnic area first. It identifies the vegetation and describes features and landmarks in the area. Then take the 5-mile hike around the entire lake. This shady stroll gives you an amateur naturalist's overview of one of the many popular Rim lakes. Look and listen for the lakeside bird life (coots, ducks, geese, blackbirds). Notice the shoreline cattail communities growing in the shallow water. This is a recreation lake—one of many that have been dammed up along the Mogollon Rim. All these lakes provide rest, recreation, and shade for the day hiker.

PART THREE

NORTHERN PLATEAU PROVINCE

Forming the Northern Plateau Province

Geology

This region, like the Central Mountains Province, is a land of contrasts. With elevations between 2,000 and 12,000 feet, the Northern Plateau hosts part of the Mojave Desert in the extreme western part, going up through every Arizona plant community to the alpine tundra on top of Mt. Humphreys just north of Flagstaff.

The Northern Plateau is a huge uplifted area—extending into New Mexico, Colorado, and Utah. It was formed by millions of years of seabed deposits stacked upon each other as water flowed in and out repeatedly over the landscape. Subsequent continental collisions pushed this large layer cake up above sea level, causing the series of plateaus that are visible today. Millions of years of wind, water, and ice erosion sculpted the soft sedimentary layers into tablelands, canyons, spires, buttes, pinnacles, arches, and mesas. The Northern Plateau bulged up high enough in places to provide hundreds of square miles of ponderosa pine forest habitat. Ancient rivers cut down through one of those plateaus to create the Grand Canyon. This kaleidoscopic landscape was then brushed with the pastel paints of two dissolved minerals—hematite and limonite. These two tints, mixed with oxygen, provided varying amounts of iron oxides that colored the sedimentary layers yellow, cream, orange, crimson, pink, and purple. Then the continental canvas was overlaid with the dark, flowing brushstrokes of lava. The final dabs of green vegetation, mixed with exotic wildflower colors, created the beauty of present-day Northern Plateau country.

The sedimentary layers get younger as you travel north up the Northern Plateau from its southern edge in Arizona to its northern boundary in Utah. Erosion aside, the Northern Plateau sedimentary layers have escaped the worst of the plate-tectonic forces and have remained level for over half a billion years—while terrain around it has been broken, tilted, pushed up, down, sideways, and out. The stable nature of the Northern Plateau has given geologists a treasure trove of opportunities to study the sedimentary processes of continent building.

There are a few areas in the Northern Plateau's western part as low as 2,000 feet, but the average elevation range is 3,000 to 5,000 feet, with sedimentary uplifts up to 8,000 feet and volcanic lava extrusions reaching to the top of Mt. Humphreys at 12,670 feet.

Strange as it seems, water is a problem on the Northern Plateau. Enough of it falls, but not enough of it stays. Most of it filters down into the sedimentary layers and becomes part of the underground supply, surfacing farther south in the Central Mountains Province in the form of springs and groundwater wells.

The Northern Plateau Province doesn't contain any large ore deposits. There is some uranium mining close to the Grand Canyon and a small amount of oil is obtained from the northeast corner of the state.

The Grand Canyon merits special note. In addition to the breathtaking views and immensity that draw upwards of 4 million visitors a year, this natural wonder is one of the great geology textbooks of the world. It represents a huge slice of the Northern Plateau layer cake and reveals almost 2 billion years of the earth's history.

When looking over the South Rim, you can see the Colorado River in many places due to the fact that the river is closer to this rim than it is to the North Rim. The dark rock layer at river level is the remnant of a 1.7-billion-year-old mountain range formed by continental collision forces. The range was subsequently eroded to a flat surface and covered with sedimentary sea and wind deposits, now visible as the colored, horizontal layers that we stare at in wonder.

The North Rim is 1,000 feet higher than the South Rim due to the tilt of the Northern Plateau from north to south. Even though looking into the same Grand Canyon, the views from the north are a new experience because of the higher, more vegetated, and cooler surroundings at the North Rim.

Climate

Part of the Northern Plateau is an arid desert—Mojave on the west and Great Basin on the east. The Great Basin desert is higher than the Southern Deserts Province to the south and therefore a bit cooler in the summer and a lot colder in the winter. It is a sagebrush desert with hundreds of square miles of nothing much more than sagebrush. The weather in the high, volcanic mountains around Flagstaff and Mt. Baldy in the White Mountains is much wetter than the lower, surrounding terrain because the elevated land masses force the rising moisture-laden air to condense into rain.

The 12,670-foot summit of Mt. Humphreys sits 50 horizontal miles south of the Grand Canyon's Colorado River, which roars along at an elevation of about 2,000 feet. That's 10,500 feet of elevation change—and weather change—and plant life change—and animal life change—in an extremely short horizontal distance.

Summer temperatures on the Northern Plateau flat areas can get above 90 degrees Fahrenheit, with glaring heat reflecting back from the bare sandstone surfaces. The absence of vegetation allows for a great range of temperatures. Without the mitigating effect of plant life to hold in the heat, the hot day's collected rays re-radiate into the atmosphere when the sun goes down. Vast expanses of hot, flat, featureless terrain soak up the sun, only to give it back at night.

On the Northern Plateau uplifts, however, the summers are cool, wet, and beautiful. They provide true escapes for folks who travel up from the hotter deserts in southern Arizona, and from the deserts of Utah.

On the level surfaces of this lonely land, summer thunderstorms can be seen for hundreds of miles as their wild winds paint the summer sky with clouds, lightning, rain, and hail, mixing the pastel-painted landscape into a constantly changing light show.

Fall is characterized by a dry transition to winter, with the sparse summer vegetation turning brown and gray and making the land even lonelier. Winters can be severe with high winds and bitter cold on both the high deserts and uplifts. The continental influences of the surrounding land masses to the north bring paralyzing snows and cold weather to the land. Since so much of the Northern Plateau is isolated Navajo and Hopi Indian land, with many families living in hogans heated only by wood fires, this severe weather can make many of the tribal families snowbound, requiring food and fuel air drops from National Guard helicopters to ensure the survival of the people and their cattle and sheep.

Pacific Northwest storms influence the Northern Plateau as they do the rest of the state. Their snow intensity determines the success of the state's two ski areas located on Mt. Humphreys north of Flag-staff and Mt. Baldy in the White Mountains. Spring brings renewal to Northern Plateau desert plant life, and once again turns the bleak sandstones to color-splotched canvases of floral delight.

Plant Life

A great percentage of the plant life of the Southern Deserts and Cen-tral Mountains provinces also occurs on the Northern Plateau. The lower-elevation, northwestern part of the province is the Mojave Desert with the characteristic creosote bush, sagebrush, Mojave yucca, and Joshua tree. Mesquite, Mormon tea, catclaw, and prickly pear are common. Parts of the Northern Plateau are covered by pin-yon, Utah juniper, banana yucca, cliffrose, and big sagebrush.

A series of elevated plateau sections—the Shivwits, Kanab, Kai-bab, and Kaibito—forms the landscape north of the Grand Canyon. These uplifts display a great variety of plant life as the elevations change from the desert grassland/sagebrush community of black sage, big sage, and sand sagebrush to the spruce-fir-aspen community characterized by Engelmann spruce, Colorado blue spruce, Douglas fir, white fir, and quaking aspen. In between exists a special plant group called the mountain grassland community, which is dominated by perennial bunchgrasses and common wildflowers such as owl clo-ver, yarrow, and dandelion.

Arizona's highest alpine tundra lies above 11,000 feet on Mt. Humphreys, where only a few grasses, herbaceous flowering plants, bristlecone pines, and dwarf junipers survive. There are places on the eastern part of the Northern Plateau where almost no plants grow. These are badlands like the Petrified Forest and Painted Desert, where soils are so sparse as to negate plant growth.

Animal Life

Many of the animal species that live in the Southern Deserts and Central Mountains provinces also live in the Northern Plateau Prov-ince.

Desertshrub and grassland communities house ringtail cats, pocket mice, packrats, jackrabbits, skunks, chuckwallas, and various other lizard species. Common kingsnakes and Mojave rattlers also in-habit these desert areas. Pinyon-juniper species include mule deer,

Striped skunk

desert cottontail, chipmunk, gray fox, and sagebrush lizard. Higher elevations provide habitat for the porcupine, golden-mantled ground squirrel, mule deer, chipmunk, and red squirrel.

The Northern Plateau is the summer range of the Wyoming elk. Bighorn sheep inhabit a few areas on the Northern Plateau (including the inner Grand Canyon). There is a buffalo preserve on a reservation in Houserock Valley on the North Rim of the Grand Canyon.

There is a special squirrel that has evolved on the Kaibab Plateau north of the Grand Canyon—the Kaibab squirrel. Evidence suggests this squirrel branched off from the Abert's squirrel as the Grand Canyon itself was formed. The endangered Gunnison's prairie dog digs his home on the plateau.

Bighorn sheep

CHAPTER 11

Flagstaff Day Hikes

Flagstaff

San Francisco Peaks Area

Mt. Elden Area

Kendrick Peak Area

Sunset Crater Area

FLAGSTAFF

The Flagstaff area was first inhabited by the Anasazi, Sinagua, and Cohonina Indians. Coronado came through the area in the sixteenth century, searching for the Seven Cities of Gold. The city was named for a very tall pine tree that was raised on July 4, 1876, and placed as a trail marker for westbound wagon trains seeking the route to California. This trail eventually became Route 66.

Flagstaff is surrounded by the largest stand of ponderosa pine forest in the country. It is what attracted loggers to the area. Mining followed with the railroad coming soon after.

Flagstaff sits at 7,000 feet elevation, at the base of the 12,000-foot San Francisco Peaks. With a population of 45,000, it is the largest city in northern Arizona.

Day hiking opportunities abound. You can explore the peaks and trails that climb remnant volcanos and take journeys through geologic time back into an explosive era of earth building or hike right into the center of an eroded cinder cone.

Mt. Humphreys, an extinct volcano that exploded millions of years ago, offers the ultimate in day hike climbing trails. Its 12,670-foot summit, the highest point in Arizona, beckons the most adventurous to its flanks.

Mt. Elden and Kendrick Peak—also volcanic mountains—afford well-maintained trails with 360-degree vistas across the Northern Plateau—all the way to the North Rim of the Grand Canyon and south to the Central Mountains Province.

Directions to all Day Hike Area Takeoff Points start at the Flagstaff Chamber of Commerce, located at 101 West Santa Fe (US 89), Flagstaff, AZ 86001. Phone: (602) 774-4505. The Chamber of Commerce is located right across the street from US 180 (Humphreys Street).

When to Go

The best hiking seasons in Flagstaff are spring, summer, and fall. Winter is usually too cold and snowy for pleasant hiking, but hikers can head south and in three hours be in the southern deserts.

Places to Visit

The *Museum of Northern Arizona* in Flagstaff was founded in 1928 to research and display the anthropology and archaeology of the Colorado Plateau. The museum is known worldwide for its collections and exhibits of Plateau Native Indian arts and lifestyles. It offers education programs for children and adults in the form of Ventures, a program of trips and treks onto the Plateau.

The museum bookstore carries an extensive collection of material about the Colorado Plateau, and is a good place to advance your understanding of the area. Call or write for current museum hours: Museum of Northern Arizona, Route 4, Box 270, Flagstaff, AZ 86001. Phone: (602) 774-5211. The museum is located on State Route 180 going north from Flagstaff to the Grand Canyon, just past the Pioneer Historical Museum.

The *Flagstaff Arboretum* is young, having been established in 1981 as a center of plant research and exhibition. It occupies 200 acres of ponderosa pine forest at an elevation of 7,150 feet.

Work at the arboretum focuses on the propagation, field testing, cultural treatment, and utilization of plants native to the Colorado Plateau, especially drought-hardy plants that can be used for ornamental, medicinal, food, or fiber-production purposes. The arboretum works with 27 species of rare and endangered plants. It also acts as a resource to the general public for assistance with gardening and landscape problems.

The arboretum includes a 5,000-square-foot horticultural center with a solar greenhouse. Guides conduct nature walks, and there is a self-guided nature trail.

Call or write for hours: The Arboretum of Flagstaff, P.O. Box 670, Flagstaff, AZ 86002. Phone: (602) 774-1441. The arboretum is located 3.8 miles off Old Highway 66 on Woody Mountain Road.

San Francisco Peaks Area

These peaks, just north of Flagstaff, are the highest mountains in Arizona—volcanic remnants of long-ago eruptions. They, along with many other remnants, dot the Northern Plateau Province in northern Arizona. The Peaks area starts at 8,000 feet and goes up to the summit of Mt. Humphreys at Arizona's highest point—12,633 feet. The area was designated the Kachina Peaks Wilderness in 1984, bringing its 18,200 acres under the protection of the Wilderness Act.

The Peaks area volcanos erupted about 2 million years ago, forming a caldera facing northeast and called the Inner Basin. Subsequent glaciation provided for a small moraine running east from the caldera. Red and black volcanic cinders cover the upper slopes, products of violent magma explosions that cooled the cinders at different temperatures and colors.

Because of their elevation and vertical relief, the San Francisco Peaks experience a wide range of weather conditions that can change in an instant. Precipitation goes from 20 inches on the lower slopes to over 40 inches on the upper slopes.

Temperatures vary greatly between day and night. They drop a couple of degrees for every thousand feet of elevation, and the wind usually picks up the higher you go. May and June are usually dry months. July and August bring summer thunderstorms—violent displays of lightning, thunder, and rain that should be avoided on the upper slopes.

Winter snows come in October or November. The hiking season slows and the skiing season begins and lasts to April–May. Day hiking usually picks up again in April–May, or when the snow melts.

Plan plenty of time for day hiking at Flagstaff altitudes. Come up a day early and get one good night's sleep before hiking the next day. Altitude sickness is a very tricky thing and can happen to anyone,

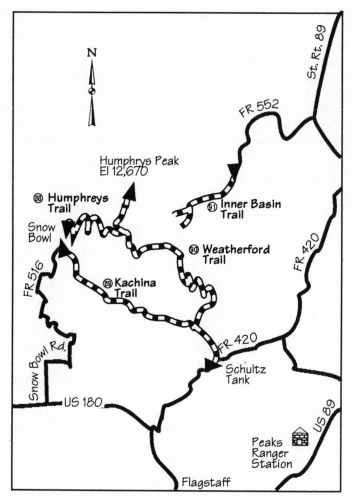

San Francisco Peaks Area

regardless of age or physical condition. Day hikes at Flagstaff altitudes are strenuous and should be planned for accordingly. Start
slowly and work up the slopes at moderate speed. Rest often and
drink water as you go.

Wind is the killer when it comes to mountain-exposure problems,
and packing a good wind/rain parka is recommended. As a matter of

fact, when climbing above treeline to the summit, take extra clothing, water, and food, plus rain gear. It is a long hike back down to treeline if weather dumps on you.

Don't move rocks or debris on the summits just to make your short stay more comfortable. Leave the terrain as you find it. Pack out other refuse you find.

Environmental Considerations: The San Francisco Peaks groundsel, *Senecio franciscanus,* is a small plant that grows above timberline on upper slopes. It grows nowhere else in the world! Therefore, hiking above timberline is restricted to designated trails only, with group size limited to nine hikers or fewer.

These peaks are of great religious significance to northern Arizona Indians. To the Navajo, they are the western cardinal point in their universe and a key element in their prayers. To the Hopi, they are the home of the Kachina Gods—the Gods that provide rain and successful harvesting of their corn.

Day Hike Area Takeoff Point Lower Snow Bowl Parking Area: From the Flagstaff Chamber of Commerce, head north on US 180 and follow it out about 7 miles to the Snow Bowl turnoff—paved FR 516. Follow FR 516 to the Snow Bowl lower parking area.

Campgrounds Bonito Campground and open National Forest camping.

88. Mt. Humphreys Trail

Time: 6 hours. *Distance:* 9 miles roundtrip. *Elevation Gain:* 3,600 feet. *Rating:* Challenging.

Trailhead: The trailhead is located at the north end of the lower parking area. Look for the sign.

High Points: This is the "high point" in Arizona, climbing to the summit of Mt. Humphreys, at 12,670 feet. Views are magnificent. It is the only day hike in this book that goes above timberline.

Hiking the Trail: Crossing the open area of the beginner's ski slope, the path heads into a forest canopy of ponderosa pine, fir, spruce, and aspen. The trail zigzags up the mountain with occasional open breaks at scree slopes that offer views of the surrounding terrain. Small meadows also open up with views to the west. As you climb higher, the Snow Bowl ski area comes into view. When you look up, you'll see Mt. Agassiz, the second-highest peak in the range.

After about 3 miles along the trail, the vegetation thins out to stunted bristlecone pines—the oldest living trees. You are now heading above timberline and into a new environment. It is still another mile to the summit and the wind can hit you hard at this altitude—especially with no vegetation to block it. At about the 3.75-mile mark, you reach the ridgeline and the junction with the Weatherford Trail. Vegetation thins out as you reach timberline, and the plants become more fragile. An hour or more of hiking along the spectacular ridgeline takes the hiker to the summit.

On a clear day, almost a quarter of the state becomes visible from the rocky summit. The hiker should see the Grand Canyon, Painted Desert, Verde Valley, Sedona, and the Hopi mesas. Small patches of snow remain on the slopes throughout the summer. Violent electrical storms can occur in any month. It's a good idea to carry snacks and plenty of water on this hike—to keep the energy level up. Return by the same route.

89. Kachina Trail

Time: 5 hours. *Distance:* 6 miles one-way. *Elevation Gain:* 100 feet. *Rating:* Moderate.

Trailhead: Look for the Kachina trailhead at the south end of the lower parking lot. The trail is best hiked one way with a shuttle to the Weatherford Trail. The shuttle requires turning right, off FR 516 and onto FR 522, at about the 2.5-mile mark. Follow 522 (Freidlein Prairie Road) for 4 miles to a parking lot, staying left on the way. The parking lot is on the left side of FR 522. A blocked road (part of the Weatherford Trail) continues north from the parking lot. Follow this on foot about one-third mile to the Kachina Trail coming in from the left.

High Points: A great forest hike on the enchanted south side of the Peaks range, exhibiting wildflowers, open meadows, aspen stands, and views south to Flagstaff and across the Northern Plateau.

Hiking the Trail: The trail starts out in a forest of fir, spruce, and aspen. It meanders along an undulating route from the parking lot to the junction of the Weatherford Trail road a few miles north of Schultz Tank. It offers a great introduction to the topography and natural history of the Peaks area, traversing through scree slopes, meadows, and stands of aspen and mixed conifers. Basaltic lava outcroppings jut out along the route. At about the 4-mile mark, Freidlein Prairie opens up with spectacular views south. Looking up, you can see massive Mt. Agassiz looming above. This is a good lunch spot. Return by the same route.

90. Weatherford Trail

Time: 10 hours. *Distance:* 15 miles one-way. *Elevation Gain:* 4,000 feet. *Rating:* Most challenging hike in this guide.

Trailhead: From the Snow Bowl parking lot, drive down FR 516 about 5 miles to Freidlein Prairie Road (FR 522). Follow 522 east for about 4 miles to a prominent parking lot on the left side of 522. This is the trailhead.

High Points: Spectacular ridgeline traverses and views of northern Arizona. Views of distorted volcanic action when this volcano erupted millions of years ago. Summit of Humphreys Peak, highest point in Arizona. A good trail for acclimatization and preparation before attempting either of the summit trails. Visible wildlife might include elk, mule deer, squirrels, Clark's nutcrackers, and Steller's jays. This is a great fall color-change hike.

Hiking the Trail: This is a long, arduous hike best attempted by those in good cardiovascular condition and with a couple of days of acclimatization to the Flagstaff altitude. The path was originally a roadbed that Model Ts could follow to the ridgeline of the Peaks. It has reverted to a trail and is quite easy to follow.

This route gives the strong hiker the best overall San Francisco Peaks area experience because it passes through so much terrain variation with so many different views. It's a long hike so bring lots of snacks and water. Bring lots of motivation also.

Walk north on the dirt road to where the Kachina Trail comes in from the left (.3 mile). Continue north across a meadow and into a shaded area, looking for a trail sign. Continue until you find a trail log book. The path leads gradually, then steeply, upward toward Doyle Saddle between Doyle and Fremont peaks. From there, you can look down into the Peaks Inner Basin to the east and out to Oak Creek Canyon and the Verde Valley 50 miles away. You'll encounter ponderosa pine, limber pine, corkbark fir, and bristlecone pine. You are walking on an extinct volcano.

Another 1.5 miles brings you to another saddle at 11,350 feet. From this saddle, you can see Kendrick Peak to the west and the Inner Basin to the east. From there, you gain the final above-timberline saddle between Mt. Agassiz and Mt. Humphreys. This is where the Weatherford Trail meets the Humphreys Trail. Continue along the ridge to the summit of Humphreys. Go down the Humphreys Trail to the Snow Bowl parking lot. This requires a shuttle to the lower parking area.

91. Inner Basin Trail

Time: 4 hours. *Distance:* 4 miles roundtrip. *Elevation Gain:* 1,500 feet. *Rating:* Moderate.

Trailhead: Drive east on Route 66 and then north on US 89 for about 12 miles to FR 552, just past the Sunset Crater turnoff. Go west on FR 552 and bear right at the Lockett Meadow sign. Continue 4.5 miles to Lockett Meadow and the Forest Service campground. Look for the trailhead sign at the northwest end of the campground. This road may be covered with snow in early spring.

High Points: Lush Inner Basin vegetation due to the moist drainages and sheltered groundcover. Picture-postcard views of the San Francisco Peaks.

Hiking the Trail: From Lockett Meadow, the trail heads toward the Inner Basin (volcanic vent) of the Peaks. The hiker is entering the mouth of the extinct volcano along this old roadbed. The road has been used by the City of Flagstaff because the Inner Basin is its watershed. Several springs permeate the basin. Huge stands of aspen cover the slopes, providing a carpet of gold in the early fall. In spring and summer, this area is covered with blue, red, and yellow wildflowers. At about 1.5 miles, you come to Jack Smith Spring, two cabins, and a trail register. This spring is a crossroads that connects FR 146 going to Shultz Pass to the left and the Bear Jaw and Abineau trails to the right.

Snow may remain in the Inner Basin through spring due to its north-slope orientation. This provides cross-country paths for early spring skiers. Black bears can sometimes be seen as they amble through the area. A hike into the Inner Basin will give the trekker unparalleled views of the whole San Francisco Peaks complex. Return by the same route.

Mt. Elden Area

Mt. Elden lies adjacent to the City of Flagstaff with many trails criss-crossing this "urban" mountain. Access is quick and easy from the city, and many folks take an after-work stroll along its flanks.

Mt. Elden looks like part of the San Francisco Peaks massif, but it is a later geologic-volcanic event. From its eastern trailhead, where most hikers start, the mountain looks like corduroy with lava projections by the hundreds covering its face. Even though an urban mountain, it is still 9,299 feet in elevation and can have severe winds and storms swirling around its summit.

Day Hike Area Takeoff Point One-half mile north of the Peaks Ranger Station: From the Flagstaff Visitor Center, follow Route 66 east about 5 miles to the Flagstaff Mall on the right. Just beyond the mall, you'll see a sign for the Mt. Elden Trailhead. Drive into the parking lot.

Campgrounds Bonito Campground and open National Forest camping.

92. Elden Lookout Trail

Time: 3 hours. *Distance:* 6 miles roundtrip. *Elevation Gain:* 2,300 feet. *Rating:* Challenging.

Trailhead: Look for the sign at the gate on the west end of the parking lot. This is the trailhead.

High Points: Open views of east Flagstaff, Sunset Crater, and the far-distant Painted Desert. Summit views of the San Francisco Peaks.

Hiking the Trail: Follow the obvious path past the turnoff to Fatman's Loop Trail. Go through the pass-through gates. About .25 mile later you'll meet the junction of the Pipeline Trail. Another .5 mile of easy gradient brings you to the other end of the Fatman's Loop Trail. This easy uphill section takes you through a pinyon/juniper and ponderosa pine forest mix. You'll also see prickly pear, hedgehog, and staghorn cactus scattered along the route. From here the trail

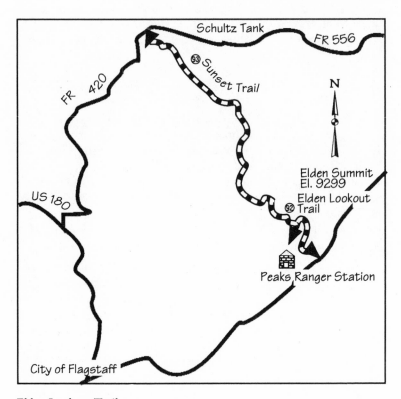

Elden Lookout Trail

becomes quite steep as it switchbacks up to the summit of Mt. Elden.
Mixed conifers of fir and pine appear as you ascend. Magnificent
views of east Flagstaff and Sunset Crater open up as you climb the
granite "staircases" of this steep day hike. Near the top of the trail,
you'll walk through an area that burned during the Radio Fire of
1977. You can see the after-fire plant succession that will soon display
aspen groves in the first step to replacing the conifer forest destroyed
by the fire. This burned-out area allows even greater views of the surrounding north country. You'll reach a sign indicating the top of Mt.
Elden. Walk another .25 mile to the lookout tower for 360-degree
views of the Northern Plateau Province with the San Francisco Peaks
massif dominating the surrounding terrain. Be on the lookout for
Steller's jays, red-tail hawks, and Clark's nutcrackers.

   Return down the trail to the parking lot.

93. Sunset Trail

Time: 4 hours. *Distance:* 4 miles one-way. *Elevation Gain:* 1,800 feet. *Rating:* Moderate.

Trailhead: From the Peaks Ranger Station, drive west on Route 66 (Santa Fe) until you reach US 180. Turn north and follow 180 for about 3 miles to the turnoff to Schultz Pass Road (FR 420). Turn right on FR 420 and drive on the paved road that turns into gravel. Follow this road for about 6 miles to a Sunset Trail sign. Turn into the parking area. The trailhead sign is located here.

High Points: Possible deer and elk sightings. Lush alpine environment. Ridgeline views of the surrounding Northern Plateau Province. Summit views from Mt. Elden.

Hiking the Trail: From Schultz Tank the path climbs up a heavily forested side canyon to a road and open area with views of the San Francisco Peaks. Climb to the top of a hill and to a trail junction. Stay left and head downhill. Be alert for deer, elk, and bird life in this rather remote ponderosa pine forest. The trail steepens as it climbs up to the ridgeline on Mt. Elden that opens views to the San Francisco Peaks and surrounding countryside. The path continues along the east edge of the Mt. Elden summit plateau and looks out across to Sunset Crater and the Bonita Lava Flow. The trail then climbs up through aspen and fir and traverses the scene of the 1977 forest fire that devastated the area. This fire almost spread into the town of Flagstaff. Although the area is making a quick comeback, it is still open and offers unlimited views across the Northern Plateau. The route continues along the crest until it ends at a junction about a mile from the lookout tower. Take the Elden Lookout Trail back down to the parking lot, where your shuttle has been parked.

Kendrick Peak Area

A short distance to the west of the San Francisco Peaks another mountain rises out of the sedimentary Northern Plateau Province—Kendrick Peak, an extinct volcano that is now part of the Kendrick Peak Wilderness Area. It offers the day hiker varied-terrain hikes with spectacular views from the ridgelines, summit, and fire tower of Kendrick Mountain.

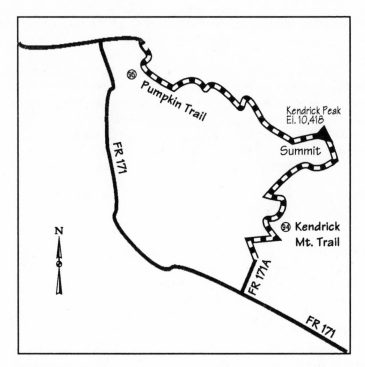

Kendrick Peak Area

Day Hike Area Takeoff Point Kendrick Mountain Parking Area: From the Flagstaff Visitor Center, take US 180 about 14 miles north (milepost 230), where FR 245 exits to the left. Take FR 245 3 miles to FR 171. Turn right on FR 171 and follow it another 3 miles to the sign for the Kendrick Trail. Turn right into the parking area.

Campgrounds Bonito Campground or open National Forest camping.

94. Kendrick Mountain Trail

Time: 6 hours. *Distance:* 9 miles roundtrip. *Elevation Gain:* 2,400 feet. *Rating:* Challenging.

Trailhead: The trailhead is located in the parking area.

High Points: Spectacular views of the Grand Canyon rim to the north and Oak Creek Canyon to the south. Views of the Northern Plateau Province for 360 degrees.

Hiking the Trail: The trail starts out as an old fire road, angling up at a comfortable rate through ponderosa pine, Douglas fir, white fir, Engelmann spruce, and corkbark fir. As you go higher, you get into the conifers and large aspen groves. Steeper switchbacks take you higher to where the road ends and a footpath takes off. Follow this old fire-tower route to the flat area below the tower, which brings you to the Old Lookout Cabin used by rangers years ago. It was built in 1911–1912 and contains a log book for you to sign. Continue climbing to the fire tower and the flat helicopter pad below it. If a ranger is on duty, he or she will probably allow you to visit the fire tower. The Northern Plateau Province spreads out in all directions. To the south, you can see Oak Creek Canyon and the lip of the province as it dips down into the Central Mountains Province. To the north, you can see the edge of the Grand Canyon and the North Rim, which is 1,000 feet higher than the South Rim. Return by the same route.

95. Pumpkin Trail

Time: 6 hours. *Distance:* 11 miles roundtrip. *Elevation Gain:* 3,100 feet. *Rating:* Challenging.

Trailhead: From the Kendrick Mountain Trail trailhead parking area, go back out to FR 171, turn right, and drive about 4 miles on 171 to FR 154. Turn right on FR 154 and drive for about 1 mile to the well-marked trailhead.

High Points: Open vistas of the Northern Plateau Province. Ranger tower on top.

Hiking the Trail: This mountain and its trails offer much the same views as Mt. Humphreys. Take plenty of water and snacks, as there is no reliable water source along the route. The trail goes along an old logging road, then goes up along a steep canyon. You will pass a pole gate where the trail ascends a ridge, turning southeast to what looks like an old helicopter landing spot. It continues through meadows and plentiful stands of aspen and conifer.

Metal signs are posted on many trees. Rock cairns appear in the many meadows that you cross along the route. After about 4 miles, the path gets steep and rough. This section is part of an old sheepherder route. You'll encounter the ruins of an old cabin along the top part of this trail at about the 5-mile mark. The lookout tower is an-

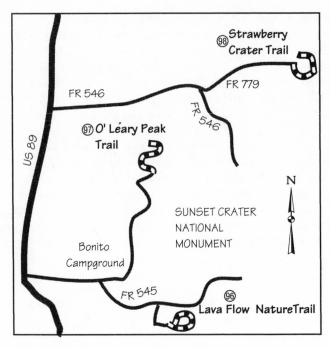

Sunset Crater Area

other .5 mile, and the trail becomes even more difficult. Return by the same route or do a shuttle and hike down the Kendrick Mountain Trail.

Sunset Crater Area

The Sunset Crater area is centered in Sunset Crater National Monument. Along with the large volcanos described in the San Francisco Peaks, Mt. Elden, and Kendrick Peak areas, this area contains almost 400 smaller volcanic eruptions as part of the largest volcanic field in Arizona. It also contains excellent short day hikes designed to familiarize the hiker with lava flows and volcanos.

The monument was established in 1930 to preserve Sunset Crater, Arizona's youngest volcano. This particular volcano is now off limits to hikers due to past overuse, but other volcanos in the area are accessible.

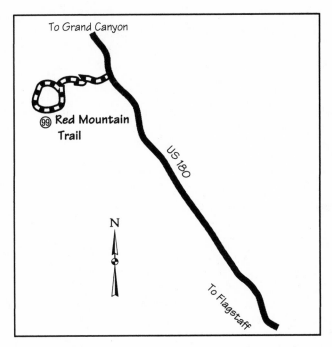

Sunset Crater Area

The eruption of the crater began in 1065 A.D. and was active for about 200 years. The ash and cinders cover an area of about 800 square miles. The eruption created the Bonito Flow, which is an a'a' lava flow characterized by rough, jagged surfaces formed from a thick, pasty, and slow-moving magma.

Nine hundred years ago, when the crater began to erupt, Sinagua Indians farmed the area. The subsequent ash-rich soil drew others to the area for its superior farming environment.

Day Hike Area Takeoff Point Sunset Crater National Monument Visitor Center: From the Flagstaff Visitor Center, take US 89 north out of Flagstaff about 10 miles to the Sunset Crater National Monument turnoff. Turn right and drive to the main visitor center. This center contains a tremendous amount of information about the Northern Plateau Province and the local volcanic fields. A visit will greatly enrich your hiking experience.

Campgrounds Bonito Campground, located just north of the main visitor center and open National Forest camping.

96. Lava Flow Nature Trail

Time: 1 hour. *Distance:* 1 mile. *Elevation Gain:* Level. *Rating:* Easy.

Trailhead: From the Sunset Crater Visitor Center, drive along the monument road (FR 545) for about 3.5 miles to Lava Flow Trail Drive. Follow it to the parking area. The trailhead is here.

High Points: A unique walk through a real lava field. Interpretive signs along the route.

Hiking the Trail: This is a self-guided loop that allows hikers to examine several volcanic features of the area. A guide booklet, keyed to the interpretive signs, is available. Part of the trail is paved for wheelchair access. Special features include lava flow squeeze-ups (thick, molten lava that once oozed through cracks of the solid lava crust) and lava tubes (a type of cave found in lava flows). This is a special one-of-a-kind trail and should be taken by every hiker who has never walked on a lava flow.

97. O'Leary Peak Trail

Time: 3 hours. *Distance:* 3 miles roundtrip. *Elevation Gain:* 750 feet. *Rating:* Challenging.

Trailhead: From Sunset Crater Visitor Center, drive back toward US 89 on FR 545 a short distance until you find the FR 545A sign on the right-hand side of the road. Turn off on FR 545A and drive along this good cinder road for almost 4 miles to a Forest Service gate located on a saddle. This is the fire-tower vehicle road but is closed for most of the year. The trailhead is at the gate.

High Points: Spectacular views of the surrounding volcanic field.

Hiking the Trail: This excellent trail winds around O'Leary Peak, giving you a 360-degree hiking panorama of the Northern Plateau Province and the local volcanic field stretching north and east from the San Francisco Peaks. The path follows a gradual but consistent climb that is well worth the effort. Corrugated metal strips line the last part of the roadbed that leads up to the fire tower. Check to see if the fire tower is occupied.

For the effort involved, this viewpoint is one of the best in northern Arizona, and it's within 750 vertical feet of your parked vehicle. This summit gives you a great overview of the Sunset Crater area with views of the crater, the San Francisco Peaks, Strawberry Crater, and all the way to the Grand Canyon. Return by the same route.

98. Strawberry Crater Trail

Time: 2 hours. *Distance:* 2 miles roundtrip. *Elevation Gain:* 500 feet. *Rating:* Moderate.

Trailhead: From the Sunset Crater Visitor Center, drive back to US 89 and turn north. Continue on US 89 about 4 miles until you get to FR 546 on the right. Turn right onto FR 546 and follow this for about 3.5 miles until you run into FR 779. Go straight on FR 779 for 2 miles, heading for Strawberry Crater. You'll reach a powerline. Go straight ahead to a cable fence and a wilderness sign. The trailhead is here.

High Points: Enchanted, dark-red lava flows. Sinaguan Indian ruins inside the crater. Walking up an actual volcanic cinder cone.

Hiking the Trail: This small, beautiful crater is located on the southwest end of the 10,141-acre Strawberry Crater Wilderness. There is a well-defined trail up through the cinders that takes you to the summit. Since this is a somewhat isolated crater, you really get the feeling of the volcanic field from this place. When standing in the inner rim by the ruins, you can imagine yourself back in ancient times, scouting for deer and elk and waiting for the rains to grow the corn.

99. Red Mountain Trail

Time: 2 hours. *Distance:* 2.5 miles roundtrip. *Elevation Gain:* 300 feet. *Rating:* Easy.

Trailhead: Go directly north on US 180 from the Flagstaff Visitor Center for almost 32 miles, looking on the left for the obvious red-faced volcanic cinder cone and the Red Mountain trail sign. Pull off on the left and park here. This is the trailhead.

High Points: Hiking into the middle of a volcanic cinder cone. Spectacular and eerie volcanic formations within the cone.

Hiking the Trail: The route follows an old jeep road that is marked with silver reflectors nailed to juniper and pinyon trees. It leaves the road in about one-third mile and continues as a path along a wash bed. The wash gradually becomes a shallow valley, flanked by black cinder mounds. You start to see strange black cinder monsters as you approach the belly of this crater. More cinder monsters greet you as you enter the center—now they are red. You can explore this strange, ghostly place to your heart's content, climbing up on some of the jumbled formations and experiencing the weird sensations that so many do when entering this sanctuary. Return by the same route.

CHAPTER 12

Grand Canyon Day Hikes

South Rim Area
  Rim Trails
  "Over the Edge" Trails

North Rim Area
  Rim Trails
  "Over the Edge" Trail

GRAND CANYON—SOUTH RIM AREA

There is only one Grand Canyon, and it's incomparable. A hiker's first view of the Canyon leaves him or her awestruck. Subsequent visits are just as awesome. The real Grand Canyon experience, however, is getting away from the crowds and getting onto some trails. The following trails offer some rim hiking "along the edges," as well as below the edge into the inner Canyon on both the North and South rims.

Day hikes don't require a permit at the Canyon. Camping does, and campgrounds are very limited. Consider camping outside the National Park at Tusayan or in the North Kaibab National Forest and driving into the park for day hikes.

The South Rim lies at an elevation of 7,000 feet. The pinyon-juniper plant community dominates the landscape on the rim edge. It is drier and hotter than the North Rim.

Grand Canyon Village has become a small city. Plane, train, car, and mule tours cover the South Rim. However, it is still quite easy

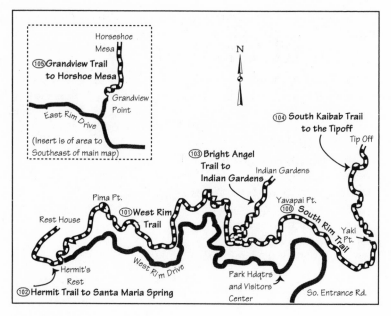

Grand Canyon South Rim Area

to get away from the crowds. Simply get into those hiking boots and head off along the rim trails or drop "over the edge" and you'll be in a world of your own.

Directions to all Grand Canyon South Rim Day Hikes start at the South Rim Visitor Center.

When to Go

Hiking seasons on the South Rim are spring, winter, and fall. Winter can be cold and snowy. Day hiking can be done between winter storms. Summers are okay for rim hiking but generally too hot for inner-canyon trekking. Check ahead for Grand Canyon weather.

Places to Visit

Tusayan, located just south of the park entrance, offers the unique experience of the IMAX Theater, which shows a mind-boggling presentation on the history of Grand Canyon exploration. Don't miss it.

The *South Rim Visitor Center* is also a must. It displays the cultural history of the Canyon and is an information center for all Canyon activities. It houses a small Grand Canyon Natural History Association bookstore.

The *Yavapai Museum* is located .75 mile east of the visitor center and features exhibits about the geology of the region. A panorama of the Canyon is visible through a large window display. Books, maps, and videos are available at the Grand Canyon Natural History Association bookstore.

Desert View is at the far eastern end of the rim and provides inspiring views of both Marble Canyon to the north and the main Grand Canyon to the west.

The *Tusayan Museum* is 3 miles west of Desert View and displays information about Anasazi life around the rim.

Rim Trails

The rim trails skirt the very edge of the Grand Canyon and are generally flat to undulating. There is one paved and one unpaved section along the South Rim.

Day Hike Area Takeoff Point South Rim Visitor Center: The entrance station to the South Rim will provide you with a map to Grand Canyon Village that tells you where the visitor center is located.

Campgrounds Mather Campground, Ten-X Campground, and Kaibab National Forest open camping.

100. South Rim Trail

Time: 3 hours. *Distance:* 3 miles. *Elevation Gain:* Level. *Rating:* Moderate.

Trailhead: The Grand Canyon Visitor Center.

High Points: A secluded, rim-edge stroll that offers unobstructed views into the central section of the Canyon's immensity.

Hiking the Trail: Follow the sign at the visitor center that leads you to the Rim Trail. The path meanders about .5 mile through pinyon and juniper to the rim itself. A junction you encounter at the rim edge gives you the choice of turning right and hiking about 4 miles on the paved path to Yaki Point or turning left and hiking along the paved path all the way to Hermit's Rest, about 5 miles along the rim. This route passes the most congested area on the rim—the "commercial district," past the concessions, El Tovar Hotel, Bright Angel Lodge, and the Kolb Studios. However, once you've passed this area, the path becomes quiet and private again as it curves north along the rim to Maricopa Point.

This paved rim trail is a great introduction to day hiking at the Grand Canyon. It gives you a feel for the rim and its vegetation. You'll see and hear scrub jays, squirrels, ravens, and rock rats. You can access this rim trail by way of the lodges as well as from the road overlooks that parallel the trail. But the best way to appreciate the hike is to start from the visitor center and do the whole route.

101. West Rim Trail

Time: 3 hours. *Distance:* 5 miles. *Elevation Gain:* Level. *Rating:* Moderate.

Trailhead: Starting from the visitor center, there are many points along the West Rim Drive that will get you onto the West Rim Trail. During the summer, a shuttle bus drops off and picks up hikers all along the route. During the winter, you can drive your own car to the many lookout points and trail contacts. Drive to the Bright Angel Lodge parking area and use the shuttle bus bench just west of Bright Angel Lodge as the trailhead.

High Points: A rim-edge path through the pinyon-juniper community, with views into the western end of the Canyon.

Hiking the Trail: The West Rim Trail is basically a continuation of the South Rim Trail. The first 1.5 miles to Maricopa Point are on the paved portion of the South Rim Trail. From Maricopa Point, the trail is a dirt path that goes along the edge of the Canyon. In many places, you have a choice of going along the edge or taking a little higher, parallel trail. You really get the feeling of being in the Canyon on this trail due to the primitive path and the absence of other people or noise. You have the option of picking up the shuttle bus at any of the overlook points: Powell Point, Hopi Point, Mojave Point, The Abyss, Pima Point, or Hermit's Rest. This is an excellent extension of the South Rim Trail for those who like level paths and are not up for the "over the edge" routes that require steep climbing.

"Over the Edge" Trails

These day hikes take you into the "real" Canyon, over the edge as it were—down into geologic time and the best of all Grand Canyon experiences. They require some steep climbing back out of the Canyon, but can be taken down partway. In fact, all you have to do is get 50 yards over the rim and you are in another world. The upper world goes away completely and you enter the past, so don't let the steepness scare you if you haven't tried the trails. Just go down a little way and back out. You can increase your experience as you feel like it. Once you go "over the edge" the first time, you'll return again and again.

Day Hike Area Takeoff Point South Rim Visitor Center: The entrance station will give you a direction map to the visitor center.

Campgrounds Mather Campground, Ten-X Campground, and Kaibab National Forest open camping.

102. Hermit Trail to Santa Maria Spring

Time: 6 hours. *Distance:* 5 miles roundtrip. *Elevation Gain:* 1,200 feet. *Rating:* Moderate.

Trailhead: From the visitor center, drive or take the shuttle bus along the West Rim Drive to Hermit's Rest overlook. There are a parking area, gift shop, and refreshment stand right at the rim. Walk west along the dirt service road located behind Hermit's Rest to the trailhead sign.

High Points: Views of the western part of the inner Canyon. A great sunset viewpoint trail.

Hiking the Trail: The route switchbacks down through the Kaibab limestone layer, then turns south through the Toroweap formation, which consists of limestones, sandstones, and siltstones. The next layer you see is white Coconino sandstone. Where this layer starts, you can look down into the drainage basin formed by Hermit Creek. As you head down, you come across the sandstone cobblestones that were used in 1912 to make a stable bed for the trail. About two-thirds of the way down through the Coconino, start looking for fossil tracks on a large, cleared slab of sandstone next to a long, well-cobbled section of the trail. An old trail, the Waldron Trail, comes in from the south and joins the main trail close to the top of the Hermit Shale formation. Look for remains of an old camp here.

The path goes down through the deep red shale of the Hermit formation, and the Dripping Springs Trail joins the Hermit from the left. The path continues into the Hermit drainage gorge and down through the red shales and sandstones of the Supai formation to Santa Maria Spring. It was built in 1913 as a cool summer rest stop. Purify any drinking water from the spring. Continue farther down if you wish, but remember, it takes three times as much effort to get back out. And three times as much water.

103. Bright Angel Trail to Indian Gardens

Time: 6 hours. *Distance:* 9 miles roundtrip. *Elevation Gain:* 3,200 feet. *Rating:* Challenging.

Trailhead: From the visitor center, drive to the Bright Angel Lodge parking area. The trailhead is just west of the Kolb Studio right below Bright Angel Lodge.

High Points: Actually entering the Canyon and becoming absorbed by the sandstones and limestones of its ancient seabed walls. The garden environment of running water within the dry Canyon at Indian Gardens. A taste of what real canyoneering is all about.

Hiking the Trail: You are at the lip of the most famous canyon in the world—one of the Seven Natural Wonders of the World. You are standing in the pinyon-juniper plant community, a semi-arid environment that receives rain in summer monsoons and winter snow.

When you look across the Canyon to the North Rim, you are looking 10 miles away. You can see Indian Gardens 3,200 feet below, and it really doesn't look that far. It is! As you look down to the gardens, you are looking down a fault zone that created Bright Angel Canyon all the way across to the North Rim. The west side of the drainage is about 200 feet higher than the east due to the fault slippage.

Be realistic when you decide how far down you want to go. The first layer you hike down through is Kaibab limestone. Notice the harder, usually multicolored, chert nodules imbedded in the limestone. They were used for arrowheads and tools by early Americans. Continue down through the Coconino sandstone, the Toroweap sandstone, and into the Hermit shale formation until you reach the Mile-and-a-Half Resthouse. You have just passed through 250 million years of geologic history. This is a good spot for a snack and rest before deciding if you want to go farther into the Canyon. In summer, there is an emergency phone and water here. This stone rest area and the Three-Mile-Resthouse, furthermore, were built by the Civilian Conservation Corps in the 1930s.

Switchbacks take you to the second resthouse, which has a phone and water in the summer also. This is a good lunch spot where you can look down the immense Redwall limestone face that extends around most of the inner Canyon. The next section, down to Indian Gardens, takes you through the 500-foot Redwall, Muav limestone, and Bright Angel shale. As you approach Indian Gardens you are hiking through basins and streambeds that support plants different from the surrounding terrain of blackbrush. You find Apache plume, mesquite, cliffrose, and single-leaf ash.

Indian Gardens itself was settled around 1300 A.D. when early Native Americans farmed the area. Take a long rest there. Get tanked up with water before the hike back out. Take at least three quarts back up in warm weather.

If you are in good shape and want an extra challenge, follow the fairly level path out to Plateau Point. From here you can see the inner gorge of the Canyon, the Colorado River, and Phantom Ranch. You will then have a good overview of the Canyon from top to bottom. Climb out at an easy, relaxed pace. Nibble on snacks and drink that water.

104. South Kaibab Trail to the Tipoff

Time: 8 hours. *Distance:* 9 miles roundtrip. *Elevation Gain:* 3,500 feet. *Rating:* Challenging.

Trailhead: From the visitor center, drive out East Rim Drive to the Yaki Point parking area. There is a portable outhouse here, but no water. The trailhead sign is obvious.

High Points: An inner Canyon experience in which you are totally absorbed by a new world of ancient rocks and erosion. Inner Canyon sandstone temples rise up above the skyline as you lose altitude down the steep trail.

Hiking the Trail: This is a steeper trail than the Bright Angel Trail, and day hikers should consider the extra effort required to get back out to the rim from the inner Canyon. A good destination for the beginning day hiker is Cedar Ridge, about 1.5 miles down the trail.

Notice the aluminum signs, describing the major geologic formations along the route. There is a pit toilet at Cedar Ridge, but no water. In fact, there is no water available on the South Kaibab at all. You must carry all you will need. Cedar Ridge gives you views of most of the rest of the trail down to the Tonto Plateau. That's 3 more miles one-way.

The next section is down the corkscrew switchbacks of the Redwall and onto the Tonto Plateau. This is decision time. The switchbacks are the most strenuous part of the South Kaibab Trail and will seem endless if you are out of energy on the way out. If you choose to continue down to the Tonto Plateau, you will find the relatively level area very enjoyable all the way to the Tipoff, where an emergency phone and pit toilet are located just past the junction with the Tonto Trail that traverses the Tonto Plateau. Once you are hiking on the Tonto Plateau, the rest of the Canyon opens up and you can appreciate the immense horizontal distances along the inner Canyon. Remember, plan for three times the amount of time and water for the return hike to the South Rim.

105. Grandview Trail to Horseshoe Mesa Campground

Time: 6 hours. *Distance:* 6 miles roundtrip. *Elevation Gain:* 2,500 feet. *Rating:* Challenging.

Trailhead: From the visitor center, drive east on East Rim Drive to the Grandview Point parking area. The trailhead is located here.

High Points: Some of the best views in the Canyon. You'll see the Colorado River as it comes south through Marble Canyon and turns west into the main Grand Canyon. Equally stunning views of the eroded formations that line the river and extend to the rim. Mining remnants on Horseshoe Mesa.

Hiking the Trail: This is a waterless trail unless you go all the way down to Miner's Spring, so take plenty of water for the return climb. This trail starts out steep and narrow and eases off on the lower part. Notice the old cribbing of logs and steel that supports the trail—remnants of days when mules climbed up the trail laden with copper ore from Horseshoe Mesa. The ore was high grade but limited in supply. Keep in mind how steep this section will be on the return climb. Horseshoe Mesa is prominent below and you can see your route all the way to the campground.

About .75 mile down, you will find a picnic site with fantastic views. This is a good lunch spot. From the picnic site, follow the trail whose tread is composed of Coconino sandstone fitted into a mosaic of blocks. More rock and steel trail cribbing is encountered as you head for the Saddle, a notch in the Coconino. You've come a little over a mile down and it's 2 more miles to the campground on a straightforward path. This is an enjoyable hike that allows you to take in both Marble and Grand Canyons. If you need water for the return climb, you must get it by scrambling 700 feet down the trail to Miner's Spring. You'll need 2 to 3 quarts of water to get back up.

GRAND CANYON—NORTH RIM AREA

The North Rim is a world unto its own, associated more with Utah than Arizona because of its isolation from the rest of the state. The North Rim is a three-and-a-half-hour drive from the South Rim, and well worth the trip. The drive itself is a wilderness experience due to the lack of habitation and facilities on this great plateau. Day hikes on the North Rim provide an even more isolated sense of wonder due to their relative inaccessibility.

The North Rim is 1,000 feet higher than the South Rim and is part of the Kaibab Plateau, one of a series of uplifts comprising the larger Colorado Plateau. It is composed of the layer-cake bedrock sediments displayed in the inner walls of the Grand Canyon. The high elevation of the Kaibab Plateau creates a Canadian-type forest community. It can snow 200 inches in heavy winters—100 inches is the norm. It is a densely forested country of Engelmann and blue spruce, ponderosa pine, white fir, Douglas fir, Gambel oak, and quaking aspen.

The forest opens up in places, providing a series of montane meadows, or "parks." In the summer, these parks are filled with the songs of the black-headed grosbeak, hermit thrush, meadowlark, western bluebird, and various hole-drilling woodpeckers. Deer, elk, mountain lions, bobcats, and rodents walk through columbine, Indian paintbrush, blue flax, yellow alumroot, and other wildflower displays.

The North Rim Lodge was built in 1928. It was destroyed by fire in 1932 and rebuilt in 1936. A small campground was established at that time. In the mid-1920s, the North Kaibab Trail was built, following old Indian trails that went down to Roaring Springs.

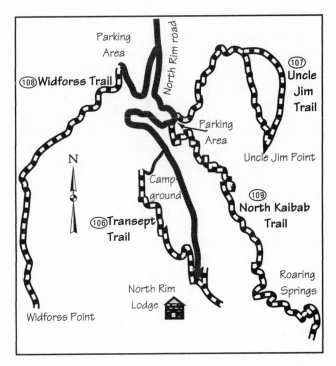

Grand Canyon North Rim Area

Directions to all North Rim Day Hikes start at the Visitor Center. The North Rim is reached by heading north on I-17 to Flagstaff. From Flagstaff, take US 89 north to US Alt 89 at Marble Canyon on the Colorado River. Follow US Alt 89 to State Route 67 at Jacob Lake. Go south on 67 to the North Rim.

This trip takes about 6 hours from Phoenix. The traveler goes from the Southern Deserts through the Central Mountains and up onto the Northern Plateau Province in a half day.

When to Go

Hiking season on the North Rim starts when State Route 67 opens from Jacob's Lake to the North Rim, usually sometime in May. The season lasts until the first heavy snow closes the road, usually sometime in November. Always check ahead in the spring and fall to the Grand Canyon Backcountry Office, phone: (602) 638-7888.

Places to Visit

Stop in at the *Kaibab National Forest Visitor Center* at Jacob's Lake, 44 miles north of the rim for information on the forest area surrounding the Canyon. Also stop at the small store across from Kaibab Lodge just outside the park boundary for information and supplies for day hiking in the area.

The *North Rim Lodge* is the focal point for all activities and information on North Rim hiking within the national park.

Rim Trails

The rim trails lead to spectacular vistas of the inner Canyon. One takes you to overlooks of the north-south Marble Canyon, the others to overlooks of the main east-west Grand Canyon.

Day Hike Area Takeoff Point North Rim Visitor Center: The entrance station to the North Rim will provide you with a map to the visitor center.

Campgrounds North Rim Campground (Grand Canyon National Park), DeMotte Park in the Kaibab National Forest, Jacob's Lake R.V. Park, and Kaibab National Forest open camping.

106. Transept Trail

Time: 1 hour. *Distance:* 1.5 miles. *Elevation Gain:* Level. *Rating:* Easy.

Trailhead: From the North Rim Visitor Center, this trail can be picked up just down the steps from the north exit of the North Rim Lodge. This is the trailhead.

High Points: Views of Transept Canyon, Zoroaster and Brahma temples. Leisurely stroll to get the feel of the North Rim.

Hiking the Trail: The path follows the edge of the Transept, a drainage into Bright Angel Canyon. It skirts this canyon and loops back into the North Rim campground area. Short off-shoot trails take you to vista points along the loop. These vistas give you a peek into the Canyon. Many paths from the campground and the cabin lodgings radiate out to the Transept Trail. The route is partly shaded by the ponderosa pine, Gambel oak, locust, scrub oak, and grasses lining its path. Deer can often be seen along this trail as it skirts the westside cabins on the rim. Return to the North Rim Lodge by way of the North Rim campground area.

107. Uncle Jim Trail

Time: 4 hours. *Distance:* 5 miles roundtrip. *Elevation Gain:* Level. *Rating:* Moderate.

Trailhead: From the visitor center, drive to the North Kaibab Trail parking lot. The trailhead is on the east end.

High Points: Leads to one of the best North Rim overlooks—west to the North Kaibab Trail and south out into the Canyon proper.

Hiking the Trail: The first mile is shared with the Ken Patrick Trail, skirting the Roaring Springs Canyon rim. A look over the edge gives you a glimpse of the North Kaibab Trail route to Phantom Ranch. Turn right at the trail sign to Uncle Jim Point. This goes a short distance before arriving at another junction, which offers two ways to Uncle Jim Point. Turn right and you'll enter an area of large locust trees, Douglas fir, and aspen groves. The trail goes across a spring-fed drainage with various seeps upstream.

When you reach the rim, there is a sharp left in the path that leads back around to the trailhead. Stay right and follow the narrow path out to the spectacular vista point amid a forest of small Gambel oaks. The views include the North Kaibab Trail to Roaring Springs, Zoroaster Temple, Brahma Temple, and Angel's Gate Temple. Be on the lookout for deer and elk as you return by the alternate route to close the loop back at the Ken Patrick Trail.

108. Widforss Trail

Time: 6 hours. *Distance:* 10 miles roundtrip. *Elevation Gain:* Level. *Rating:* Moderate.

Trailhead: From the visitor center, drive back on the North Rim road, about 1 mile past the North Rim campground turnoff, and look for the Widforss Trail sign by the dirt road that turns off to the left. Follow the dirt road for another mile to the parking area on the left. The trailhead is here.

High Points: A delightful walk through mixed vegetation along the North Rim's most popular backcountry day hike. Great views of Brahma, Buddha, and Zoroaster Temples.

Hiking the Trail: The path climbs from a meadow by the parking area and winds along for about 100 yards before entering a forest of ponderosa pine, blue spruce, Engelmann spruce, white fir, Douglas fir, and quaking aspen. After about a mile, the trail edges out to the rim and exposes the immensity of the inner Canyon. It takes your breath away. A look over the edge at many overlooks shows you how fast the vegetation changes on the inner Canyon slopes—exposed to more sunlight than the sheltered forest. Gambel oak, cliffrose, and pinyon-juniper inhabit the sunny slopes and ledges. The path continues along the rim of Transept Canyon, then angles away from the rim and crosses several wetter ravines.

The difference in vegetation is striking. In the ravines you can find aspen, wild strawberries, and many other streamed microhabitats. The path continues across the ponderosa forest to Widforss Point, a delightful picnic spot and overlook. Return by the same route.

"Over the Edge" Trail

There is only one practical day-hike route "over the edge" on the North Rim—the North Kaibab Trail.

Day Hike Area Takeoff Point North Rim Visitor Center: The ranger at the entrance station will give you a map of the North Rim that will direct you to the visitor center.

Campgrounds North Rim Campground, DeMotte Park in Kaibab National Forest, and open Kaibab National Forest camping.

109. North Kaibab Trail

Time: 6 hours. *Distance:* 10 miles roundtrip. *Elevation Gain:* 3,600 feet. *Rating:* Challenging.

Trailhead: Drive 2 miles north of the North Rim Lodge on the rim road and look for the parking area to the North Kaibab Trail. Park in the lot provided for hikers. There is no overnight camping here—only day use.

High Points: Dramatic vegetation change on the steep descent to the springs. Cross-canyon views all the way to the South Rim.

Hiking the Trail: This trail leads the hiker through one of the most spectacular displays of geologic history anywhere on earth. The trail follows a geologic fault that occurred during the Kaibab Plateau uplift.

The hiker also descends through different plant communities on the way to Roaring Springs—getting warmer and drier with descent. "Drier" is a key word here, accentuating the need for carrying at least three quarts of water on a warm day and filling the canteens up at the bottom for the return hump. The South Rim can be seen across the Canyon, along with the San Francisco Peaks north of Flagstaff.

The Supai Tunnel was blasted through sedimentary rock for this trail in the 1930s. When you reach it, you are entering the drier part of the Canyon—the pinyon-juniper plant community.

The Bridge in the Redwall is the next manmade object, constructed after the 1966 flood that destroyed part of the trail. Roaring Springs is the obvious lunch break. Water can be obtained from the springs by climbing up to them.

Index

About the Author

Dave Ganci teaches Outdoor Recreation courses at Yavapai Community College in Prescott, Arizona. He also coordinates day hikes for the college Elderhostel program—a recreation program for folks over 60.

He has three books in print: *Desert Hiking, Desert Survival,* and *Hiking the Southwest.*

He is a desert warfare consultant to the Department of Defense, conducting escape/evasion and survival courses for military Special Warfare groups.

Dave holds an undergraduate degree in geography and a graduate degree in recreation from Arizona State University.

He spends a lot of time out on Arizona's trails, recording the natural history of the surrounding areas.

He spent two years hiking all the trails in this book, and considers the hikes among the best in the state.

Dave owns and runs Wild Places, a tour company that takes folks out to explore the beauties and adventures of Arizona's remote backcountry.